JOHN W. SPANIER

THE
TRUMAN–MacARTHUR
CONTROVERSY
AND
THE KOREAN WAR

The Norton Library

W · W · NORTON & COMPANY · INC ·

NEW YORK

To My Parents

Books That Live
The Norton imprint on a book means that in the publisher's
estimation it is a book not for a single season but for the years.
W. W. Norton & Company, Inc.

PRINTED IN THE UNITED STATES OF AMERICA

3 4 5 6 7 8 9 0

PREFACE

It is the purpose of this book to examine the nature of the controversy between President Truman and General Douglas MacArthur, which began shortly after the outbreak of the Korean War and reached a climax when the President relieved MacArthur of his commands. To accomplish this, an analysis has been made of the basic decisions which American policy-makers had to make during the Korean War. The most important of these was the decision to accept the Communist challenge and repel the North Korean invasion by force. The others were: the neutralization of Formosa; the Inchon landing; the crossing of the 38th Parallel; the "home by Christmas" offensive; the decision *not* to extend the war to China after Communist China's intervention; to condemn Peking as an aggressor; and MacArthur's dismissal. This analysis will bring out clearly the policy differences which separated Truman and MacArthur, how these differences arose, and why they developed to the point where the President had no choice but to dismiss his field commander.

The aim of this book, however, is not only to explore the Truman-MacArthur controversy; more fundamentally, it is to analyze the problems of civil-military relations during a limited war. For it is the author's belief that the Korean War raised the question whether the conduct of a limited war is in fact compatible with the time-honored principle of civilian supremacy over the military. The reason for this belief, and the framework within which the Truman-MacArthur controversy will be analyzed, is set out in detail in the introductory chapter.

Since 1959, when this study was first published, events have reinforced the author's conviction that limited war is a fact of life in the nuclear age. In the longer perspective that time now offers, it seems even more clear that the limited objectives of civilian leaders during the Korean War were more realistic than the demands for a total military offensive — and all the risks that that entailed — in some military quarters. For this edition, Chapters I and XIV have been somewhat revised to try to explain the enchantment of some Americans with the paper tiger of "total" victory and to reflect recent debate on the use of nuclear weapons. The revision in no way reflects a change in point of view.

It is with great pleasure that I thank the following cartoonists and their newspapers for permitting me to include their cartoons in my book: Paule Loring, of *The Providence Evening Bulletin,* and Vicky, of the London *Evening Standard,* formerly of the *News Chronicle.* At the same time, I would like to acknowledge my thanks to Alfred A. Knopf, Inc., for permission to quote passages from General Court-ney Whitney's *MacArthur: His Rendezvous with History;* to Time, Inc., for permission to quote from President Truman's *Memoirs;* and to Mr. Joseph Alsop, Mr. Walter Lippmann, and the *New York Herald Tribune* for permission to reproduce a number of passages from the columns of these two distinguished political analysts.

I particularly wish to express my gratitude to two of my former teachers at Harvard University: William Y. Elliott, who first stimulated my interest in the problems of formulating and administrating Ameri-can foreign policy; and Henry A. Kissinger, my senior-year tutor, who encouraged my interest in military affairs, and focused it on postwar American military strategy.

J. W. S.

CONTENTS

CONTENTS

LIST OF ILLUSTRATIONS

PART ONE

THE KOREAN WAR
JUNE 1950 TO NOVEMBER 1950:
THE PERIOD OF
NORTH KOREAN AGGRESSION

KOREA

scale (miles)
0 20 40

CHINA

U.S.S.R.

CHONGJIN

HYESANJIN

PUJON RES.

SINUIJU
CHANGJIN RES.
ONJONG
UNSAN

PORT ARTHUR
ANJU
DAIREN

HUNGNAM

SEA

OF

JAPAN

WONSAN

PYONGYANG

cease
fire line

38°
CHUNCHON

SEOUL
INCHON

YELLOW

SEA

TAEGU

PUSAN

MOKPO

CHEJU

MacARTHUR RETURNS

A few minutes after midnight, April 11, 1951, the White House announced that it would hold a press conference at 1:00 A.M. As the reporters gathered, they wondered what could be so important that they should be called to a conference during the night. They soon found out: President Truman had relieved General Douglas MacArthur of all his commands — as Supreme Commander, Allied Powers; Commander in Chief, United Nations Command; Commander in Chief, Far East; and Commanding General, U.S. Army, Far East. The President's statement read in part:

With deep regret I have concluded that General of the Army Douglas MacArthur is unable to give his wholehearted support to the policies of the United States Government and of the United Nations in matters pertaining to his official duties. In view of the specific responsibilities imposed upon me by the Constitution of the United States and the added responsibility which has been entrusted to me by the United Nations, I have decided that I must make a change of command in the Far East. . . . It is fundamental . . . that military commanders must be governed by the policies and directives issued to them in the manner provided by our laws and Constitution. In times of crisis, this consideration is particularly compelling.

There are few principles to which Americans are more devoted than the principle of civilian control which the President mentioned. Yet, in April 1951, General MacArthur, dismissed from his commands for publicly challenging and opposing the policies of his government, was received home with great popular acclaim while Harry Truman was burned in effigy. The consequent Truman-MacArthur controversy — which had actually begun shortly after the outbreak of the Korean

War and was only climaxed by MacArthur's dismissal — opened what one astute observer of the national scene has called the gravest and most emotional constitutional crisis that the United States has faced since the Great Depression. The issue at stake was no less than the continuation of civilian supremacy and of the President's authority as Commander in Chief and chief diplomat to determine the nation's foreign policy. Or, more succinctly, the authority of the United States government was at stake. The central question was who was President — Truman or MacArthur.

The national mood by April 1951 was one of anger and helplessness. The outpouring of emotion for MacArthur, who over and over again insisted that there was no substitute for victory, was in a sense a cry for the man who could "deliver his children" from the seemingly endless and indecisive Korean War — as well as a cold war which allowed the country neither to enjoy peace nor to mobilize its full resources for a war that would once and for all eliminate the cause of the nation's troubles. While MacArthur was not to reap the reward of this feeling — for however belligerent Americans may at times seem, they entrust their political leadership only to "safe" generals who, like Dwight D. Eisenhower, have been "civilianized" — the issue he raised was fundamental to the future conduct of American foreign policy: how can civilian supremacy over the military establishment be maintained in limited wars? MacArthur may have precipitated the crisis which resulted in his dismissal, but the circumstances out of which this crisis grew were not as unique as MacArthur's personality. On one hand, the Korean War was in many respects likely to prove to be a model for future wars. The atomic bomb had made the world safe only for limited wars. Total wars, like World War II, had been outmoded by technology. On the other hand, the American temperament and military tradition were hostile to the concept of limited wars. In these circumstances, other civilian-military conflicts might arise again if a general who disagreed strongly with Administration policy were to look for political support in the opposition party. To be sure, the field commander of a limited engagement might not himself precipitate a conflict with his political superior. The opposition party, seeking office and eager to exploit popular frustration with a seemingly never-ending and indecisive war, might initiate the attack on the conduct of the war, particularly if it were a protracted guerilla war. Americans like to have their boys brought "home by Christmas." Wars have to be ended quickly either by victory or by withdrawal.

The political-psychological shortcoming of American democracy in these circumstances is obvious. But the opportunities open to the opposition party, once American forces are directly involved on a large scale, are promising. And any general who disagrees vigorously with Administration policy, whether he is in the field or a member of the Joint Chiefs of Staff, is likely to be drawn into this partisan struggle; a resulting division between Republican and Democratic generals cannot but weaken civilian control and direction of foreign policy.

Yet limited conflicts — be they conventional military engagements, unconventional or guerilla wars, or threatened nuclear "confrontations" — are the only feasible forms of conflict in the nuclear era. Total war is tantamount to mutual annihilation and World War III is merely a pseudonym for suicide. All-out war has become an "irrational" instrument of national policy, for nations do not generally defend their "national interest" by immolating themselves. This is why the emphasis of military strategy has shifted from fighting an all-out war to preventing the eruption of such a catastrophe. The principal purpose of military policy is deterrence rather than defense after the initiation of hostilities. Deterrence is achieved by threatening the opponent with utter devastation — "megadeaths" in the strategists' vocabulary, virtual annihilation in plain English — if he should dare to launch the knockout blow. Defense after a nuclear strike would be futile; if war were to break out, a nuclear holocaust would be unavoidable.

If the United States can ensure that neither the Soviets nor the Chinese will seek to transform the *status quo* into a *status quo minus* by means of total war, it cannot prevent such a transformation by threatening to respond to limited challenges with strikes against Moscow and Peking. Unless the United States is able to react to such challenges — which are at the very heart of Communist strategy — with equally limited responses, it will confront a truly agonizing dilemma: total war with its suicidal risks, or inaction and surrender. A series of limited challenges can thus turn the balance of power against the West in a piecemeal fashion. This tactic, commonly referred to as the salami tactic, seeks to slice off one piece at a time; no one piece is so large that it will be missed particularly. But in the end the salami will nevertheless have disappeared. A strategy of all-out nuclear war to deter such nibbling lacks credibility to an opponent; he simply will not believe that the American propensity for committing suicide is that high. The fact that the Soviets were willing to risk launching the North Korean army to invade South Korea, even at a time when the United States was immune to attack, is ample evidence that Moscow believed that Washington would not precipitate a total war over a limited challenge.

Yet the essence of the limited challenge — and response — is that the *political* objectives sought or defended remain limited. The objective of total war is the complete destruction or surrender of the enemy's military forces and the overthrow of his government — the enemy's unconditional surrender. In limited conflicts, neither the total defeat of the opponent's armies nor the elimination of his government are sought. The aim may be a particular piece of territory, but more likely it is a political or psychological advantage. Yet, from the American point of view, these advantages may have a profound bearing on the distribution of power by affecting Communist willingness to probe "soft spots" along the Sino-Soviet periphery, the cohesiveness of America's alliances, and even the present, or future, positions of presently nonaligned nations. If limited wars are defined primarily in terms of limited political objectives — rather than, say, the limited area in which the battle is fought — it is at all times vital to remember that these objectives are limited not by choice but by necessity. It is the desire to avoid a nuclear catastrophe that dictates these political limitations. Both parties to the conflict therefore deliberately hobble their power; they never resort to their "Sunday punch." It is, of course, easy to assert that limited wars are bound to escalate into total war because the losing side will prefer escalation to defeat. The fact that all postwar conflicts have remained limited is evidence, however, that all the major actors on the world scene, particularly the United States and the Soviet Union, wish to avoid total war. Indeed, the ability of both powers to expand hostilities gives both of them the strongest possible incentive to avoid an escalation, at least escalation into total war. No nation seeks to avoid a limited defeat by initiating an all-out war from which no survival at all is possible.

Nevertheless, the experience of the Korean War is not likely to change the American people's disinclination to fight less than total wars, to abstain from wars that cannot be converted into moral crusades for righteous causes. This preference to fight for total military victory springs from a deeply ingrained American attitude which abhors "power politics." [1] The employment of power, which Americans tend to identify with military force, is condemned as sinful. The American credo is that man is a rational and moral creature who can settle his differences with his fellow men through the use of reason and moral suasion. The normal relations among men, whether among individuals or men organized into states, are peaceful and harmonious. Conflict is a deviation from this norm, primarily the result of wicked (i.e., undemocratic) statesmen: autocratic rulers, like Kaiser Wilhelm II, or totalitarian tyrants, like Hitler or Stalin. Conflict and war, in short, stem from undemocratic political systems. "Power politics" is an instrument of selfish and tyrannical rulers who seek their own personal advantage. War, to them, is a great — and profitable — game. But to the man who has to fight and risk injury, if not death, war is a dangerous and unpleasant "sport." The ruler who is not held accountable to his people must consequently be a warmonger; by contrast the "man in the street," who has to suffer the cruelties of war, is by nature peaceful. The dichotomy is simple: undemocratic states are warlike and evil; democratic nations, in which the rulers are responsible to the governed, are peaceful and moral. It follows logically that the use of force in peacetime is not permissible since force is morally corrupting.

But once the United States is provoked into violence by despots, the employment of force *can* be justified, but only in terms of universal moral principles. This evil instrument, war, can be rendered legitimate only if the nation at war pursues noble purposes and completely destroys the enemy who threatens the integrity, if not the existence, of these principles. American power must be "righteous power"; only its full exercise can ensure salvation or an absolution of sin. The national aversion to violence thus becomes transformed into a national glorification of violence, and our wars become ideological crusades to make the world safe for democracy — by democratizing it. Once that goal has been achieved, the United States can again withdraw into itself, secure in the knowledge that American deeds have again proven to be "good works."

This traditional American depreciation of power has resulted in a clear-cut distinction between war and peace. Peace is characterized as a state of harmony among nations. Power politics is regarded as abnormal and any resort to violence, as completely unjustifiable on moral grounds. Once war erupts, however, force must be used to destroy the enemy completely. The total application of force can then be justified; only force used without limit can destroy the evil and immoral opponent. Force is legitimatized because it is the means of eliminating power politics. The aim of war, succinctly, is to end all wars. This all-or-nothing approach to foreign policy is nowhere more appropriately revealed than in that uniquely American genre, the Western. The hero of a Western is self-reliant, courageous, and patriotic; he always knows what is right and wrong, good and evil; he is always on the side of fair play, justice, and virtue. In his consuming passion for justice and morality, the cowboy pursues the outlaw and "shoots him dead." This is typical of the American approach to war once the nation has been provoked: shoot the enemy dead and thereby solve the problem. Moreover, the enemy is evil and his death is therefore socially beneficial and morally justified.

Once war has occurred, logic dictates that force must be administered by the specialists of force, professional soldiers. Just as the physician has the responsibility of curing a malady, so the military man treats the disease of war. After the diplomats have failed to preserve the peace through reason and appeals to morality, the military "doctors" take charge. The American attitude toward war, in short, has regarded the military as a politically neutral weapon whose operations should be guided solely by its own professional rules and imperatives. The military officer is a nonpolitical man who conducts his campaign in a strictly military and technically efficient manner. His only aim is victory, his sole criterion the destruction of the enemy's forces. Just as in peacetime force cannot be justified, so in wartime "political interference" with the military conduct of the campaign cannot be warranted. As MacArthur explained it:

The general definition which for many decades has been accepted was that war was the ultimate process of politics; that when all other political means failed, you then go to force; and that when you do that, the balance of control . . . the minute you reach the killing stage, is the control of the military. A theater commander, in any campaign, is not merely limited to a handling of his troops; he commands that whole area politically, economically, and militarily. You have got to trust at the stage of the game when politics fail, and the military take over, you must trust the military. . . .[2]

Thus there is a direct clash between the notion of limited war with its limited *political* objectives and the inclination to fight total wars for total *military* victory and the enemy's unconditional surrender. In these circumstances, there is ample opportunity for conflict between the Commander in Chief and Chief diplomat — the President, who is charged by the Constitution with the responsibility for the nation's foreign and military policies — and a field commander claiming that there is no substitute for a complete military victory. Furthermore, the field commander may in such an instance expect political support. The failure to prosecute the war until the enemy has been totally defeated may create widespread frustration. In terms of the nation's image of itself as a noble and selfless crusader on behalf of moral principles, it would have failed to achieve its stated purpose, namely, complete punishment of the aggressor. In the resulting mood of disillusionment the possibility of conflict between a President and a Congress in which the opposition party holds a majority or sizable minority of seats is hardly remote. For only during a total war is the separation of powers between the Executive and Congress subordinated to the conduct of the war; short of such an all-out engagement, partisan politics is unlikely to be eliminated. Bipartisanship may eliminate some of the excesses of interparty strife and bring the President the strong support he needs when at a critical time he speaks and acts abroad in the name of the United States; but the desire for political office cannot await the termination of the cold war, or even the completion of its warmer interludes. However regrettable the fact may be, foreign policy cannot be neatly isolated from public opinion and party fortunes. Partisan advantage and foreign affairs are inextricably interwoven. External policies impinge at almost every point on domestic matters; differences over the latter are bound to affect the former. Moreover, even if it were possible to separate domestic politics from foreign policy, it is too much to expect the political conflict between the two major parties to limit itself to domestic issues at a time when the survival of the United States dwarfs every other question. By bringing differences over foreign policy to the people, the party system offers them in the external realm, as in the internal one, the only relatively effective means through which they can channel their opinions and moods; in fact, changes in the public mood may take place long before the parties respond to them. Nor is it unimportant to remember that the party in power is reluctant to share its successess with its political opponents, lest it not receive full credit from the electorate; likewise, the opposition party wishes to have a free hand to exploit the foreign-policy blunders of the Administration.

It is all very well to say that the "national interest should be placed ahead of partisan advantage" and that "politics should stop at the water's edge," but these maxims are general, and usually pious, appeals which lack specific content. The "national interest" is nowhere written down like the Ten Commandments and can be interpreted in different ways in various situations. Both political parties, not surprisingly, identify their views with the national interest. For politics to stop at the water's edge, foreign policy would have to stop there too. "Hot" war political unity does not carry over into a "cold" war. When the United States is attacked, the national interest is easily discernible. The nation maximizes its strength and concentrates on the task of totally defeating the enemy. In "peacetime," when a particular limited conflict is part of a larger conflict, opinions on what the national interests may be are bound to differ. Partisan differences are inherent in the nature of democratic government. The opposition party will naturally be tempted to exploit a limited war which has become unpopular, as the Korean War did when it increasingly was referred to as "Truman's war."

It was hardly surprising that General Eisenhower, in campaigning for the Presidency in 1952, vowed that, if elected, he would "go to Korea." For implicit in this statement was the promise of ending the Korean War — and perhaps in some voters' minds, ending the cold war itself. Nor was it surprising that having concluded one limited war, the Eisenhower Administration refused in 1954 to intervene in Indochina after the French defeat at Dienbienphu. Although Eisenhower himself had called Indochina of "transcendent importance" to American security, he was unwilling to risk becoming involved in an unpopular war.

More characteristic of the American tradition was the Eisenhower-Dulles policy of massive retaliation. In effect, it rejected the concept of limited war by threatening to respond to both total and limited attacks with massive retaliation against Moscow and Peking. Thus it reasserted the traditional attitude of total abstinence or total commitment to total war, despite the fact that the Korean War had dramatically demonstrated that the threat of an all-out nuclear war did not deter a less-than-total challenge. Korea was, in effect, ignored as if it had never happened. There were to be no more "half wars," as MacArthur called them. Psychologically, massive retaliation responded perfectly to the American mood of the early fifties.

The fundamental issue posed by the Truman–MacArthur controversy, then, is whether the conduct of limited warfare is compatible with continuing civilian supremacy over the military. Since Americans have long regarded the principle of civilian control as one of the unquestioned tenets of their democratic system, they have rarely doubted its future efficacy. They believe that the constitutional and institutional safeguards which the Founding Fathers wisely provided for this contingency will preserve this control. These prerequisites are:

1. The heads of the government are civilians and are the representatives of a majority of the citizens, to whom they are accountable and by whom they may be removed in the normal functioning of existing legal and political processes.
2. The professional heads of the armed services are under the control of the civilian leadership of the government in a manner which is both constitutional and effective.
3. The departmental management of the military establishment is under the authoritative direction of civilians who coordinate all phases of the program and are themselves responsible members of a responsible administration.
4. Elected representatives of the people make general policies, including such things as the decision about war, the voting of money and men for military purposes, and the granting of whatever emergency powers may be required; also, they are able to exercise an ultimate and general control over those responsible for the execution of policy.
5. The courts are in a position to hold the military accountable for the protection of the basic democratic rights of the people of the nation.[3]

The Korean War demonstrated rather convincingly, however, that even though the principle of civilian control is enshrined in the Constitution, enacted in legislative statutes, and reflected in the administrative organization of the federal government, civilian supremacy cannot be guaranteed by these formal and legal mechanisms alone. Indeed, civilian control resulted not from formal rules and prescriptions but rather from the absence of an active and sustained foreign policy. In short, wisdom of constitutional provisions has been confused with the beneficial results of geographic isolation, primitive technology, and power politics. American isolationism, rendered possible by wide oceans to the east and west, weak neighbors to the north and south, and the *Pax Britannica,* made it unnecessary to maintain large-scale military forces and possible to exclude military leaders from the highest councils of gevornment. Extra-constitutional factors, in other words, were responsible for the preservation of civilian control; the Constitution itself remained almost untested.

American dreams of political and military isolation ended once and for all with the collapse of the European balance of power in 1940.

The constitutional principle of civilian supremacy also lay shattered; civilian control during World War II was largely absent. President Roosevelt recognized his lack of expertness in military matters and relied almost wholly upon the advice of his Chiefs of Staff. Although the President believed strongly that civilians should exercise political authority, he subscribed to the traditional view that once war had begun, it should be directed by military technicians isolated from allegedly irrelevant "political" conditions. The military leaders held the same opinion: their services were politically neutral instruments whose operations should be guided solely by the rules of war. Victory on the field of battle was their only objective. The effect of this sharp separation of political and military affairs, and the subordination of the former to the latter, meant that the direction of American policy was left to General George C. Marshall, the Army Chief of Staff, and his colleagues.

The State Department was thereby relegated to a minor role. This was partly due to President Roosevelt's habit of circumventing diplomatic channels by meeting and writing personally with Prime Minister Churchill and Premier Stalin and partly due to Cordell Hull's lack of personal qualifications and temperament for the job of Secretary of State. But another factor was more important: the State Department was simply not equipped to take the lead in formulating political policy and providing the political framework for a military strategy aimed at establishing a postwar balance of power in Europe and Asia. For two decades it had devoted itself almost exclusively to economic matters. America's business was business, not "meddling" in other peoples' affairs; the State Department's principal occupation was to open, and keep open, channels of trade. The resultant political inactivity in world affairs, with the exception of Latin America, had not prepared the department's personnel for a task of this magnitude. Secretary Hull concerned himself with only two problems, both of which divorced diplomacy from force: the United Nations Organization and the Free French force led by General Charles de Gaulle. To the extent that the department became involved with the daily conduct of the war, it served as an auxiliary arm of the military.

Congress, with its grant of special wartime authority to the President, also abandoned its control over the executive branch. Theoretically, of course, it still possessed a check in the power of appropriation, but the budgets were not subject to effective supervision. Total war demands total mobilization; the resources of the entire nation are harnessed to defeat the enemy. The emphasis is not on saving dollars but on developing sufficient military strength, not on balancing the budget but on matching the hostile armies. Opposition to expenditures under these circumstances could easily be made to appear as a hindrance of the war effort and therefore as unpatriotic; few Congressmen were willing to incur the voters' wrath in this way.

Perhaps during World War II it was at least feasible, even if not desirable, for the military leaders to make the major decisions: to concentrate upon the military defeat of the Axis powers; to defeat Germany and Italy before Japan; to enforce unconditional surrender upon all three; and to postpone all political decisions with regard to the postwar settlement until after the end of hostilities. This policy could at least be defended upon two expectations. First, the position of the armies at the conclusion of the war would define the new political situation; and second, the Allied armies, particularly the American forces, would occupy Japan and enough of western and central Europe to permit the creation of a favorable new balance of power.

The Korean War was not, however, the major foreign-policy problem of the United States. The military response to events in Korea, therefore, could not be determined solely in terms of conditions on the battlefield, and the field commander could not be allowed the same degree of discretion that he had in World War II. Military operations had to be closely controlled and politically supervised. Rarely, indeed, did military considerations determine military actions: not the decision to rescue South Korea from North Korean aggression; nor the decision to cross the 38th Parallel; nor the decision to maintain the limited character of the war after Communist China's intervention. Civilian policymakers were always keenly aware that just as events outside of Korea directly affected and even dictated policy in Korea, so military operations in Korea had or could have serious consequences in other parts of the world. It was the total political framework of American foreign policy which influenced American policy in Korea and made it necessary in the Administration's opinion both to fight in Korea and to limit the war; the security of Western Europe and the desire to prevent the disintegration of NATO, for instance, played a determining role in both of these decisions.

It was thus during the Korean war that the constitutional and institutional prescriptions for civilian control received their first real test — and, in fact, they almost failed to withstand the strain. Admittedly, the problem was of a somewhat different nature than during World War II. Under Roosevelt, the Chiefs of Staff had no alternative but to fill the vacuum created by the abdication of civilian responsibility for the formulation of political and military strategy; the civilian authorities were, in short, responsible for the abandonment of civilian control. Under Truman, political and military policies were closely coordinated; one of the outstanding characteristics of the American government's conduct of the Korean War was the over-all agreement between the State Department and Defense Department on the relationship between military strategy and political objectives, on the respective contribution of Europe and Asia to our national security, and on the role of our allies and the United Nations in American policy.

The principal threat came instead from the field commander, who openly challenged the President's authority as Commander in Chief and chief diplomat. As General Marshall, Secretary of Defense at the time of General MacArthur's dismissal, expressed it: "What is new and what has brought about the necessity for General MacArthur's removal is the wholly unprecedented situation of a local theater commander publicly expressing his displeasure and his disagreement with the foreign policy of the United States." Ironically, MacArthur's disagreement with the Administration did *not* stem from "strictly military" considerations, as is so widely believed. Most commentators on the Korean War have taken MacArthur's definition of war at its face value. For instance, Robert Endicott Osgood, in his brilliant critique of the American total-war approach to foreign policy, has summed up this widely accepted interpretation of MacArthur's conduct of the Korean War:

Whereas the Administration imposed definite restraints upon the military effort in the light of superior political considerations, MacArthur was temperamentally incapable of tolerating these restraints if they conflicted with his single-minded determination to meet with "maximum counterforce" in order to secure a clear-cut military victory. . . . Any deviation from that indispensable military objective for political reasons constituted "appeasement." [4]

Paradoxically, MacArthur was one of the few American soldiers who did not subscribe to the view that military men should isolate themselves from all "unprofessional" political factors; he was not imbued with the belief that the total defeat of the enemy forces was the only goal. MacArthur was very much aware that war was a political instrument. Though he usually talked as if the term "victory" held only military substance, not political content, this was only a shrewd means to maximize popular and political support and to legitimize his "democratic heresy," defiance of civilian authority. The fact that he talked in purely military terms is, however, in itself significant, particularly since he was using these terms to undermine the authority of the government. Yet, whether his reason for opposing official policy was political or military, MacArthur — that most "military" of military men — was acting in a most unmilitary fashion. It is true, as MacArthur said, that war is the "ultimate process of politics." But it is not true, as he claimed, that when "politics fail, the military take over." War, as another military officer, Prussian General Karl von Clausewitz phrased it, is the continuation of politics by other means. Military conflict, he asserted, has its own grammar but not its own logic; the logic is that of politics. Force is the handmaiden of diplomacy; military expediency does not usually determine political strategy. "The subordination of the political point of view to the military would be unreasonable, for policy has created war; policy is the intelligent faculty, war only the instrument, and not the reverse. The subordination of the military point of view to the political is, therefore, the only thing which is possible." [5]

Inherent in this definition of war as a political instrument is the demand for civilian control of the military. The soldier, it is true, can win or lose a policy, but it is not for the soldier *as* a soldier to make the final decisions. In a democracy, this is the task of those who have been charged by the people with the responsibility of charting the nation's course. In the United States it is the President and his chosen advisers who, both formally and effectively, determine the over-all "grand strategy" which the country pursues. The military man executes their orders. This is his duty. He is, so to speak, a military "civil servant," a nonpartisan career officer who implements state policy. He may not openly question that policy while he is still in command. As a soldier, he must obey his orders; obedience is the cardinal requisite of the military profession. If he cannot accept the orders he has received, he must resign; that is his responsibility as a moral being. If he will not resign, he must be dismissed. Civilian control of the military and Administration conduct of foreign policy demand no less. For the issue is *not* whether the soldier's policy is right or wrong. The issue is whether he is properly implementing the policy of his government.

II

THE NORTH KOREAN ATTACK:
COMMUNIST "LIBERATION" AND
AMERICAN "CONTAINMENT"

The North Korean Democratic People's Army launched its offensive against the Republic of Korea at four o'clock, Korean time, on the morning of June 25, 1950. After an opening two-hour artillery barrage, North Korean troops, spearheaded by approximately one hundred Soviet T-34 and T-70 tanks, crossed the 38th Parallel at three separate points; at the same time, several amphibious landings were carried out along the east coast.[1] The United Nations Commission on Korea made an immediate on-the-spot investigation, and on June 26 forwarded these conclusions to Secretary-General Trygve Lie: first, that the actual progress of the North Korean army's operations demonstrated a well-planned, concerted, and full-scale invasion of South Korea; second, that the South Korean forces had been deployed on a wholly defensive basis all along the 38th Parallel; and third, that they had been taken by complete surprise, since intelligence sources had not alerted them to the imminence of an invasion.[2]

Three days later the acting chairman of the commission furnished the United Nations Security Council with further supporting evidence. The day before the North Korean attack, United Nations field observers had returned from a trip along the 38th Parallel, and in their report they had concluded that the South Korean army was organized entirely for defense and was in no condition to carry out a large-scale attack against North Korean forces. This conclusion was based on a number of observations: that the parallel was guarded on the southern side by small bodies of troops located in scattered outposts, and that no concentrations of troops or massing for attack were visible at any point; that at "several points," North Korean forces were in "effective possession of salients on the south side of the parallel," but that there was no evidence that the South Korean army had taken any steps or made any preparations to eject North Korean forces from any of these salients. "So far as equipment of South Korean forces [are] concerned, in absence of armour, air support, and heavy artillery, any action with object of invasion would, by any military standards, be impossible . . . There is no indication of any extensive reconnaissance being carried out northward by the South Korean Army nor of any undue excitement or activity at divisional headquarters or regimental level to suggest preparation for offensive activity. Observers were freely admitted to all sections [at the] various headquarters including operations room." [3]

The attack upon South Korea came as a shock to the American government, for the Communist aggression took place in an area which the Administration had long considered as being of secondary strategic significance. This evaluation of Korea's contribution to American security had first been analyzed in 1947. In September of that year, the President had instructed Secretary of State Marshall to request the Joint Chiefs of Staff's estimate of the importance of further military occupation "from a point of view of military security of the United States." In his reply, Secretary of Defense Forrestal stated that the troops and bases in Korea were of minor strategic value for American security. The Joint Chiefs, of whom General Eisenhower was the unofficial chairman,[4] reasoned that in the event of war American troops stationed in Korea would constitute a military liability, since they could not be maintained on the peninsula without substantial reinforcements prior to the attack. Furthermore, any American offensive launched on the Asian continent would in all likelihood bypass Korea. If, of course, an enemy "were able to establish and maintain strong air and naval bases in the Korean peninsula, he might be able to interfere with communications and operations in East Asia, Manchuria, the Yellow Sea, Sea of Japan and adjacent islands." But such interference would require large air and naval forces in an "area where they would be subject to neutralization by air action. Neutralization by air action would be more feasible and less costly than large-scale ground operations."

The Joint Chiefs had, therefore, recommended that the 45,000 troops then stationed in Korea should be evacuated, since they could be used more profitably elsewhere. The withdrawal of these forces, they had concluded, would not impair the military position of the United States in the Far East "unless, in consequence, the Soviets establish military strength in South Korea capable of mounting an assault on Japan." [5] Although General MacArthur could not later recall whether he had "recommended" the withdrawal or had merely "concurred" in it, there could be little doubt that he had been in accord with this retraction of American power from the Asian mainland. For MacArthur, like the Joint Chiefs, had never favored the commitment of American ground troops to fight a land war on the continent of Asia; in his famous phrase, anyone who advocated such a course should have his head examined. Korea, in particular, was militarily vulnerable to Russian land power, and in a major war American forces would be trapped. Moreover, in September 1947, "There was nothing peculiarly threatening at that time in Korea when the decision was made to get out." [6] The result was that MacArthur too had excluded Korea from the American defense perimeter. "Now the Pacific has become an Anglo-Saxon lake and our line of defense runs through the chain of islands fringing the coast of Asia. It starts from the Philippines and continues through the Ryukyu archipelago which includes its broad main bastion, Okinawa. Then it bends back through Japan and the Aleutian Island chain back to Alaska." [7] Although MacArthur has since claimed that in delineating the United States defense perimeter he had merely been defining his responsibilities as prescribed for him by Washington, his statement does not seem to be in contradiction with the opinions he expressed during the Congressional inquiry investigating his dismissal.

Three specific reasons lay behind the Joint Chiefs' memorandum. First, the postwar economizing of the military budget left the United States with a widely dispersed skeleton military establishment which was threatened with even further cuts. The soldiers' professional reflex was to pull back their scattered units from exposed areas and concentrate them in a few areas of major strategic interest.

The limitation of military funds was imposed upon the Administration by the 80th Congress which convened in Washington on January 3, 1947. The Senate was divided into 51 Republicans and 45 Democrats, the House into 245 Republicans and 118 Democrats. The President and the Democratic party had been repudiated at the polls during the mid-term election. As the Representatives and Senators met for the new session of Congress, the question was not, as one writer phrased it, whether Mr. Truman would or could lead the United States to accept the burden of grave world responsibilities, but how far

Congress would roll back New Deal legislation, cut appropriations for the armed forces and foreign relief, and carry the United States back to prewar political and economic isolation.[8]

Republican intentions were stated by House Speaker Joseph Martin in his opening address to the assembled Representatives: a sufficient reduction in government expenditures to allow for a 20 per cent income-tax reduction. When it was rumored that the President would submit a $41 billion budget, Republican leaders suggested a minimum cut of $7 billion; and when the President submitted a $37.5 billion budget, Republicans denounced it as extravagant and proceeded to cut it down to size — $31.5 billion. Secretary of War Patterson warned that the proposed cut in the military budget might make it necessary to withdraw American troops from Germany and Japan; and James Forrestal, then Secretary of the Navy, announced that the cut would render the navy practically impotent. The House was not alarmed; neither was the Senate, although the Senate did restore $1.5 billion to the budget.

A few days after the Senate restoration, Senator Henry Cabot Lodge compared his party's ravenous attack upon the President's budget to "a man wielding a meat ax in a dark room [who] might cut off his own head." The army quickly fell victim to this ax. General Marshall recalled during 1951 that the army had been so small in the years before the outbreak of the Korean War that there were only one and one-third divisions in the United States; the Chiefs of Staff had so few troops at their command that they were even worried about obtaining enough men to guard air strips at Fairbanks, Alaska! "We had literally almost no military forces outside of our Navy and outside of an effective but not too large Air Force, except the occupation garrisons, and . . . even in Japan they were only at about 60 per cent strength."[9]

The second reason which accounted for the withdrawal of American forces from Korea was the Joint Chiefs' single-minded preoccupation with total war. This left Korea militarily dispensable within the global pattern of American security, since in an all-out war the fate of Korea would be decided in other theaters of war; Soviet occupation of Korea would not raise Korea's strategic significance since the peninsula could be neutralized by American air and sea power. This concentration of the Joint Chiefs on a total-war strategy was directly related to the congressional economy drive; for the legislative determination to pare military funds to a minimum and balance the budget forced each of the services to choose from among the available weapons those which would deter or win the ultimate and most calamitous contingency: total war. The resulting strategy of "massive retaliation" was based upon four assumptions: one, that the only form of future war would be a total war, which would be precipitated by a direct Soviet attack upon the United States or America's "first line of defense" in Western Europe; two, that deterrence or victory could be achieved by air striking power and its ability to inflict maximum damage and destruction; three, that the Russians would not risk the use of force, even in limited engagements, before they possessed a sizable atomic stockpile, sufficient means to deliver it, and an adequate defense against American bombers; and four, that the almost complete reliance upon one branch of one service was considerably less expensive than large balanced forces. Needless to say, this strategy warmed congressional hearts; but the result of this "bigger bang for a buck" policy was a severe cut in the navy's and particularly the army's strength.

The last reason for the Joint Chiefs' recommendation for an early evacuation of Korea was their fear that the continued lack of progress toward a free and independent Korea might in the coming months give rise to violent disorders which would place the occupation forces in an untenable position. "A precipitate withdrawal of our forces under such circumstances would lower the military prestige of the United States, quite possibly to the extent of adversely affecting cooperation in other areas more vital to the security of the United States." [10] In addition, as General MacArthur emphasized, the South Korean government had itself exercised considerable pressure for the removal of our military forces at the time.[11]

The State Department was receptive to the Joint Chiefs' recommendation: it accepted their argument about the danger of dispersion; it shared their predisposition to think of Korea's importance only in terms of a total-war strategy; it was well aware of the strong South Korean wish for an early end of the occupation; and it knew from the Soviet announcement in December 1948 that the Russians had withdrawn their troops from North Korea. If under these circumstances, the department had advocated the further maintenance of American forces in Korea, despite the almost unanimous desire of the South Korean people for an end of the occupation, the United States would have been placed in an untenable propaganda position.

It was left to Secretary Acheson to give public expression to the

Joint Chiefs' thinking in his celebrated speech before the National Press Club on January 12, 1950. He began by defining the American defense perimeter in the Pacific. It ran, he said, from the Aleutians (outside the Kuriles) [12] to Japan, through the Ryukyus (Okinawa) to the Philippines. In this strategic island chain, the United States possessed immediate responsibilities and the power to act. Beyond this defense perimeter, however, the United States had no specific obligations. Washington could not, therefore, guarantee areas lying outside this American chain against military attack; proposals to this effect were neither sensible nor necessary within the "realm of practical relationship." The Secretary did, however, qualify these remarks. While the United States could not furnish such nations the devotion, determination, and the will to fight, our assistance could be effective when it was the missing component in a situation that could otherwise be solved; under such circumstances, American help could lead to accomplishments which in its absence could not be achieved.

Should an attack, therefore, occur on areas outside the defense perimeter, the initial reliance had to be on the people attacked. Their resistance would spark the commitment of the entire civilized world acting under the Charter of the United Nations; and the charter, Acheson reminded his listeners, had not proven itself a weak reed to lean upon for any people who were determined to protect their independence against external aggression.[13]

In actual fact, the absence of pledged American military support to resist North Korean aggression left South Korea highly vulnerable. Her forces were only lightly armed; the United States had equipped them with neither tanks, heavy artillery, nor planes. These weapons were deliberately withheld because the Truman Administration believed that if the South Korean government of Syngman Rhee possessed them, it would attempt to carry out its oft-repeated threat to unify the country by force. But these weapons were also unfortunately the precise weapons which the Korean Republic's army would need to fend off a Communist attack. Even the military equipment that was to be furnished under the Mutual Defense Assistance Act of 1949 was only just beginning to be delivered at the time of the North Korean aggression. In short, South Korea's forces were prepared primarily for dealing with internal revolt, not with external assault; consequently, South Korea offered itself as an attractive vacuum for Communist expansion. In this context, Secretary Acheson's implied promise of aid through the United Nations was no barrier to Soviet temptation. The leaders in the Kremlin were aware that the United Nations could not act without American leadership; without American power, the international organization would be impotent. And American military strategy had already excluded South Korea from the defense perimeter.

Did Acheson's speech, then, "invite" the attack upon South Korea, as so many of the Secretary's critics charge? The very fact that the critics ask this question shows that they assume that if the Secretary had not publicly broadcast the outlines of the Pacific defense perimeter, the Soviets would have remained completely unaware of our decimated army, our preoccupation with total war, and inflexible military strategy; that they would not have learned of the Joint Chiefs' reluctance to commit their troops on the Asian continent, of the few troops at their command, and their emphasis upon stationing these troops in areas considered more vital to American security in an all-out war than Korea. The truth is that the Soviets would have been aware of these factors even if Secretary Acheson and General MacArthur had never publicly defined the defense perimeter. Both men were only verbalizing the basic American strategy of total war, in terms of which Korea was indeed outside the defense perimeter; both were expressing a military doctrine that had not calculated on the kind of military challenge with which the Communists faced the United States on June 25, 1950 — a less than all-out challenge by a Soviet satellite in Asia against an American friend, whose strategic importance was not "worth" the price of total war. In short, it was not American words but American policy that probably encouraged the Communists to believe that the United States would not defend South Korea. And in the formulation of this policy the Republicans too played their role, albeit a negative one.

North Korea's aggression thus caught the American government completely unaware — so much so, in fact, that the Administration received the first news of the attack not from the military personnel or foreign service officers in Korea, but from the United Press news service. The American government had for several months admittedly recognized the capability of the northern regime to strike southwards; and intelligence to this effect had been reported to the State Department by its own representatives, the Department of the Army, the Central Intelligence Agency, and the Far Eastern Command. But these agencies had not believed that the North Koreans intended an immediate attack; the Communists had not yet exhausted all the potentials of psychological and guerilla warfare, political pressure, and intimidation in their efforts to undermine the young Republic. Acheson cited that MacArthur's intelligence had reported the spring or summer of 1950 as possible dates for an invasion of South Korea; but each time the General had attached comments — even as late as March 25 — that such an attack was unlikely, and that the "most probable course of North Korean action this spring or summer is furtherance of its attempt to overthrow the South Korean Government by the creation of chaotic conditions in the Republic through guerrilla activities and psychological warfare." Fifteen days earlier, on March 10, MacArthur had noted that the Soviets "probably will be content to wait a while longer and let South Korea ripen for future harvest."

> Secretary Acheson . . . Therefore, you would have had reports that this attack was going to occur and the intelligence of the Far East believed that was not the case.
> Senator Bridges. Well [from October 12, 1949, to March 25, 1950], Mr. Secretary, the record shows — even the record that you read here shows — that they reported there was to be an attack in June, even though they did qualify it afterwards. That would be a fair analysis; would it not?
> Secretary Acheson. Not only qualified it; they said it is believed that it will not occur. That is a little more than a qualification.[14]

Louis A. Johnson, Secretary of Defense at the time the Korean War broke out, supported Acheson's testimony: "Wolf," he said, had been cried so often in the intelligence reports that it was difficult to know what to believe. Consequently, nothing had put "us on notice that anything was going to happen in Korea."[15]

Shortly after the North Korean attack, the columnists Joseph and Stewart Alsop wrote that "the Kremlin-sponsored attack on Korea has knocked the basic assumption underlying American policy into a cocked hat. This assumption was that the Kremlin was not now ready, and would not be ready for some years, to risk a world war. Yet the Kremlin has clearly and consciously risked a world war. This in turn means Washington had been mistaken about Soviet capabilities and intentions. Thus a new and unexpected situation has arisen."[16] In a similar vein, James Reston of the *New York Times* wrote that until June 25 the Administration had believed that the Russian leaders would limit their activities to the exploitation of domestic miseries and grievances but would "hesitate to use force, at least until they were at the top of their military strength, some time between 1952 and 1954." [17] American policy had been prepared only for an all-out challenge by a surprise Soviet attack upon the United States or Western Europe at some future date. It has not unjustly been claimed that if the Korean War had not broken out, American strategists would never have believed that a less than total challenge would have been possible.

The North Korean attack, therefore, presented the United States with an attack for which it was strategically unprepared. What would the Administration do? Was South Korea's independence "worth" the cost of total war? If not, could the United States respond to this limited challenge with an equally limited response? Had the Communists not actually faced the government with an unsolvable dilemma: either to respond by total war — which seemed unlikely — or not to respond at all? Were our divisions in Japan not under-manned and "undertrained"? Could Japan be left denuded of its occupation troops? And even if this risk were taken, could the forces reach Korea in time and in sufficient numbers to stop the speedy southward drive of the North Korean army? If this task were impossible, would it not be better to allow South Korea to fall and disclaim its "strictly military" importance, rather than sacrifice American troops and prestige in a battle that could not be won? To sum up, did Korea all of a sudden assume such vital importance in the pattern of American defense and security that it was worth the risk of committing MacArthur's troops?

Inherent in this question which suddenly confronted the Administration was the assumption that the Kremlin had deliberately and cold-bloodedly "unleashed" its puppet. Since there was no direct evidence to support this contention, however, it was at least logically possible that the North Koreans had initiated the attack without Russia's knowledge and blessings, and maneuvered the Soviet leadership into a position where it had no choice but to back their move. Several reasons might have been advanced to lend this point of view some credence. First, that outright aggression was a departure from the standard Soviet technique of seeking control through subversion; the United States government's own intelligence reports had shown that the Communists were generally successful in their campaign of undermining South Korea. Second, that only a few days before the outbreak of hostilities, a new South Korean legislature had assembled with a large anti-Rhee majority; there was thus the possibility that the Rhee government might soon be reconstituted and become more amenable to "negotiating" with the North Koreans over the question of unification. And third, that the Soviet Union was absent from the United Nations Security Council; it was, therefore, in no position to veto a possible American countermove.[18]

The Administration, by never considering these views, implicitly rejected them. It is not difficult to see why. It was, of course, true that the Rhee government was unpopular; the recent elections attested that fact. Similarly, it was widely known that the morale of the South Korean army was low and defection and desertion commonplace. As Hanson Baldwin, military correspondent of the *New York Times,* wrote a few days after the North Korean attack, the "questionable political and military reliability of the Army and police forces are the greatest weaknesses of the defending forces against Soviet domination." [19] In these circumstances, the attack was in accord with Communist political tactics — to use force to administer the *coup de grâce* to a nation whose people had already been sufficiently weakened by internal subversion, economic distress, and political instability. Moreover, it seems fantastic to suggest that the careful and long-range planning which preceded the well-coordinated invasion of South Korea could have entirely escaped the attention of the approximately 3,500-man Russian military mission; if the United States could prevent Syngman Rhee from launching a war against the Russian satellite, the Soviets with their far tighter control of the northern regime could surely prevent Kim Il Sung, North Korea's Premier, from initiating a massive invasion of an area in the American sphere of influence. Finally, the continued Soviet boycott of the Security Council proves less that the Russians had not intended the war than Russian confidence that the United States would not defend South Korea. The Soviet leaders had ample evidence to support this confidence; "if they interpreted America's conduct of foreign policy in terms of their own standards, they could hardly have reached any other conclusion than that the United States would acquiesce in a limited move of a satellite army into a minor strategic position, just as a chess player must accept the maneuver of a pawn when he is in no position to prevent it." [20]

The real point is not Soviet innocence but miscalculation. The attack upon Korea had at one stroke altered the whole basis upon which the Joint Chiefs of Staff had based their earlier recommendations. Their analysis of Korea's strategic value had been in terms of global warfare. But the cold war focused attention upon the wider political and military implications of a Communist occupation of South Korea and the threat that this would pose in the Far East.

John Foster Dulles, chief architect of the forthcoming Japanese peace treaty and the principal Republican adviser to the Secretary of State, saw these consequences clearly. According to his interpretation, the North Korean aggression was inspired by the Soviet desire to prevent the resurgence of Japan as a great industrial and military power on the side of the United States and the Western world. Since the Soviet Union held the Sakhalin Islands just to the north of Japan and Korea was close to Honshu, the southernmost island of Japan, Russia's strategic move would place Japan "between the upper and lower jaws of the Russian bear" — or, in the more deadly metaphor, Russia would point a dagger right at the heart of Japan.[21] This fear was reportedly shared by MacArthur's headquarters in Tokyo. At the time of the North Korean attack, Marguerite Higgins of the *New York Herald Tribune* wrote that thoughtful people in Tokyo believed the establishment of Communist power within one hundred miles of Japanese shores would encourage serious political disturbances.[22]

Mr. Dulles suggested further that, in his opinion, the Soviet leaders might have attempted to forestall Japan's rearmament because they believed that history might soon repeat itself. He recalled that during the Russo-Japanese War of 1904–1905, the Japanese, controlling Korea, had captured Port Arthur (150 miles to the west of Korea) and had threatened Vladivostok (75 miles to the east of Korea). "Russian analyses of the cause of Russia's failure in the war ascribe it largely to the very fact that Japan controlled the Korean peninsula. Ever since, Russian strategists sought that control for Russia." [23] But this objective might remain beyond their grasp if Japan were allowed to rearm in alliance with the United States; indeed, under these circumstances, they had to expect increased Japanese-American pressure on North Korea and China. The United States, as Dulles phrased it, "had turned from what had seemed a policy of drift, and we were developing policies which would give hope to these nations whose independence was endangered by a new form of international slavery." Referring to his recent trip to Japan with Secretary of Defense Johnson and General Omar N. Bradley, Mr. Dulles concluded that the United States had shown "that we did not admit that the Soviet had veto power over that future and could perpetuate a do-nothing policy which would enable communism to make great underground gains."

In 1949 continental China had fallen under the Communist domination. The United States was now bent upon the task of creating a situation of strength in the Pacific by rearming Japan. Could this Soviet attempt to undermine American policy in Asia, therefore, be allowed to go unchallenged? Mr. Dulles thought not. If the government could not hold and repulse the North Korean attack, American armed forces should be sent to their aid, "even though this risks Russian counter moves. To sit by while Korea is overrun by unprovoked armed attack would start a disastrous chain of events leading most probably to world war." [24]

President Truman and his advisers also saw the refusal of the United States to rescue South Korea as the beginning of a series of events which would inevitably end in global war; for to stand by while South Korea fell would demonstrate to the world that Washington was either afraid of Russian power or unconcerned for the safety of its allies and that its guarantees of help to preserve its allies' national integrity and political independence were valueless. Admittedly, no treaty of alliance had ever been signed between the United States and South Korea, but few could doubt that the youthful Republic was under American protection and that Washington had a moral obligation, if nothing else, to come to its assistance. The United States had pledged itself in Cairo in 1943 to establish an independent Korea after its liberation from Japan; although the Russians had two years later endorsed this Anglo-American promise at Potsdam, the sweep of Soviet military operations into Manchuria during the closing days of the war and the entry of Soviet forces into Korea two days after Japan surrendered on August 10, 1945, had made it impossible to fulfill these promises. The nearest American troops at the time were in Okinawa, 600 miles away, and in the Philippines, 1,500 to 2,000 miles away! The establishment of the 38th Parallel, therefore, originally decided upon for purposes of dividing the task of disarming the Japanese between the Russians and ourselves, at least preserved the freedom of South Korea.

In addition to this moral commitment, the United States shared its responsibility for the preservation of South Korea with the United

Nations. The State Department had first attempted to negotiate the implementation of the Cairo and Potsdam agreements on a bilateral basis; after this had failed, the department in late 1947 had presented the issue to the United Nations and called upon that organization to sponsor a free election throughout all Korea. The General Assembly had thereupon established a Temporary Commission on Korea and charged it with holding and supervising such an election; the Soviet refusal to grant the commission access to the northern half of the country had, however, limited the election to the lower part of the peninsula. Afterwards, the United States, Nationalist China, England, and France had recognized South Korea as the official Republic and had acknowledged the elected government of Syngman Rhee as its legitimate representative. The United States had also extended economic, technical, and military aid to bolster the non-Communist government and help the Korean people establish a democratic society.[25] As recently as two weeks before the invasion, Mr. Dulles had reaffirmed American responsibility for South Korea in a speech to the Korean Parliament:

The American people give you their support, both moral and material, consistent with your own self-respect and your primary dependence on your own efforts.

We look on you as, spiritually, a part of the United Nations which has acted with near unanimity to advance your political freedom, which seeks your unity with the north and which, even though you are technically deprived of formal membership, nevertheless requires all nations to refrain from any threat or use of force against your territorial integrity or political independence.

The American people welcome you as an equal partner in the great company of those who comprise the free world, a world which commands vast moral and material power and resolution that is unswerving. Those conditions assure that any despotism which wages aggressive war dooms itself to unutterable disaster.

The free world has no charter, but it is no less real for that. Membership depends on the conduct of a nation itself; there is no veto. Its compulsions to common action are powerful, because they flow from a profound sense of common destiny.

You are not alone. You will never be alone so long as you continue to play worthily your part in the great design of human freedom.[26]

The North Korean attack, therefore, presented the United States with a dilemma of "put up or shut up"; the Communist aggression was a test of the value of American promises. If under the threat of force the United States abandoned Korea, our European allies, ever alert to signs of a resurgent American isolationism, would believe that they too would be abandoned in a similar crisis. They would dismiss American treaty pledges as unreliable and turn to neutralism as a means of solving their predicament; in this state, they would be subject to increasing Russian pressure and eventual domination.

The President and Secretary of State were determined to forestall such a disaster for two reasons. First, Europe and its dependent areas provided the Strategic Air Command with bases. If these bases were lost, SAC's effectiveness would be greatly, perhaps fatally, reduced; for its supply of expensive intercontinental jet bombers was limited and its main reliance was placed on medium-range bombers. As late as July 10, 1951, SAC possessed only eighty-seven B-36 bombers ready for action; sixty more were being modernized and the production rate was only two or three a month.[27] Also, of course, the nearer the bases were located to the potential enemy, the less time it would take to destroy him, and the greater the savings on the wear and tear of planes and crews.

More important, American independence and security required that the United States maintain a balance of power in the interior of Europe to check any nation which possessed ambitions to conquer the sea-bordering states as a prerequisite to first eliminating England and then proceeding to world conquest. During most of the nineteenth century, this balance had been safeguarded by the English navy. During the twentieth century, as British power declined, the United States had been forced to fight two major wars to help England preserve this equilibrium. In the post-World War II days of long-range bombers, schnorkel submarines and guided missiles, the American stake in Europe was even more vital. Western Europe controlled the sea gateways vital to American security — the English Channel, the Skagerrak, and the Strait of Gibraltar; it possessed the largest number of skilled workers, technicians, and managers outside of the United States; it maintained the second greatest concentration of industrial power in the world; and lastly, it exercised control over most of the strategic raw materials the United States needed to maintain its military strength and capacity to wage war (rubber, tin, copper, zinc, mercury, cobalt, tungsten, chrome, graphite, and uranium). American security, therefore, demanded the preservation of the Western alliance.

If NATO were allowed to disintegrate, a radical shift would take place in the global balance of power — a decided shift toward Russia.

American security would then be at best very precarious and could be maintained only by the organization of our society as a "garrison state"— a condition incompatible with any interpretation of the "American way of life." At worst, it would place the United States at the mercy of a Soviet bloc in control of almost the entire Eurasian continent.

The implication of American inaction was thus very grave for the future of national security and independence, particularly since President Truman and his advisers saw in the North Korean attack an uncomfortable resemblance to the Nazi and Fascist aggressions of twenty years earlier; and their memory of the outcome of Britain's and France's attempts to appease Hitler and his fellow dictators — Munich and the Second World War — intensified their belief in the folly of leaving South Korea to fend for itself. As one reporter summed up the opinion of sources close to leading American officials: they "were certain that the North Korean attack was being viewed as a test of the countries, including the United States, that are standing up against Communist expansion. In such a light, the march across the North-South Korean border would appear similar to the attacks that Hitler used to make to feel out the opposition." [28] In short, the President and other top policy-makers viewed Stalin's challenge as a Hitlerian test of American determination and will-power to resist Communist military expansion; Korea was their "Rhineland." The analogy was decisive, for they believed that Stalin, like Hitler before him, would not be satiated if he were allowed to devour his single "situation of weakness" in peace; rather, his whetted appetite would proceed to devour other areas.[29]

From this generalized interpretation of dictatorial behavior, the President and his advisers drew the conclusion that if the Soviet challenge were not met, if the United States failed to measure up to the Russian test, the leaders in the Kremlin would have succeeded: in demonstrating to the world their own strength and resolution, and conversely, American fear and unreliability; in disintegrating the Western alliance; in forestalling the creation of a situation of strength in the Pacific; and in frightening the leaders of the neutralist nations of Southeast Asia and the Middle East. The resulting power vacuums would provoke further acts of aggression and render World War III inevitable — under the most trying of all circumstances: a heavily diminished political prestige, a shattered moral position, and a disadvantageous and isolated strategic position. A stand had, therefore, to be taken.[30] "Firmness now would be the only way to deter new actions in other portions of the world. Not only in Asia, but in Europe, the Middle East, and elsewhere the confidence of peoples in countries adjacent to the Soviet Union would be very adversely affected, in our judgment, if we failed to take action to protect a country established under our auspices and confirmed in its freedom by action of the United Nations. If, however, the threat to South Korea was met firmly and successfully, it would add to our success in opposition to the aggressive moves of the Communists. And each success, we suggested to our allies, was likely to add to the caution of the Soviets in undertaking new efforts of this kind. Thus the safety and prospects of the free world would be increased." [31] The commitment of American armed forces was inherent in this line of reasoning.

The President and all of his advisers were thus unanimously agreed that the North Korean invasion must be repulsed. There was from the beginning, in the President's words, an "almost unspoken acceptance on the part of everyone that whatever had to be done to meet this aggression had to be done. There was no suggestion from anyone that either the United Nations or the United States should back away from it. This was the test of all the talk of the last five years of collective security." [32] No one doubted that force would have to be employed. The only question was whether the South Korean army would be capable of halting the North Korean offensive with only American air and naval support or whether United States ground forces would also have to be committed to the battle. On the Sunday evening of the attack, June 25, Admiral Sherman, Chief of Naval Operations, and General Vandenberg, Air Force Chief of Staff, both thought that naval and air forces might suffice; General Collins, the Army Chief of Staff, said that troops would have to be employed if the South Korean army were destroyed.

No one, however, was yet sure whether the South Korean army needed such assistance; neither the President nor his advisers were that Sunday evening aware of the extent of South Korea's collapse. The President, therefore, directed General MacArthur to send a survey party to Korea to estimate the magnitude and character of the military effort which would be required of the United States to stop and repel North Korea's aggression. Meanwhile, the military situation was rapidly deteriorating. On Monday, General MacArthur informed the President: "South Korean units unable to resist determined North Korean offensive. Contributory factor exclusive enemy possession of tanks and fighter planes. South Korean casualties as an index to fighting have not shown adequate resistance capabilities or the will to fight and our estimate is that a complete collapse is imminent." The President immediately ordered MacArthur to use American air and naval power to support the South Korean army; American forces were, however, to limit their operations to the area below the 38th Parallel. News of this decision was officially released early next morning.[33]

On June 29, MacArthur flew to Korea to inspect the situation for himself. What he saw was disquieting. The South Korean army, he cabled Washington immediately upon his return to Tokyo, was in utter confusion. Its supplies and equipment had been abandoned or lost and its capacity for united action was lost. Consequently, a grave danger existed of a further breakthrough. "If the enemy advances continue much further, it will threaten the Republic." MacArthur added that the only assurance of holding the Han River line and regaining the lost territory was through the commitment of American ground combat troops; the continued utilization of the air force and navy was ineffective without the support of land forces. Accordingly, he stated, that if he received authorization, he would immediately move a United States regimental combat team to Korea as the nucleus of a possible build-up of two divisions for an early counteroffensive.[34]

Mr. Truman immediately gave his consent.[35] In an official press release on June 30, the President announced that he had lifted his previous restrictions on the air force and navy: "he had authorized the United States Air Force to conduct missions on specific military targets in Northern Korea wherever militarily necessary and had ordered a Naval blockade of the entire Korean coast." The release ended with this terse sentence: "General MacArthur has been authorized to use certain ground units." [36] All three branches of the American armed forces were now committed.

Uncertainty over the degree of the South Korean collapse was, according to several close observers of the Washington scene, not the only reason for the delay in committing American ground forces. Apparently, until June 29, Washington hoped that Moscow could be prevailed upon to withdraw the North Korean army. If Moscow had "unleashed" the North Koreans in the belief that the United States lacked determination to respond to its move, an American show of force would encourage the Soviets to pull their satellite back to the 38th Parallel, just as a French and British show of force in 1936 would have compelled Hitler to withdraw from the Rhineland. This aim had reputedly been the objective of the first United Nations Security Council resolution calling upon the North Koreans to withdraw, and of the President's statement the next day promising vigorous support for the Security Council's effort to terminate this serious breach of the peace. Mr. Truman's statement concluded with this significant paragraph: "Those responsible for this act of aggression must realize how seriously the Government of the United States views such threats to the peace of the world. Willful disregard of the obligation to keep the peace cannot be tolerated by nations that support the United Nations Charter." [37] Though the President's words were at the time widely interpreted in both the United States and in Western Europe as an indication of irresolution or aid short of war,[38] Beverley Smith was later told that the President had on the same morning walked over to the big globe in his office, pointed to Korea, and said: "This is the Greece of the Far East. If we are tough enough now, there won't be any next step."

The President's announcement on June 27 that he had ordered American air and naval forces to assist the South Korean forces was interpreted by the Alsop brothers along the same line: "The purpose of President Truman's decision is simply to persuade the Kremlin that the United States means what it says. It is hoped that the Kremlin, convinced that the United States means business, will soon call off its puppets." [39] Support for this point of view also comes from the strong note which the Administration sent to the Soviet government shortly after it had directed American forces into Korea. "In view of the universally known fact of the close relations between the Union of Soviet Socialist Republics and the North Korean regime, the United States Government asks assurance that the Union of Soviet Socialist Republics disavows responsibility for this unprovoked and unwarranted attack, and that it will use its influence with the North Korean authorities to withdraw their invading forces immediately." [40] According to one observer, who interviewed the leading officials who had participated in the decision to fight in Korea, this note was to "give Russia an opportunity to retire gracefully from the chessboard

in case it was sufficiently moved by the show of American determination." [41]

The Soviet Union did not, however, call off its satellite. Instead,
in its reply of two days later, the Russian government laid the blame
for the war on the provocation of the "South Korean authorities and
upon those who stand behind their back." It stated that it considered
the events in Korea to be part of the internal affairs of Korea, and it
declared its opposition to foreign intervention in the domestic concerns
of other nations.[42] Nevertheless, the Soviet note was received with
relief in Washington. In Secretary Acheson's opinion, it indicated that
the Soviet Union would not intervene in the war.[43]

The Russian note thereby opened the way for the commitment
of American ground troops, for it ended Washington's fear that the
attack on Korea was merely a diversionary action. "I wanted to take
every step necessary to push the North Koreans back behind the 38th
parallel," Mr. Truman recounted later. "But I wanted to be sure that
we would not become so deeply committed in Korea that we could not
take care of such other situations as might develop." The President's
natural concern lest that happen was enhanced by reports that the
Chinese Communists had been massing troops on the Chinese mainland opposite Formosa; that the Soviets were active near the Yugoslav
border; and the possibility that the Soviets might move against Iran,
Germany, and Northern Europe.[44]

The President's anxiety that the United States might not be able to
counter Russian thrusts into these other areas even inclined him
initially to accept Nationalist China's offer of 33,000 of its "best
equipped" troops — although these troops would require extensive
American logistical support. The employment of Chiang's troops in
Korea would minimize the commitment of American troops there and
allow them to be employed in other trouble-spots in case of emergency.
But Secretary Acheson urged that the Nationalist troops should concentrate on their task of defending Formosa; the Joint Chiefs also
opposed the acceptance of Chiang's offer because of the doubtful
value of his soldiers. The President gave in: "I was still concerned
about our ability to stand off the enemy with the small forces available
to us, but after some further discussion I accepted the position taken
by practically everyone else at this meeting [of June 30]; namely, that
the Chinese offer ought to be politely declined. I then decided that
General MacArthur should be given full authority to use the ground

forces under his command" — not merely the two divisions that Mac-Arthur had suggested in his cablegram of the day before, but all of the troops stationed in Japan.[45]

Thus the employment of "certain supporting ground units" was not decided upon until after the North Koreans had shown no inclination to halt their attack; not until after the Soviet Union had refused to "use its influence" with Pyongyang, but had at the same time shown no inclination to intervene or strike elsewhere; and finally, not until after Washington had received General MacArthur's personal estimate that the South Korean army had disintegrated and that the situation could be saved only by American troops.

Commitment of these American troops was the decisive step in stemming the North Korean advance. The brilliant and unorthodox defensive tactics employed to achieve this aim have nowhere been more dramatically described than by General MacArthur himself:

. . . I felt that it was entirely problematical whether we could save any remnants of the South Korean Army or establish any position in Korea.

My directives were to establish a beachhead in the neighborhood of Pusan and to take such steps as I felt I could within the means I possessed to support the Korean Government and help maintain the South Koreans.

I was reminded at the time that my resource for the time being was practically limited to what I had and that I must regard the security of Japan as a fundamental and basic policy.

I threw in troops from the Twenty-fourth Division by air in the hope of establishing a locus of resistance around which I could rally the fast retreating South Korean forces.

I also hoped by that arrogant display of strength to fool the enemy into the belief that I had a much greater resource at my disposal than I did.

I managed to throw in a part of two battalions of infantry, who put up a magnificent resistance before they were destroyed — a resistance which resulted, perhaps, in one of the most vital successes that we had.

The enemy undoubtedly could not understand that we would make an effort with such small force.

Instead of rushing rapidly forward to Pusan, which he could have reached within a week, without the slightest difficulty, he stopped to deploy his artillery across the Han River.

We had destroyed the bridges. It took him days to do that.

We gained 10 days by that process, before he had deployed in line of battle along the 150-mile front with Suwon as the pivotal point.

By that time, I had brought forward the rest of the Twenty-fourth Division, under General Dean. I gave him orders to delay the advance of the enemy until I could bring the First Cavalry Division and the Twenty-fifth Division over from Japan.

He fought a very desperate series of isolated combats in which both he, and a large part of that division, were destroyed.

By that time we had landed the Twenty-fifth Division at Pusan, and it was moving forward by rail. And we had landed the First Cavalry Division on the east coast, and they moved over and formed a line of battle. I do not think that the history of the war will show a more magnificent effort against what should have been overwhelming odds as those two divisions displayed.

By that time the Eighth Army Command had moved over under a very indomitable leader, General Walker. From that time on I never had the slightest doubt about our ability to hold a beachhead. And on July 19 in the first communiqué that I recall I issued, I predicted that we would not be driven into the sea.[46]

This communiqué was a tribute to both MacArthur and Truman: to the General's skill and daring in stemming the onrushing North Korean army by unorthodox means; and to the President's instinct to make the right decisions on the big issues. The North Korean army was well organized, trained, and lead; it had quickly shattered its opponent. Could American forces get to Korea in time and in adequate numbers to stem the North Korean drive? Were American troops sufficiently trained to hold and repulse the Communist army, part of which had been trained and tested during the Chinese civil war? If in the crucible of battle the answers to these questions had been in the negative, American prestige would have received a shattering blow. But the President acted, in the words of the *New York Herald Tribune* front-page editorial on June 28, "with magnificent courage and terse decision . . . This position had to be taken. The jubilation in the Soviet satellite press over the first successes of the Korean invasion, the dispirited reaction from all peoples who have looked to United States support in their battle for freedom, is sufficient indication of what would have been bound to follow if the United States had supinely accepted this as one more victory for Communist armed infiltration. The President has refused so to accept it; his is an act of statesmanship and this newspaper believes that it is a basic contribution toward genuine peace in our disturbed and distracted world." The overwhelming number of Americans agreed.

Actual commitment of American forces was authorized by two resolutions passed by the United Nations Security Council. The first of these was passed on June 25. Its purpose was to induce both parties to terminate their hostilities and to restore the *status quo,* for having noted that the armed attack upon the Republic of Korea constituted a breach of the peace, it called for the immediate cessation of hostilities and withdrawal of North Korean forces to the 38th Parallel, requested the United Nations Commission to submit its recommendations and to keep the Council informed of the resolution's implementation, and called upon all members to assist in the execution of the resolution and to refrain from giving assistance to the North Korean government.[47] This resolution did not, therefore, sanction the use of force. This was provided for in the second resolution, approved on June 27 and called by Warren Austin, the American Ambassador at the United Nations, the "logical next step." It noted that the North Korean authorities had not desisted from their attack upon South Korea, and therefore recommended that all member states "furnish such assistance to the Republic of Korea as may be necessary to repel the armed attack and to restore international peace and security in the area." [48]

Two events preceded the passage of the second resolution: the warning of the United Nations Commission in Korea to the Security Council on June 26 that its call for a cease-fire and withdrawal of North Korean troops might soon prove to have been an "academic" exercise; [49] and more important, President Truman's receipt on the same day of General MacArthur's first report predicting the "complete collapse" of the South Korean army. The President had immediately directed MacArthur to use American air and naval forces to support the South Korean troops. "The attack upon Korea makes it plain beyond all doubt that Communism has passed beyond the use of subversion to conquer independent nations and will now use armed invasion and war . . . A return to the rule of force in international affairs would have far-reaching effects. The United States will continue to uphold the rule of law." [50]

American forces were, in short, sent into Korea before the passage of the June 27 resolution recommending all United Nations members to furnish the assistance necessary to repel the North Korean attack. In this sense, the Security Council decision was merely a retroactive approval of a *fait accompli.* Nevertheless, in the American government's opinion, the failure of the North Koreans to comply with the Security Council's call of June 25 for a cease-fire and withdrawal of troops, and South Korea's imminent collapse, rendered immediate American armed assistance both legitimate and absolutely necessary. The spirit of the United Nations Charter came before the narrow legal interpretation of its articles.

Only the Soviet Union and its satellites questioned the American action: "It is known that the Government of the United States had started armed intervention in Korea before the session of the Security Council was summoned to meet on June 27, without taking into consideration what decision the Security Council might take. Thus the United States Government confronted the United Nations with a 'fait accompli,' with a violation of peace." The Russians also questioned the legality of the American move on the basis of Article 27, paragraph 3, of the United Nations Charter which read, "Decisions of the Security Council on all other (except procedural) matters shall be made by an affirmative vote of seven members including the concurring votes of the permanent members." The Soviets pointed out that two permanent representatives had, however, been missing: Communist China, "the legitimate representative of China," and the Soviet Union, who had absented herself in protest against the exclusion of Communist China. Thus, "the resolution which the United States is using as a cover for its armed intervention in Korea was illegally railroaded through the Security Council by a gross violation of the Charter of the United Nations organization. This only became possible because gross pressure by the United States Government on members of the Security Council converted the United Nations organization into a kind of a branch of the State Department of the United States, into an obedient tool for the policy of the American ruling circles, who acted as violators of peace." [51]

The American reply was that the permanent members, including the Soviet Union, had on many occasions in the past refrained from voting on substantive issues without raising any questions over the legality of the action taken. Abstention did not, therefore, constitute a veto; and absence, the State Department claimed, was equivalent to abstention. In any case, Article 28, paragraph 1, of the United Nations Charter obligated every member of the Security Council to have a representative present at all times so that the Council could function continuously. The Soviet Union could hardly violate this provision while at the same time benefiting from another section of the Charter. As to Communist China, a decision that it should replace Nationalist China as a permanent member on the Security Council could only be taken by the Council itself; the Council had not yet taken such a decision.[52]

The absence of the Soviet Union from the Security Council, therefore, made it possible for the Council to act quickly and arrive at its decisions without protracted debate; nevertheless, the logical assumption that the United States would not have responded to the Communist challenge in Korea if the Soviet Union had been present at the council table and cast a veto does not follow. If the North Korean attack were as grave a menace to American security as the President and his advisers claimed it was, and if the Communist aggression threatened to upset the balance of power in Asia and in Europe as the Administration contended it would, then the containment of Soviet expansion could hardly have been abandoned simply because of a Russian veto. If the Soviet Union had been present at the council table and cast a veto, the Western powers would probably have invoked Article 51, which allows for the individual and collective self-defense of United Nations members in case of United Nations inaction, and sought sanction for its action from a special session of the General Assembly. Prime Minister Clement Attlee suggested this very possibility in his statement to the House of Commons on July 5, 1950:

The ordinary principles of international law recognize that any State which is attacked has a right to defend itself, and that any other State has a right to assist the State which is the subject of aggression.

The Charter of the United Nations has not taken away this inherent right. On the contrary, it expressly states in Article 51 that "nothing in the present charter shall impair the inherent right of individual or collective self-defense if an armed attack occurs against a member of the United Nations, until the Security Council has taken the measures necessary to maintain international peace and security." It is true that Article 51 only mentions in this connection an armed attack against a member of the United Nations, and the Korean Republic is not a member. But the purpose of Article 51 is not to create a new right but merely to make it clear that an inherent right vested in every State is not prejudiced . . . The only limitation which is put on the right of self-defense (and the right to receive assistance from others) was that which it expressly states in the words "until the Security Council has taken the measures necessary to maintain international peace and security."

All the Powers which are parties to the North Atlantic Pact have recognized expressly that the right of collective self-defense referred to in Article 51 applies in the case of attacks against States which are not members such as Italy and Portugal . . . The broad principle is that all states may be endangered if the aggressor is allowed to get away with the fruits of aggression in any part of the world.[53]

The Prime Minister's words make it clear that the Korean War was undertaken by the United States and her allies to protect their *selective security,* to preserve the global balance of power against the Soviet

Union, and to prevent the disintegration of this republic's principal shield of defense, the North Atlantic Alliance. President Truman later emphasized that the American government had regarded "the Korean situation as a symbol of the strength and determination of the West." [54] It was no mere accident that of the fourteen nations whose troops were fighting in or on their way to Korea by the end of 1950, ten were allies of the United States and members of either NATO — or a group closely cooperating with NATO — or the British Commonwealth: Australia, Belgium, Canada, France (which then had 80,000 troops fighting in Indochina), Greece, the Netherlands, New Zealand, Turkey, the Union of South Africa, and the United Kingdom (which had 25,000 troops fighting in Malaya, considerable responsibilities in other parts of the world, and like France, had an economy which could not afford the same quantities of guns and butter as the American economy). Two more of the fourteen countries, Thailand and the Philippines, were close friends of the United States, one being in fact a vital link in the Pacific defense perimeter; the remaining two countries were Columbia and Ethiopia. [55]

The predominantly Western nature of this enterprise was further emphasized by the attitudes of three other groups toward North Korea's aggression. The first of these groups included the Latin American nations, most of whom of course endorsed the American decision, although they did not send more than token contributions because of their limited resources and more immediate domestic involvements. The second group embraced members of the Afro-Asian block who, while they expressed their disapproval of North Korea's use of force, were nevertheless determined not to become involved in the cold war. The last group consisted of the Soviet bloc, which condemned the American action as aggression, illegal and unwarranted interference in the internal affairs of Korea. [56]

Why then did the United States government seek United Nations authorization for its decision to fight in Korea? The answer seems to be twofold. First, the United Nations had been intimately concerned with the birth of the young state — as Ernest Gross, American deputy representative at the United Nations, stated, the North Korean attack was an "invasion upon a state which the United Nations itself, by action of its General Assembly, had brought into being. It is armed aggression against the Government elected under United Nations supervision. Such an attack strikes at the fundamental purposes of the United Nations Charter. Such an attack openly defies the interest and authority of the United Nations." [57] Second, one of the aims of United States foreign policy was to associate its cold war policies with the humanitarian and symbolic values of the international organization. It is traditional for nations to justify their policies in this manner; and this propensity is particularly marked in American policy. The American depreciation of power and unwillingness to recognize and accept power as a factor in human affairs makes it psychologically necessary to rationalize actions in the international arena in terms of ideological objectives and universal moral principles; American power must be "righteous power," used not for purposes of "power politics" and selfish national advantage, but for the peace and welfare of all mankind.

Thus the role of the United Nations was confined to authorizing and recommending action to its members, lending its good name to the Western powers' effort to contain the expansionist aims of the Kremlin, conferring its blessings on their undertaking, and allowing the United States and her allies to justify their policy in terms of the organization's global symbols. This function of the United Nations was by no means an unimportant one; perhaps it was an inevitable one, given the global character of the bipolar conflict between the Western powers and the Soviet bloc. But it must be recognized for what it was: a marginal role. In fact, the United Nations function was precisely the one which would have fallen to the international organization if the action in Korea had been undertaken under Article 51 of the Charter.

The important decisions during the Korean War were arrived at not in Lake Success, but in Washington, Tokyo, and after Communist China's intervention, in London. Arnold Wolfers has realistically emphasized that "the character of the action in Korea must be judged by the decisions and acts of the United States and its associates. It would seem permissible, in fact, to concentrate on the conduct of the United States, because the other nations which made contributions to the defense of South Korea might conceivably have done so as friends and allies of the United States . . ." [58] Nowhere is this predominantly American influence better demonstrated than in the influence of American domestic politics on the unilateral American decision to neutralize Formosa, or more aptly symbolized than in the appointment of General Douglas MacArthur as the United Nations Commander.

III

DOMESTIC POLITICS AND FORMOSA;
THE REPUBLICAN DRANG NACH WESTEN

The Korean War was from the beginning deeply embroiled in American politics. The reason was that since late 1949 and early 1950 the American people had become increasingly dissatisfied with the Administration's foreign policy. This dissatisfaction, which lent itself dramatically to partisan exploitation, was the product of four circumstances: the containment policy, which was emotionally and psychologically incompatible with the traditional American approach to foreign relations; the collapse of Chiang Kai-shek's Nationalist government, which convinced many Americans of the failure of Administration policy — a conviction which was shortly to be confirmed by Russia's explosion of her first atomic bomb and the outbreak of the Korean hostilities; the resumption of the foreign policy leadership of the Republican party by the conservative and predominant wing of the party in the two houses of Congress; and the strong belief of this orthodox wing that the opposition party's real business was to oppose, on both domestic issues and foreign affairs. The result: the American people in 1950 felt and expressed an intense bitterness against the Administration for having involved them in a cold war to which no one saw a speedy conclusion and for having pursued a containment policy which in Asia seemed to have failed miserably. After a lengthy isolation from world affairs, there were naturally strong feelings of nostalgia for the more carefree days before World War II; the public's disposition was to complain and criticize. By articulating these complaints and criticisms, the Republican opposition garnered widespread popular support because it expressed incisively the mood of frustration, weariness, doubt and fear of the American people. The vital decisions of the Korean War were thus bound to be affected by this interplay between party politics and the people's mood.

Much of the frustration was undoubtedly the result of the people's adjustment to their new role of world leadership. Traditionally, the United States had whenever possible abstained from involvement in foreign affairs. Attention had instead been focused on domestic development. The business of America had been America — not foreign countries. Occasionally, of course, foreign affairs had interrupted this intense preoccupation with domestic concerns. Then the matter had been quickly settled: if a Latin American state "misbehaved," a few thousand marines soon "corrected" the misdeeds of the offender; or if, as in this century, Germany twice set out to conquer continental Europe, the nation harnessed all its resources, maximized its military strength, and crushed the enemy in the shortest possible time. Whatever the technique employed, the main point was that the conflict was settled quickly and completely. Only if the external crisis were solved immediately and totally could the American people return to their more important tasks: internal development and earning a livelihood; in this context, foreign affairs were regarded as an annoying — but only temporary — diversion.

Containment ran directly contrary to this national experience in foreign policy. The Administration's aim was not the destruction of Russia and its satellites, but the creation of a balance of power to effect the "containment" of further Soviet attempts to expand. The objective of the United States government was not to erase the Soviet Union by a swift war, but to accept the basic fact of coexistence. Truman and Acheson sought only to strengthen the United States and its allies in order to improve the terms of coexistence and possibilities of survival, not to end the Soviet threat once and for all. And they sought to achieve these aims not by war but through costly economic means; and not alone, but with the aid of allies who were not always in agreement with American policy and at times even in opposition to it.

Emotionally, this policy was frustrating because it was "defensive" and "negative," leaving the initiative to the Soviet Union. To be sure, the short-term aim of containment was to deter the Russian leaders from attempting to achieve world domination by resort to total war and to lead them instead to the negotiating table to settle all outstanding East-West differences; and the long-term objective was to increase the stresses and strains within Soviet society to such a degree that its leaders would have to moderate their aims or witness the disintegration of their political system. But actually these two aims were coincidental. The Administration did not expect to achieve the first objective before the realization of the second objective. To negotiate with the Russians, Secretary Acheson said in February 1950, was like dealing with a force of nature. "You can't argue with a river, it is going to flow. You can dam it up, you can put it to useful purposes, you can deflect it, but you can't argue with it . . . so far as agreement is concerned, I think we have discovered that even the simplest thing growing out of the war, which is to make peace . . . has become impossible." In short, only negotiations could end the cold war; and the cold war could not be ended until the Communists had in effect ceased being Communists. The Soviet threat thus promised to be a lasting one! [1]

The frustrations of containment were bad enough; but failures made it intolerable. This was especially the case with China. Americans had long regarded China as their special ward. Whereas American foreign policy toward Europe during the last fifty years had been limited to two short but decisive military interventions occasioned by Germany's threats to the European balance of power, American involvement in the Far East, and particularly in China, had been active since the turn of the century. The original interest in China had not been political but commercial; China had promised to be a huge market for American products. But our policy toward China had not been devoid of a large element of altruistic intent: a genuine interest in the welfare and Christian salvation of the Chinese people. In fact, the United States had long regarded itself as the protector of China from foreign exploitation and invasion. Through the Open-Door policy, whose aim had been to prevent Great Britain, France, Russia, Germany, and Japan from shutting out American commerce and to obtain an equal opportunity to sell on the Chinese market and invest in the Chinese economy, the United States had become politically committed to preserve the territorial integrity and political independence of China. But the American people had never been prepared to fight for this objective. The result had been that the United States had really failed to protect China from external pressures and invasions: the Russians had established a sphere of influence in Manchuria about 1900; the Japanese had replaced the Russians as the actual rulers of this strategic area after the Russo-Japanese War. During and after World War I, Japan had expanded its influence and control over China, and in 1931 Japan had initiated the Sino-Japanese War to consummate its long-run ambition to turn China into a Japanese vassal or colony. The Open-Door policy, then, had been largely a verbal policy which the United States had never intended to support by military means. Americans had never understood, however, that words by themselves had been insufficient to preserve the political independence of China — indeed, that since they had been unprepared to fight for this aim, the United States had usually disregarded this commitment whenever Russia or Japan had challenged it. Americans had even then believed that words were a substitute for an effective policy; out of this arose the illusion that the United States had long been China's protector and friend, extending to the Chinese people the bountiful benefits of Western Christianity, political ideals, science, and medicine.

Americans were, therefore, shocked by Chiang Kai-shek's collapse in 1949 and the Communist control of the Chinese mainland. They were totally unprepared for the propaganda emanating from Peking accusing the United States of being "the Chinese People's Implacable Enemy . . . a Corrupt Imperialistic Nation, the World Center of Reaction and Decadence . . . a Paper Tiger and Entirely Vulnerable to Defeat." They had expected that a "loyal" and fundamentally democratic China, grateful to America for past protection and help, would emerge from World War II as a strong friend of this country, and a powerful and reliable ally in the Far East. The failure of these expectations, as announced in the State Department's White Paper on China in August 1949, came as a deep shock to the American public — a shock which was all the deeper since the Administration had failed to prepare public opinion for this disaster. All of a sudden, the relative security which had been founded on the successful application of containment to Europe — the Truman Doctrine, the Marshall Plan, and the Berlin Airlift — seemed to have disintegrated. It seemed as if the United States had stemmed the Communist menace in Europe only to allow it to effect a breakthrough in Asia. The resulting insecurity and anxiety was further heightened by two other events: the news in September 1949 that Russia had exploded her first atomic bomb and thereby shattered the American monopoly of the weapon widely regarded as the principal deterrent to a Soviet attack; and the conviction in early 1950 of Alger Hiss — followed shortly thereafter by other revelations of espionage by Klaus Fuchs and Judith Coplon — which suggested continued Soviet espionage in high places.

Coinciding with these events was the decline of bipartisanship in foreign affairs. "For some time," the Washington *Star* noted in an editorial in late 1949, "there has been a restless stirring in the Republican ranks, a rising revolt against the 'me-tooism' which some hold responsible for the succession of G.O.P. disasters at the polls. And there is more than a suspicion that some influential Republicans have been playing with the idea of carrying this revolt to the extent of junking the bipartisan foreign policy in the hope that some partisan advantage could be salvaged from the resulting discord." [2] Senator Arthur H. Vandenberg, the leading advocate of such bipartisan cooperation, in a letter to his close friend and foreign policy adviser, John Foster Dulles, detected the same tendency within GOP ranks. He was "getting sick and tired," Vandenberg wrote, "of the increasingly persistent attempts to support the fiction that bipartisan foreign policy is entirely 'me-too' on the part of its Republican participants." The Senator thought this idea clearly mistaken:

> To me "bipartisan foreign policy" [he wrote to a constituent on January 5, 1950] means a mutual effort, under our indispensable two-Party system, to unite our official voice at the water's edge so that America speaks with maximum authority against those who would divide and conquer us and the free world. It does not involve the remotest surrender of free debate in determining our position. On the contrary, frank cooperation and free debate are indispensable to ultimate unity. In a word, it simply seeks national security ahead of partisan advantage. Every foreign policy must be *totally* debated . . . and the "loyal opposition" is under special obligation to see that it occurs.[3]

Nonetheless, despite Vandenberg's ideas, his removal from the Senate through illness, together with the defeat of Senator Dulles in a special New York election, left the congressional leadership of the Republican party on matters of foreign policy and the determination of electoral strategy for the coming mid-term election in the hands of the traditional and predominantly middle-western conservatives, who constitute the majority of Republicans in Congress.[4]

Ever since 1948, these leading Republican politicians of the party's orthodox wing, headed by Senators Robert Taft, Kenneth Wherry, and Styles Bridges, had attributed the defeat of Thomas E. Dewey's presidential aspirations to his "me-tooism" in domestic and international affairs. These men were convinced that policies which bore the Administration's trademark were credited by the electorate to the party in power and not to the opposition which had supported them. Three lost presidential elections seemed to them sufficient proof.

Consequently, they believed that the politically profitable course was not to support the President's various programs but to attack them, and thereby to develop an alternative set of measures to submit for the voters' approval at the next election. Nor was their conviction that the opposition's real business is opposition limited to matters of domestic concern; for they did not believe that they were likely to capture a clear and conservative majority in Congress — or put one of their own kind into the White House — on the strength of their conservative domestic record. They were thus eager to discover and exploit issues of foreign policy. Twenty years of opposition added to this eagerness. The frustrations of containment, the fall of China, the loss of the atomic monopoly — soon to be followed by the Korean War — made it easy to exploit the public's fears, doubts, and anxieties during the second session of the 81st Congress.

This determination to attack the foreign policy record which the Administration had built up with the cooperation of Senator Vandenberg and liberal Republicans was, however, the offspring of more than political expediency and hunger for office. It was also a matter of strong conviction; for the conservative elements in the Republican party were absolutely convinced that the "New Deal" Democratic majority aided by the eastern wing of their own party were destroying the political and economic foundations of the country, and that this process could be halted and reversed only by the restoration to power of the heirs and custodians of the "true" Republican tradition.

This tradition embodied the philosophy of nineteenth-century liberalism: a belief in a strong legislature and a weak executive, in a maximum of political and economic freedom and a balanced budget; it abhorred Big Government which gave the executive branch the power to intervene in business; it disapproved of high taxes which allegedly destroyed the spirit and initiative of private enterprise; and it equally opposed large government expenditures and the threat of inflation which purportedly provided the government with an additional pretext for the imposition of controls on the economy. To the Taft Republicans the preservation of their ideal, the late nineteenth-century American political and economic system, was the necessary prerequisite to all foreign and domestic policies and legislation. Since they were firmly convinced that an active and costly foreign policy bred Big Government, a strong presidency, high taxes, and economic controls even more powerfully than the New Deal, they opposed both;

indeed, they tended to see both as Democratic plots to destroy the private enterprise which they saw as the foundation of America's greatness and as Democratic means to substitute a socialist economy and political dictatorship for the traditional democratic system.

Consequently, the orthodox Republicans did not first assess the international situation and then decide whether American security could afford to dispense with greatly increased national expenditures for economic and military aid, large-scale rearmament, or a greater exercise of the President's discretionary powers; they simply assumed that America and the Western hemisphere were essentially secure and self-sufficient. To have assumed otherwise would have been tantamount to accepting the Democratic contention that the United States was *not* secure, and that the nation could achieve a measure of security only through the possession of a powerful and expensive military establishment, the adherence of allies who however needed economic aid to help them recover from the destruction of World War II, and an active foreign policy, formulated and executed by a strong President. Conservative Republicans could not accept this Administration viewpoint; for to have done so would have compelled them to vote for measures which, because they taxed the economy "too" much or extended the President's powers "too" far — the "too" being defined at a low order of magnitude — they considered a threat to the American economy and democracy. Thus, to preserve the foundations of the American political and economic system, "true" Republicans would have to replace the "internationalists" who now dominated both the legislative and executive branches; the term "internationalists" applied not only to Democrats but also to the liberal Republicans, whom the orthodox regarded as heretics.

That the conservatives in the Republican party should turn their attention to the Administration's Far Eastern policy in preparation for the November election is hardly surprising. The China issue was particularly attractive for domestic exploitation, since the Republicans had remained uninvolved in the Administration's formulation of policy. For the most part, American policy toward China had been conducted by the executive branch — during World War II by President Roosevelt, and afterwards by General Marshall. Republicans, by not being consulted, were thereby allowed to stand aside and wait for the Administration to make mistakes that could be profitably exploited. Periodically, the GOP politicians would, of course, remind the public that they were not being consulted and go on record for substantial aid to Chiang; but purportedly they knew full well that the Administration, deeply involved in the reconstruction of Europe, would hesitate to spend too many of its precious dollars in a situation which it deemed had been rendered beyond help by Chiang Kai-shek's own ineptitude.[5] Bipartisanship was therefore limited to Europe; the result was that at each turn in their China policy the Democrats handed their opponents an issue of great political capital.

Not that the Administration's explanation of Chiang's collapse lacked persuasiveness. The United States, it claimed, had done all in its power to bolster Chiang's position. It had supplied him with approximately two billion dollars in grants and credits since V-J Day; this total had not even included the one billion dollars of military and civilian surplus stock which the Nationalists had procured for $232,-000,000.[6] "It has been urged," the State Department declared editorially in its White Paper on China, "that relatively small amounts of additional aid — military and economic — to the National Government would have enabled it to destroy communism in China. The most trustworthy military, economic, and political information available to our Government does not bear out this view . . . Our military observers on the spot have reported that the Nationalist armies did not lose a single battle during the crucial year of 1948 through lack of arms or ammunition."

Chiang, according to this official explanation, had only himself to blame for his predicament. He had failed to eliminate the extensive corruption and incompetence in his administration; he had refused to reform his government along democratic lines and curb the arbitrary activities of the secret police; and he had been incapable or unwilling to carry out certain long overdue social reforms, particularly land redistribution and a lowering of the excessive tax burden which fell almost exclusively on the peasants. The State Department recalled the words that Lieutenant General Albert C. Wedemeyer, the staunch supporter of the Chinese Nationalist leader, had spoken to the Chinese in 1947:

I believe that the Chinese Communist movement cannot be defeated by the employment of force. Today China is being invaded by an idea . . . The only way in my opinion to combat this idea successfully is to do so with another idea that will have stronger appeal and win the support of the people. This means that politically and economically the Central Government will have to remove corruption and incompetence from its ranks in order to provide justice and equality and to protect the personal liberties of the Chinese people, particularly the peasants. To recapitulate, the Central Government cannot defeat the Chinese Communists by the employment of force, but can only win the loyal, enthusiastic, and realistic support of the masses of the people by improving the political and economic situation immediately. The effectiveness and timeliness of these improvements will determine in my opinion whether or not the Central Government will stand or fall before the Communist onslaught.[7]

Chiang had failed to heed these wise words of his friend. The consequence was that he alienated the sympathy and support of the Chinese people and left them no alternative but to turn to the Communists for relief from their poverty and misery. As Secretary Acheson summed it up, the Kuomintang's "leaders had proved incapable of meeting the crisis confronting them, its troops had lost the will to fight, and its government had lost popular support. The Communists, on the other hand, through a ruthless discipline and fanatical zeal, attempted to sell themselves as guardians and liberators of the people. The Nationalist armies did not have to be defeated; they disintegrated." History had again proven that "a regime without faith in itself and an army without morale cannot survive the test of battle." Acheson's conclusion was clear and succinct: "The unfortunate but inescapable fact is that the ominous result of the civil war in China was beyond the control of the government of the United States. Nothing that this country did or could have done within the reasonable limits of its capabilities could have changed that result; nothing that was left undone by this country has contributed to it. It was the product of internal Chinese forces, forces which this country tried to influence, but could not. A decision was arrived at within China, if only a decision by default." [8]

The validity of the Administration's explanation of Chiang's collapse may be left to the historian; we need only note that the Administration had committed one grave error which left it open to partisan attack. At no time had it associated leading Congressional Republicans with its policy regarding China. It would have been wise to have done so for two reasons. First, this would have enabled the Administration to forestall the massive assault upon its China policy; Republicans could hardly have launched a full-scale attack upon a policy which they had helped formulate. Second, such cooperation would probably not have wrought fundamental changes in American policy, since few of the most prominent Republicans in Congress had any constructive alternative program to offer. In a report which he had submitted in 1948 to the Senate Foreign Relations Committee, Senator Vandenberg had called China a "maze of imponderables," and declared that it was impossible to know the quantity and type of aid necessary to restore a stable and independent China. After Mr. Truman's re-election, Vandenberg re-emphasized this point when he wrote that the situation in China had deteriorated "to such a tragic extent that it is exceedingly difficult to know just what we can *effectively* do at this final moment in the crisis. The mere appropriation of money . . . is sheer waste of our substance. Furthermore . . . the Nationalist Government has failed to reform itself in a fashion calculated to deserve continued popular confidence over there or over here." And when former Republican presidential candidate Alf Landon denounced bipartisan cooperation for stilling Republican voices on China, Vandenberg answered that "Mr. Landon may be of the opinion that we 'gulled' Republicans should have yelled our heads off about China and the Generalissimo during the past year or two, but in my opinion it would only have precipitated and underscored a discussion of Chiang's weaknesses and would have nullified any remnant of his prestige. It is easy to sympathize with Chiang . . . But it is quite a different thing to plan resultful aid short of armed American intervention with American combat troops (which I have never favored and probably never shall)." [9]

These observations by Senator Vandenberg show that his evaluation of Chiang's effectiveness and morale was similar to that of the Administration; and that the Administration's failure to formulate and implement its China policy in the same bipartisan fashion as its policy toward Europe was a cardinal error. Not until late 1948 or early 1949, when it was too late to save Chiang, did the critics of the China policy raise their voices and call for a vast new aid program. If before this time, President Truman and Secretary Acheson had sought the cooperation of Senator Vandenberg and his followers, Senators Taft, Wherry, Bridges, and Knowland would not have been in such an advantageous political position to attack the Administration's policy after it had become apparent that it was too late to help Chiang; orthodox Republicans could no more have launched a frontal assault upon an unsuccessful bipartisan Chinese policy than upon a successful bipartisan European policy.

It may be quite correct, as Secretary Acheson observed, that the

United States did everything within "reasonable limits of its capabilities" to bolster the position of the Nationalist government, and it may be quite true that the American people would in all likelihood have refused to sanction the measures necessary to ensure Chiang's survival — the spending of large additional sums of money, the command of the Nationalist army by American officers, and the probable intervention in China of remobilized American land, sea, and air forces. But at no time had the Administration shown itself willing to debate openly the importance of China within the pattern of American security as it had debated the importance of Europe within the scheme of American defense; at no time was the American public given the opportunity to discuss the issues and weigh the alternatives. If it had been afforded that chance and if Acheson's estimate of the willingness of the American people to support such a program had then proven correct, the Administration, after Chiang's downfall, would have possessed the freedom of action to initiate its new policy toward Communist China — namely, to exploit the alleged clash of national interest between Communist China and Soviet Russia and turn this conflict to the United States' advantage.

The possibility of converting Mao Tse-tung to Mao Tse-tito had first been advanced by the majority of the American Far Eastern "experts" who met at the State Department in early October 1949 to advise the Secretary on a new policy toward Communist China. They had held that "the burden of proof that communism in China is merely another brand of Russian is on the person who makes that allegation." The Chinese Communist government, they predicted, would be "distinctly Chinese." Only Bernard Brodie, whose major interest is weapons technology and military strategy rather than Far Eastern politics, argued that the postwar experience with Communism in Europe had shown that the cultural pattern of a people upon whom Communism is imposed had very little relevance, since Communism relied heavily on coercive techniques. He advocated that the United States, therefore, face up to the unpleasant fact of conflict with a powerful Sino-Soviet bloc.[10]

Secretary Acheson presented the Administration's official thinking on the China problem in a speech which he delivered on January 12, 1950, before the National Press Club. During the course of his address, the Secretary declared that American policy toward China was based upon the traditional principle that any nation violating the integrity of China was an enemy of the people of China and acting in a manner contrary to our interests. This doctrine was still the "first and the greatest rule in regard to the formulation of American policy toward China," and it reflected America's concern for the national freedom and independence of the Asian countries. The Secretary stressed that this concern was not the product of a mere anti-Communism but of a deep and historic faith in the dignity and right of all nations and peoples to develop in their own way, to make their own errors, and to reach their own triumphs.

This common faith in national independence, Secretary Acheson said, forged the chief link between the United States and Asia. But Russia had long cherished ambitions which encroached upon this freedom. "The attitude and interest of the Russians in north China, and in . . . other areas as well, long antedates communism. This is not something that has come out of communism at all. It long antedates it. But the Communist regime has added new methods, new skills, and new concepts to the thrust of Russian imperialism. This Communist concept and techniques have armed Russian imperialism with a new and most insidious weapon of penetration."

Soviet imperialism did not constitute a menace solely to the non-Communist nations of Asia; it presented a dire threat even to Communist China. The central theme of Secretary Acheson's speech was the conflict of interests between Russia and China. His basic supposition was that, irrespective of the ideological character of the regime ruling China, the traditional geopolitical conflict between the two neighbors would continue. The Kremlin, armed with new powers, "is detaching the northern provinces [areas] of China from China and is attaching them to the Soviet Union. This process is complete in outer Mongolia. It is nearly complete in Manchuria, and I am sure that in inner Mongolia and Sinkiang, there are very happy reports from Soviet agents to Moscow." Secretary Acheson emphasized that "this fact that the Soviet Union is taking the four northern provinces of China is the single most significant, most important fact, in the relation of any foreign power with Asia."

This analysis indicated that the United States must disentangle itself from Chinese politics, and thereby forestall the growth of anti-American sentiments among the Chinese people. Chinese attention would then focus on the detachment of the northern provinces from their country, and the attachment of these areas to the Soviet Union. These Russian actions would unveil Soviet purposes more fully than any American speeches; they would unmask Communism as an agent of Russian imperialism. ". . . We must not seize the unenviable position which the Russians have carved out for themselves," said the Secretary of State. "We must not undertake to deflect from the Russians to ourselves the righteous anger, and the wrath, and the hatred of the Chinese people which must develop." [11]

Acheson predicted that Russia's appetite for a sphere of influence in Manchuria and Northern China would alienate Chinese nationalism. The long-run implications of this thesis are enormous. The first of these implications maintains that if Peking were genuinely concerned with the preservation of China's national interest, it would resist Soviet penetration. Mao Tse-tung, chairman of the Chinese Communist party, might therefore be a potential Tito. The second implication of the Secretary's speech was that if Mao Tse-titoism failed to develop, if Mao and his colleagues remained subservient to Soviet Russia, they would lose the support of the Chinese people. Since its leaders had shown that they served not the interests of China but those of another nation they would be identified with foreign rule. This "foreign domination," Acheson said, was still hidden behind the façade of a crusading movement, whose roots were indigenous and national. But given time, "the profound civilization and the democratic individualism of China will reassert themselves and she will throw off the foreign yoke." [12] Whichever of these two developments occurred, the United States could only gain from the antithesis between Communism and Chinese nationalism.

This policy could not, of course, be initiated with any degree of success until the United States had dissociated itself from Chiang's government and Formosa had fallen. Until that point the United States would remain identified, however slightly, with Chiang. The first attempt of the Administration to disengage itself from Chiang came with the release of the White Paper, which argued that the Nationalist government had lost control of the Chinese mainland despite adequate American economic and military aid. The clear implication was that, since Chiang was no longer worthy of American support, American recognition of Chiang's government as the official government of China should be withdrawn; conversely, that the Chinese Communists should be recognized as the official government, both as a matter of fact and as a gesture of friendship. In a closed meeting with the Senate Foreign Relations Committee in early January 1950, Acheson apparently sounded its members out on a number of problems, one of which was the recognition of Communist China. The Secretary of State emphasized that the Communists now controlled all of China except a few isolated areas. Partly because he was unsure whether the new government would protect the safety of American citizens and live up to its obligations under international law, and partly no doubt to soothe his listeners, Acheson suggested that there was "no need for haste in recognizing" China's new leaders.[13]

Actually, Acheson expected time and events to take care of the problem of recognition. These would have left the Chinese Communists as the only rulers of China, since Formosa was expected to fall during 1950. From October 1948 to January 1950, Acheson later testified, the United States had not possessed sufficient troops to commit to the defense of the island, even though its strategic importance was recognized. The policy was, therefore, that the State Department should try, by diplomatic and economic means, to keep Formosa from falling into hostile hands; but by August 1949 even this policy was no longer possible.[14] The Joint Chiefs of Staff supported the State Department estimate that while Formosa had strategic importance for the United States, its significance was not sufficient to warrant occupation by American troops. On October 12, 1949, a unanimous interdepartmental opinion among the Army, Navy, Air Force, and State Department concluded that Formosa would be conquered by the Chinese Communists before 1950 had reached its end.[15] Colonel McCann of the Central Intelligence Agency even expressed the belief that the Communists could take over the island without a full-scale invasion. Two factors, in the Agency's opinion, offered the Communists fruitful ground for their subversive techniques: first, the lack of discipline and low morale of the Nationalist troops, the result of past defeats and inadequate leadership; second, Chiang's administration of the island since V-J Day earned him the "earnest hatred" of the population.[16]

After the Nationalists had in December 1949 deserted the Chinese mainland for Formosa, however, Secretary of Defense Johnson requested the Joint Chiefs of Staff to review the Formosa situation, and they recommended the sending of a fact-finding commission to the island. The State Department disagreed with the Defense Department proposal: "We took the attitude," Secretary Acheson said, "that since the very statement of our problem indicated that this could not be successful, and that only the interposition of armed forces of the United States could save the island, what we would be doing would be making an effort here which was by hypothesis ineffective, and we would involve ourselves with further damage to our prestige and to our whole position in the Far East." [17] Consequently, on December 22, the President told Secretary Johnson that while he "did not disagree with the military considerations . . . he wasn't going to argue with me about the military considerations but that on political grounds he would decide with the State Department." [18]

A week later, the National Security Council formally recommended this decision to the President. President Truman made his decision public on January 5, 1950:

> The United States has no predatory designs on Formosa or any other Chinese territory. The United States has no desire to obtain special rights or privileges or to establish military bases on Formosa at this time. Nor does it have any intention of utilizing its armed forces to interfere in the present situation. The United States Government will not pursue a course which will lead to involvement in the civil conflict in China.
> Similarly, the United States Government will not provide military aid or advice to Chinese forces on Formosa. In the view of the United States Government, the resources on Formosa are adequate to enable them to obtain the items which they consider necessary for the defense of the Island. The United States Government proposes to continue under existing legislative authority the present ECA program of economic assistance.[19]

Secretary of State Acheson elaborated on these remarks during a press conference held later the same day. He explained that the President's phrase "at this time" did not qualify, modify, or weaken the fundamental policies set forth in the rest of the President's declaration. It was a recognition of the fact that, in the unlikely and unhappy event that our forces might be attacked in the Far East, "the United States must be completely free to take whatever action in whatever area is necessary for its own security."

Acheson made it plain, however, that the President's decision had not been based on strategic considerations. "The underlying factors in the decision are not in that area. They have to do with the fundamental integrity of the United States and with maintaining in the world the belief that when the United States takes a position it sticks to that position and does not change it by reason of transitory expediency or advantage on its part." In making this statement, Acheson was referring to the wartime promise, made to China at Cairo in 1943 and at Potsdam in 1945, that all territory stolen from her by Japan would be returned after the war. The fact that the Chinese Nationalists had now been defeated by the Chinese Communists did not change the American position; the promise had been given to China, not to one of the two principal political parties.

Hence American forces would not be used to defend Formosa; nor would the Chinese Nationalists obtain American military advice or assistance. Chiang, Acheson stressed, had sufficient reserves on Formosa and he had "very considerable" military equipment which he had received from the United States since 1948. "That [sufficient military forces and equipment on the island] is not where the difficulty lies in maintaining the Island by the forces on it. It is not that they lack rifles or ammunition . . . That is not the trouble. The trouble lies elsewhere, and it is not the function of the United States nor will it or can it attempt to furnish a will to resist and a purpose for resistance to those who must provide for themselves." If, for Chiang, January 5, 1950, signaled the beginning of the end, the American government offered no condolences; Chiang, it held, had only himself to blame for his predicament.[20]

Chiang's doom and the fall of Formosa were regarded with so much certainty in Washington that the State Department had already prepared and distributed an information paper to be used as a guide for information officers on what they were to say after the Chinese Communists had overrun the islands. Their task, they were told, was to counter the "false impression" that Formosa's loss "would seriously damage the interests of either the United States or of other countries opposing communism." [21]

The State Department took this attitude not because it actually advocated the fall of Formosa, as its critics vehemently charged; the reason was that the department hoped to minimize the damage to American prestige and the morale of other nations when Formosa fell. As Acheson explained:

> . . . if a captain in command of a company finds that the companies on either side of him are falling back and taking punishment, what he says to his men is, "Don't give it a thought. It doesn't matter at all. You are doing fine. Dig in. Hold it. It is all right."
>
> You are all familiar with Mr. Churchill's great statement in 1940 that the British would fight on the beaches, fight in the streets, and fight in the hills. I don't think any of you thought that that was a scientific report on the military programs of the British General Staff . . .

. . . I don't know any other attitude which would be sounder to take if you believed, as we did believe — and rightly believed — that an event was going to happen which would be damaging to our prestige, than to say, "Keep your chin up; it doesn't matter; this isn't important; we will go ahead and deal with it in some other way." [22]

The information document, prepared in December 1949, was leaked by General MacArthur's headquarters in Tokyo on January 3, 1950,[23] and precipitated an attack upon the Administration's Far Eastern policy by Congressional Republicans determined to commit the United States to the defense of Formosa and nonrecognition of Peking. Senator Knowland immediately made public a letter from former President Hoover which urged the United States to pursue a policy of nonrecognition toward the new Chinese regime, to continue its support of Chiang Kai-shek's government, and to give it naval protection if that were needed. Mr. Hoover then outlined the objectives he believed to be desirable: to build an anti-Communist wall in the Pacific; to defend Japan and the Philippines; to guard against Chinese legations and consulates in the United States — "and such countries as agree with us" — from being turned into nests of Communist conspiracies; to prevent the addition of another Communist member to the Security Council of the United Nations; to eliminate the danger of Chinese Communist participation in the formulation of the Japanese peace treaty; to maintain a symbol of resistance which would give us "a better basis for salvation in southeastern Asia"; and finally, to preserve "a continued hope of sometime turning China in the paths of freedom again." [24]

Senator Knowland then bitterly denounced the Administration for its unwillingness to help the Nationalist regime to survive, and he pointed out the discrepancy between the government's policy of containing Communism in Europe and permitting it to expand in Asia where, in Knowland's opinion, it "has made gains . . . which many times offset the losses of Communism in Europe." [25] Senator Taft, who had also called for the naval defense of Formosa on January 3, seconded this theme.[26] In order to contain Communist imperialism in Europe, he said, the United States had on several occasions risked a war with the Soviet Union by telling it "this far you shall go and no further"; but in the Far East the Administration was unwilling to draw such a line to protect Chiang, even though there "is not the slightest evidence that Russia will go to war with us because we interfere with a crossing to Formosa. It is hardly possible to see how the

Chinese Communists by themselves can begin a war against the United States, or why they should do so." Formosa, he continued, "is a place where a small amount of aid and at a very small cost, can prevent the further spread of Communism." Such a policy, Senator Taft continued, did "not commit us to be backing the Nationalist Government in any prolonged war against the Chinese Communists. We can determine later whether we ever wish to recognize the Chinese Communists and what the ultimate disposition of Formosa shall be."

The President had said that the United States was unwilling to involve itself in China's civil war — but had he not involved this country in similar conflicts in Greece, in Korea, and several other places? Mr. Truman had stated that the government would not provide any more military aid or advice to the Nationalist forces — but was this not "curiously inconsistent" with the policy he pursued in every other part of the world? "The question of the containment of Communism is largely a practical one," Senator Taft concluded. "The only reason so much heat has been engendered about the Formosa situation is the bitter resentment of the State Department and its pro-Communist allies against any interference with its policy of liquidating the Nationalist Government. No two men are more familiar with the Far East than General MacArthur and former President Hoover, and both of them are able to see the obvious military and political facts of the situation. Here is a small area of the world, where, with no difficulty or expense, we could prevent the spread of communism to an island which might be of great strategic value and whose people desire to be independent." [27]

Senator Alexander Smith supported Taft's demand that "under no condition" should the United States allow Formosa to fall into the hands of the Chinese Communists or under the domination of Russia. He even suggested that the United States take over control of the island under a United Nations trusteeship. He argued that although the United States had agreed to return Formosa to China after the defeat of Japan, the peace treaty with Japan had not yet been signed. Technically, therefore, the island was still part of Japan and the "logic of the situation" suggested that the United States should be in "friendly and peaceful occupation" of the island until its ultimate sovereignty was determined.[28]

The Republicans did not, however, limit themselves to demanding the defense of Formosa and the nonrecognition of Communist China.

They also created a political atmosphere in which any Administration moves to abandon Chiang and establish diplomatic relations with Mao Tse-tung would have been widely regarded as "un-American" and "pro-Communist"; this they accomplished by charging that the New Deal administrations of Franklin Roosevelt and Harry Truman had deliberately or unwittingly "sold China down the river." The Republicans rejected the official explanation that the Nationalist defeat was due to the social ferment among the Chinese masses, particularly among the peasants who constituted 80 per cent of China's population, or to the low Nationalist morale, ineptness, and repressive policies, or the superior Communist organization, direction, morale, and ability to identify themselves with the people's aspirations; nor did they accept the Democratic contentions that the Chinese revolution had been in progress already for over two decades, that the Chinese Communists were an indigenous party, or that Russia had not become a Pacific power at Yalta but had for 300 years shared a common frontier with China. Chiang's collapse, the Republicans charged, was due to Presidents Roosevelt and Truman, and Secretaries of State Marshall and Acheson and their foreign service advisers, who had attempted to force Chiang into a coalition government with the Communists, betrayed him at Yalta, and withheld arms from him in his fight with Mao.

The Republican thesis was simplicity itself: America's Chinese policy had ended in Communist control of the Chinese mainland; the State Department and the Administration leaders were responsible for the formulation and the execution of policy; thus the government must be filled with Communists and "Communists sympathizers" who "tailored" American policy to advance the Soviet Union's global aims. General Patrick Hurley, who during World War II had been sent to China by President Roosevelt to mediate between the Nationalists and Communists, typified this conspiratorial attitude in his denunciation of the White Paper. "The paper," he said, "is a smooth alibi for the pro-Communists in the State Department who have engineered the overthrow of our ally, the Nationalist Government of the Republic of China, and aided in the Communist conquest of China." [29] Hurley, as a friend of President Roosevelt, at least did not accuse him; most conservative Republicans were less sensitive. Roosevelt was to them the symbol of the "pro-Communists" in the American government.

For these "pro-Communists" were the same "New Dealers" who for twenty years had been undermining American institutions at home by stifling private enterprise with tax rates, inflationary controls, and general intervention in the business sphere; the same "liberals" who during the war had trusted Stalin in the naïve hope that they could win his goodwill for a long era of postwar peace by converting him from a Communist to a democrat; the same "progressives" who had conducted American policy in a pattern fitted to Communist aims; the same "internationalists" who had "sold out" not only China but also Eastern Europe; and the same "do-gooders" who were now wasting American resources by huge "give-away" programs which would further weaken the traditional American economic and political system.

It was these attitudes which brought together men of such different character and background as Senators Robert Taft and Joseph McCarthy. Most observers of American politics have usually failed to understand how the senator from Ohio, with his sensitive concern for the liberties of his fellow countrymen, could not only condone but actually support the unscrupulous senator from Wisconsin; they view this period of Taft's political life as a temporary aberration from the norm, and view it uncomfortably and with distaste. In fact, the alliance was entirely logical, for both men viewed foreign policy as an instrument by which the New Dealers intended to complete the design they had been contemplating and pursuing for two decades — a socialist America. The McCarthy slogan, "twenty years of treason," might have been an extreme phrasing, but it was implicit in the conservative Republican position. The Taft Republicans did feel that the New Deal Democrats — the majority Democrats — had betrayed the country by their "un-American" views and behavior; and the intensity with which they felt this was evidenced by the vehemence of their attack upon the Truman Administration's Far Eastern policy.

The result of this onslaught was a stalemate between the two major political parties.[30] The Democrats were unwilling to make any commitments to Chiang, except to provide him with some economic aid; since this minimal American commitment at least assured continued identification of Chiang with the United States and thwarted the recognition of the Communist regime for the time being, the Republicans demanded this economic aid as the lowest price for their support of Administration policy in other areas. Their ability to attack and hamper the Administration's policy toward Western Europe was their sanction. If the Democrats could not be bothered with containing

Communism in Asia, Republicans would not concern themselves with containing Communism in Europe. Indeed, in the general atmosphere of distrust and suspicion which the Republicans had first created and then exploited, the Democrats could not have afforded to discard Chiang completely or to establish any relations with Communist China. The Republican explanation of the fall of China gained widespread acceptance as revelations of Communist espionage in the government became known; perhaps the government and the State Department were full of subversives. Harry Truman's outright dismissal of legitimate criticisms of existing security regulations as "red herrings" only furthered the acceptance of the belief that the United States was being betrayed from within. To have abandoned Chiang and established diplomatic relations with Communist China under these circumstances would have been tantamount to political suicide.

The resulting inflexibility imposed upon the Administration's policy by this domestic deadlock made it impossible for the government to initiate its policy of exploiting the purported conflict of interests between Communist China and the Soviet Union, and surrendered the initiative in the Far East to the Communists. In this situation, ironically enough, only the Chinese Communists, by eliminating Chiang, could help American policy-makers out of their dilemma.

Unfortunately, the Communists chose to exercise their initiative in a manner which upset the Administration's calculations. They attacked not Formosa, but Korea. Formosa was immediately neutralized by assigning the Seventh Fleet the double mission of, first, protecting the island from invasion by the Chinese Communists, and second, of preventing Chiang from launching any attack upon the mainland. In the official statement announcing this decision, the President defended his act in military terms. The occupation of Formosa, he said, "would be a direct threat to the security of the Pacific area and to United States forces performing their lawful and necessary functions in that area." Later the President elaborated on his statement: the American action was a matter of elementary security at a time when peace and stability in the Pacific area had been seriously disturbed by the attack on Korea. Under such circumstances, attacks elsewhere in the Pacific would have enlarged the Korean crisis and made it more difficult for the United Nations to carry out its obligations.

Neutralization, the President continued, did not, however, mean that the United States possessed any territorial designs on Formosa or sought any special position or privileges on the island. Nor would neutralization prejudice Formosa's political status; this issue could be settled peacefully once peace had been restored. During the brutal and unprovoked aggression on Korea, the question would simply have to be held in abeyance to guarantee the security of American forces.[31]

Whether or not considerations of strategy were the primary reason for the defense of Formosa, domestic politics would have forced the Administration to adopt the same policy. For political unity during this crisis facing the United States was considered highly desirable; and this the Administration achieved. When shortly after the North Korean attack, Senator James Kem took the floor of the upper house to denounce the Communist aggression as "the harvest of the tragic transactions at Yalta in 1945" and to question the constitutional authority of the President "to make an armed attack," Senator Knowland, one of the Administration's most bitter critics on Far Eastern policy, quickly stood up to interrupt. The President's statement, Knowland said, "had drawn a line in the Far East which was essential to be drawn some time . . . I believe that in this very important step which the President of the United States has taken . . . he should have the overwhelming support of all Americans regardless of their partisan affiliation." Later, when Senator Wherry also questioned the President's authority to send troops into Korea without congressional authorization, Knowland tersely replied that the President had the authority as Commander in Chief: "Certainly the action which has been taken to date is not one which would have required, or one in which I believe it was desirable to have a declaration of war, as such by the Congress of the United States. What is being done is in the nature of a police action"! The President had had to act quickly or have been too late.[32]

The most important symptom of the restoration of political unity came, however, from Senator Taft in a speech in which he, on the one hand, showed his devotion to the conspiratorial interpretation of American Far Eastern policy, and on the other, approved — although not without qualification — the Administration's stand in Korea. The present crisis, Taft asserted, was the result of "the sympathetic acceptance of communism as a peace-loving philosophy." The Administration was responsible for the North Korean attack for three reasons: first, because "we agreed to the division of Korea along the thirty-eighth parallel giving the Russians the northern half of the country . . . in line with a very foolish policy which paid for Russian assistance against Japan, which we did not need . . ."; second, because we had not furnished the South Koreans with the necessary arms to guarantee their external security; and third, because "the Chinese policy of the administration gave basic encouragement to the North Korean aggression. If the United States was not prepared to use its troops to give military assistance to Nationalist China against Chinese Communists, why should it use its troops to defend Nationalist Korea against Korean Communists?" This policy, Taft continued, was moreover in line with Secretary Acheson's "defense perimeter," from which he had excluded both Formosa and Korea. "With such a reaffirmation of our Far Eastern policy, is it any wonder that the Korean Communists took us at the word given by the Secretary of State?"

In now defending Korea and protecting Formosa, the President had totally reversed Acheson's "defense perimeter" policy. Taft suggested that "any Secretary of State who has been so reversed by his superiors and whose policies have precipitated the danger of war, had better resign and let someone else administer the program to which he was, and perhaps still is, so violently opposed."

Taft, however, approved of the Administration's stand in Korea, for it was in line with the "much more determined attitude against communism in the Far East" which he had urged for so long. "It seems to me that the time had to come, sooner or later, when we would give definite notice to the Communists that a move beyond a declared line would result in war. That has been the policy which we have adopted in Europe . . . I believe the general principle of the policy is right," although, he added cautiously, he was unsure whether the President had chosen the right place or time to declare his new policy. The President could be the only judge of that, since he possessed the information necessary to make such a decision.

But, Taft concluded, it should be noted that the President had not consulted Congress before authorizing the use of force in Korea; it was his opinion that the President had acted without legal authority by usurping his powers as Commander in Chief. But, Taft quickly added, "I may say that if a joint resolution were introduced asking for approval of the use of our Armed Forces already sent to Korea and full support of them in their present venture, I would vote in favor of it." Taft had squared the circle in what for him was a mild speech.[33]

These words of "Mr. Republican" signaled the Administration's success in re-establishing political cooperation during the Korean crisis. Truman had made decisions on Korea, and particularly on Formosa, for which the conservative Republicans felt they deserved much of the credit; for six months, they had been urging a tougher policy in the Far East. The President had now adopted their policy. By his actions, Harry Truman had restored bipartisanship; not only that, he had for the first time applied it to the Far East. But this bipartisanship was inherently unstable, for the political unity produced was not positive, the result of common political convictions and a shared outlook on foreign policy. It was a negative unity, the product of external crisis. The parties did not really cooperate; they merely declared a temporary truce. And this truce could not have been converted into a genuine peace, since the price the Republicans demanded for their support of Democratic foreign policy was an all-out commitment to Chiang Kai-shek. Since the Administration was unwilling to pay this price, the Republicans were soon to return to the attack. The moment for this renewed offensive came when General MacArthur began to voice his own policy differences with the government.

IV

MacARTHUR, FORMOSA, AND INCHON: THE MANY-SPLENDORED GENERAL

President Truman officially appointed General MacArthur as the first United Nations Commander in history on July 8, 1950, the day after the United Nations Security Council passed its third resolution on the Korean crisis, recommending that all members providing military forces and other assistance pursuant to the Council's resolutions of June 25 and 27 "make such forces and other assistance available to a command under the United States"; requesting the United States to designate the command of such forces; authorizing the unified command to fly the United Nations flag "at its discretion" during the course of its military operations; and requesting the United States to provide the Council with reports "as appropriate on the course of action taken under the unified command." [1] The form of the United Nations and the substance of American power and predominance had now been completely identified. The United States Far Eastern Command had been transformed into the "unified command"; but General MacArthur's chain of command continued to run via the Joint Chiefs of Staff to the President.

This chain of command was not slated to be a smooth one. For MacArthur was no ordinary general, who simply executed the orders he received from his superiors. MacArthur was a powerful Pacific force in his own right. On the eve of the Korean War, the General already held a number of formidable commands. He was the Supreme Commander for Allied Powers (SCAP) in Japan. In this capacity he was solely responsible for the implementation of allied occupation policy. Since the United States was the major occupying power, allied policy was essentially American policy. This in turn meant that MacArthur was the real ruler of 83,000,000 Japanese. Only rarely did Washington overrule its proconsul; on no occasion, certainly, did the

President openly reprimand MacArthur as he was to do during the Korean War. MacArthur's implementation and frequent formulation of the successful occupation policy with minimal interference from Washington was symbolized by the fact that several of the functions he shouldered are normally reserved for heads of state. The Japanese government, for instance, had no diplomatic relations with other nations except through SCAP. A foreign diplomat assigned to Tokyo was accredited to SCAP, not to the Emperor, and it was MacArthur who received him. MacArthur's long exercise of almost absolute power over a great foreign nation was unique in the annals of American history. At times, indeed, it seemed as if the General were a mid-twentieth-century spiritual descendant of such former Viceroys of India as Clive or Warren Hastings, ruling an Asian people in the imperial tradition of Western benevolent despotism.

MacArthur also held the position of Commander in Chief, Far East (CINCFE). This command gave him authority over all United States army, navy, and air forces under the Far Eastern Command. This command embraced Japan, the Philippines, the Ruyuku Islands, the Marianas, Guam and other island groups; it excluded Korea. Lastly, MacArthur was the Commanding General, United States Army, Far East. In this role, his operational responsibility overlapped his position as CINCFE.

In addition to his military responsibilities, MacArthur held the confidence of conservative Republican circles, among whom he was highly regarded. He had been President Hoover's Chief of Staff. During that period, in the midst of the depression, he had dispersed the "radical" bonus army on the Anacosta Flats in Washington. Although he had done this on orders from his civilian superiors, his dashing performance in glittering uniform and polished boots had gained him the support and respect of an influential and major segment of conservative opinion. During World War II, he had vigorously opposed President Roosevelt's Europe-first strategy. In this opposition MacArthur had received the support of many Republican isolationists who preferred to fight a "nationalist" war in the Far East to an "internationalist" war in cooperation with Great Britain and the Soviet Union in Europe; in this manner, these isolationists had also been able to express their hostility and resentment toward Roosevelt without at the same time appearing to impede the war effort. In 1944, some of these Republicans led an abortive MacArthur-for-President movement, which MacArthur helped to destroy by an amazing display of political ineptness.[2]

After the war, as the virtually omnipotent ruler of a nation half the size of the United States, MacArthur had become increasingly critical of the Administration's policy toward China. As the American proconsul in Japan, MacArthur was naturally very concerned about Japan's future. In his opinion, Japan could not re-establish its economic recovery and great-power status without China's food and raw materials for manufacturing purposes and the Chinese market on which to sell its products; in 1947 he had prophesied that if China went Communist and expanded into the neighboring countries, Japan would some day have to "beg" the Communists to allow it to enter the Iron Curtain. When Chiang did collapse, MacArthur thought that our failure to give him effective support would turn out to be "the greatest blunder in the history of the United States";[3] and he believed that this blunder had been committed largely because of the Administration's continued pre-occupation with Europe.

The reason for MacArthur's lack of concern for Europe is clear from a statement he made during World War II. In it, he described Asia and its future in apocalyptic terms: "Europe is a dying system. It is worn out and run down, and will become an economic and industrial hegemony of Soviet Russia . . . The lands touching the Pacific with their billions of inhabitants will determine the course of history for the next ten thousand years"![4] In accordance with this point of view, MacArthur had recommended that the second front be established in the Pacific, not in Europe. Roosevelt had sent him a message on May 6, 1942, explaining his inability to furnish him with the reinforcements MacArthur had requested because "I find it difficult this spring and summer to get away from the simple fact that the Russian armies are killing more Axis personnel and destroying more Axis material than all the other twenty-five United Nations put together. Therefore, it has seemed wholly logical to support the great Russian effort in 1942 by seeking to get all munitions to them that we possibly can, and also to develop plans aimed at diverting German land and air forces from the Russian front." MacArthur had replied that he agreed "with the President as to the predominant importance of the Russian front. It is vital and nothing should prevent its maximum support. Only limited assistance, however, can be transported there so that the necessity for a second front is self-evident. That front should be in the Pacific area. Nowhere else can it be so successfully launched and nowhere else will it so assist the Russians. The Siberian pressure now exerted upon him by Japan will be at once released, permitting him either to utilize the Siberian resources in direct support of his European front or to join his allies in the Pacific attack" (the desirability of which MacArthur had first recommended to Washington on December 10, 1941, and which he continued to recommend until the end of the Pacific war).⁵ Since Europe was destined to be the industrial frontyard of Russia, anyway, MacArthur contemplated the loss of Europe with equanimity. When the President and General Marshall rejected his recommendation, MacArthur bitterly condemned their Europe-first strategy as inspired by Russian Communists and British imperialists. MacArthur's postwar criticisms of the Administration's foreign policy still reflected the same attitude.

Republicans were, therefore, delighted by MacArthur's appointment as United Nations Commander. They were also reassured because it put "one of their own kind" in charge of implementing American policy. This would make it impossible for the Administration to "sell out" Chiang Kai-shek and "appease" the Chinese Communists. Several clashes over Formosa were soon to show how close MacArthur was to the right-wing Republican position and how far the Administration and he were apart on Asian policy.

Though the United States was now committed to the defense of Formosa and protection of Chiang Kai-shek's government, the Administration wished to minimize this commitment, for two reasons. First, it believed the principal sources of Asian unrest stemmed from the tragic poverty of her peoples and their rejection of Western colonialism.⁶ Since Chiang had forfeited the loss of his popular support by his unwillingness or inability to cater to the desires of his peasant masses for social change and a better future, American help, and particularly American military intervention, would not only alienate the masses of China but generate bitter anti-American and anti-Western resentment among all the peoples of Asia. For they would regard American intervention on Chiang's behalf — particularly if this effort were to culminate in his imposition upon the Chinese people — as a reassertion of Western dominance and colonialism. North Korea's aggression, American domestic politics, and military security had made it impossible to pursue further the policy of disengagement from the Nationalist leader after June 25; nevertheless, close relations with Chiang were to be avoided.

In the second place, if the commitment to defend the Nationalist government on Formosa were to be maximized or to last beyond the duration of the Korean War, it would be difficult to unroll the new China policy: to detach Mao Tse-tung, from Moscow and use him to counterbalance Soviet power in the Far East. Instead, it would drive Communist China and the Soviet Union closer together and perhaps precipitate either a global war with the two largest and strongest Communist powers, or at least a Far Eastern war with the new Chinese regime. The latter course would serve Soviet purposes well, because it would divert scarce American resources from Europe and leave that much more vital area exposed to the Red Army. The Administration, realizing that Chiang's only salvation lay in provoking such major hostilities, was most anxious to keep its involvement with him very limited.[7] Our allies shared these thoughts and fears with equal intensity and apprehension; in fact, they had already dissociated themselves from the unilateral American decision to neutralize Formosa and protect Chiang.[8]

The first step which the American government took in accordance with this policy of limiting its commitment to the Nationalist Chinese was to decline the Nationalist's prompt and substantial offer of 33,000 of their "best equipped troops" for the fight in Korea. The President was at first inclined to accept this offer, but Secretary Acheson and the Joint Chiefs dissuaded him. The Secretary argued that Nationalist China was different from other United Nations members and that it was incongruous to send the Seventh Fleet to protect Formosa and at the same time strip it of its defenders; the use of these troops might, moreover, tempt Peking to enter the war and inflict heavy losses upon Chiang's troops, thereby reducing his ability to defend the island from invasion in the future. The Joint Chiefs in their turn pointed out that Chiang's troops were of questionable value; they believed that they would be as helpless against the North Koreans as the South Koreans had been. In addition, the transportation and logistical support they would require could be used to better advantage in the transportation and logistical support of our own troops.[9] As MacArthur phrased it in his support of the Joint Chiefs, the Chinese Nationalist contingent would be an albatross around our neck.

The second step which the Administration undertook to avoid

any further international complications arising from its protection of Formosa and Chiang Kai-shek, was to welcome United Nations considerations of the Formosa question and to propose an on-the-spot investigation by the international organization. The American government made this offer in response to Communist China's accusations that the United States' neutralization of Formosa constituted "armed aggression" against the territory of China and a violation of the United Nations Charter.[10] In a letter to Secretary-General Trygve Lie, Ambassador Austin clarified the American position in these seven points: first, that the United States had not encroached upon or committed aggression against China; second, that the United States action had been taken because the island was in itself in conflict with the mainland, that the Chinese Communists threatened the security of the forces operating in Korea; third, the United States action was an impartial neutralization designed to preserve peace and that this country did not covet the island for itself; fourth, that the United States action was taken without prejudice to the future political settlement of Formosa's status; fifth, that the United States had an ancient record of friendship for the Chinese people, unlike the Soviet Union; sixth, that the United States would welcome United Nations consideration of the Formosa case and suggested an on-the-spot investigation; and seventh, that the United States would not be diverted from repelling aggression in Korea, which the United Nations had condemned.

The opposition to these Administration efforts to minimize its temporary role in defending Chiang was led by General MacArthur. The General, who wanted a "stronger" pro–Chinese Nationalist and "more active" anti–Chinese Communist policy, was concerned because the President's order to neutralize Formosa gave the Communist forces and installations on the Chinese mainland "complete immunity" in their preparation for an attack against the island. "They were also thereby promised United States naval protection for their entire coastline, so that they could release defending forces for employment anywhere else in Asia." MacArthur later claimed that it was this protection which made it possible for the Chinese Communists to release the two field armies which spearheaded their intervention in North Korea.[11]

The first open conflict over Formosa came during General MacArthur's visit to Formosa on July 31. The initiative for this trip had come from Washington.[12] In its note to the Nationalist government declining the offer of Chiang's troops, the Administration had said that it could make no final decision until General MacArthur's headquarters had conferred with the Nationalist authorities on the defense of the island.[13] MacArthur had himself suggested that he personally go to Formosa and explain to Chiang why his offer was unacceptable. As the General testified later, for a period of ten days prior to his trip he had been receiving messages from the Joint Chiefs expressing their grave concern over the situation in Formosa. So he had decided to see for himself.[14]

Upon his return to Tokyo, MacArthur issued a statement in which he emphasized the military nature of his talks with Chiang and stated that arrangements had been completed for the effective coordination of Chinese and American forces in case of attack upon the island. Prevention of such an invasion, he said, was the mission assigned to him. In concluding, the General warmly praised the Nationalist leader, whose "indomitable determination to resist Communist domination arouses my sincere admiration. His determination parallels the common interests and purpose of Americans, that all people in the Pacific should be free — not slaves." [15]

The distress this statement caused in Washington and allied capitals was sparked by Chiang Kai-shek's declaration on May 1 that his talks with General MacArthur had laid the foundation for the joint defense of Formosa and "Sino-American military cooperation." The Nationalist leader more than implied that the "American" in "Sino-American" referred specifically to General MacArthur. Half of the communiqué was devoted to an expression of admiration for MacArthur "for his determined leadership in the common fight against totalitarianism in Asia and for his deep understanding of the menace of communism. Now that we [Chiang and his government] can again work closely together with our old comrade in arms," victory was assured.[16]

Secretary Acheson immediately cabled William Sebald, the State Department officer attached to MacArthur's staff, requesting him to send Washington details of the General's talks in Formosa "in the light of their vital relationship to overall policy formulation." [17] Sebald wired back that he had not been taken along by MacArthur on this trip; prior to his departure, the General had informed him that the meeting with Chiang would be strictly "nonpolitical." And upon his return, MacArthur had again emphasized the same point: he had been most meticulous in confining the talks to "military problems of a technical nature." Sebald added that MacArthur had expressed special concern over the possibility that his task of defending Formosa would be adversely affected by the "unfriendly" attitude of the State Department's Formosan representatives toward Chiang. The clear implication was that the United States should establish closer and more cordial diplomatic relations with Chiang as a prerequisite to the successful military defense of the island.

The outcome was that the President dispatched one of his most trusted subordinates, Averell Harriman, to brief the General. Harriman pointed out the basic conflict of interest between Chiang and the United States. Chiang's ambition was to reconquer the mainland, a task he could achieve only if the United States were involved in a full-scale war with the Communist regime. MacArthur answered that he recognized that Chiang's ambition could not be fulfilled, but added — probably facetiously — "it might be a good idea to let him land and get rid of him that way." Harriman's comment to the President on MacArthur's suggestion was that the General "did not seem to consider the liability that our support of Chiang on such a move would be to us in the East . . . I pointed out the great importance of maintaining UN unity among the friendly countries, and the complications that might result from any mis-steps in dealing with China and Formosa." MacArthur, however, assured Harriman that "as a soldier" he would support the President's policy toward Formosa — although Harriman thought "without full conviction." MacArthur was too strongly pro-Chiang and thought that "we should back anybody who will fight communism"; conversely, he would "never" recognize the Chinese Communists since this would strengthen their prestige. It should be America's objective to destroy that prestige.[18]

After Harriman's departure, MacArthur issued another statement. He disclaimed that his visit to Formosa had included any discussion of nonmilitary matters. He said that his trip to Formosa to discuss the island's defense had been formally arranged and coordinated beforehand with all branches of the American and Chinese governments; that his talks had not been concerned with any such subjects as the future of the Chinese government or developments on the Chinese mainland, or "anything else outside the scope of my military responsibility . . . " and that a full report of the results of his visit had been submitted to Washington.

His concluding words were harsh: the purpose of his trip, he said, had been "maliciously misrepresented to the public by those who invariably in the past have propagandized a policy of defeatism and appeasement in the Pacific. I hope the American people will not be misled by sly insinuations, brash speculations and bold misstatements invariably attributed to anonymous sources, so insidiously fed them both nationally and internationally by persons 10,000 miles away from the actual events, if they are not indeed designed, to promote disunity and destroy faith and confidence in American purposes and institutions and American representatives at this time of great world peril." That MacArthur's strong language was aimed at his superiors in Washington cannot be in doubt.[19]

These words did little to reassure the President. Truman was forced to agree with Harriman's conclusion that MacArthur did not recognize "fully the difficulties, both within the world and within the East, of whatever moves we make within China in our position with the Generalissimo in Formosa."[20] On August 14, therefore, MacArthur received a further directive from the Secretary of Defense. In it, he was informed that he was not to authorize any Nationalist attack on the mainland: "the most vital national interest requires that no action of ours precipitates general war or gives excuse to others to do so."[21] MacArthur wired back that he thoroughly understood the presidential decision of June 27 "to protect the Communist mainland."

As memories of this visit began to fade and the American proposal for a United Nations investigation of the Formosa case calmed allied fears and soothed neutralist suspicions, MacArthur sent the Veterans of Foreign Wars a lengthy message which was to be read on August 28 at their annual encampment. The purpose of his message, MacArthur claimed, was to correct the "misconceptions currently being voiced concerning the relationship of Formosa to our strategic potential in the Pacific." MacArthur suggested that Formosa was the fulcrum of the American island chain ringing the Asian mainland from the Aleutians to the Marianas. From this defensive perimeter, the United States could by air power dominate every Asiatic port from Vladivostok to Singapore and prevent any hostile movement into the Pacific. Any attack from the Asian continent would have to be an amphibious operation, but no such effort could succeed against American air and naval supremacy based on the island defense perimeter. Under such conditions, the Pacific no longer represented "menacing avenues of approach for a prospective invader — it assumes instead the friendly aspect of a peaceful lake." This line of defense was a natural one and could be maintained with a minimum of military effort and expense.

But in the hands of a hostile power, MacArthur continued, Formosa would become an unsinkable aircraft carrier and submarine tender. It would then "either counter-balance or overshadow the strategic importance of the central and southern flank of the United States front-line position," for it would constitute a salient in the very center of our defense perimeter. He concluded his strategic lesson with this grave warning: "If we hold this line we may have peace — lose it and war is inevitable."

Then switching from the strategic to the political, MacArthur attacked the argument that an American defense of the island would alienate the sympathies and support of the peoples of Asia. This "threadbare argument" came only from those who advocated appeasement and defeatism. "Those who speak thus" he said,

do not understand the Orient. They do not grant that it is in the pattern of the Oriental psychology to respect and follow aggressive, resolute and dynamic leadership to quickly turn on a leadership characterized by timidity or vacillation — and they underestimate the Oriental mentality. Nothing in the last five years has so inspired the Far East as the American determination to preserve the bulwarks of our Pacific Ocean's strategic position from future encroachment . . . To pursue any other course would be to turn over the fruits of our Pacific victory to a potential enemy. It would shift any future battle area 5,000 miles eastward to the coast of the American continent, our own home coast.[22]

This message was sent to press associations, newspapers and magazines as a "routine courtesy,"[23] though this courtesy was not extended to either the State or Defense departments. When President Truman learned of the existence of MacArthur's message, he ordered it withdrawn. By then it was already on the newstands.

The political overtones of MacArthur's messages shocked Washington. MacArthur had, first of all, strongly implied that the United States should maximize its commitment to Chiang. The Nationalist leader, MacArthur later testified, was to the average Asian a symbol of an invincible determination to resist the advances of Communism.[24] The United States should therefore give him its vigorous support and not undermine him; ". . . we have not improved our position," he had told Harriman, "by kicking Chiang around, and [he, MacArthur] hoped that the President would do something to relieve the

SPECIAL GALA-PERFORMANCE OF
THE EAGLE HAS TWO HEADS
(FOR ONE DAY ONLY)

VICKY

strain that existed between the State Department and the General-issimo." [25]

In case the Administration might not agree with his estimate of Chiang's potential as a leader in the fight against Communism, Mac-Arthur had again emphasized that strategic reasons alone provided sufficient ground for defending Chiang's island-bastion. These two reasons were of course closely related, since in MacArthur's view the prerequisite for a successful defense of the island was a closer harmony between Washington and Taipei. As MacArthur had already privately informed the State Department,[26] and had told Harriman during the latter's visit, the allegedly hostile attitude of the department's representatives toward the Nationalist government might hamper the close military cooperation essential for the accomplishment of his mission. In short, American security demanded more cordiality with and greater confidence in Chiang.

The Administration was also disconcerted by MacArthur's indirect suggestion that the United States wholeheartedly acknowledge Communist China as its enemy. In his message, he had referred several times to a "power unfriendly to the United States" and a "military power hostile to the United States"; only one nation could qualify for these labels. MacArthur had previously told Harriman that he would never recognize the Chinese Communists, even if he had to veto their admission into the United Nations. Recognition would strengthen Mao Tse-tung's prestige; it was in America's interest to destroy that prestige.[27] This judgment was both unwelcome and unacceptable to the Administration and its allies, since they believed that Mao's regime was potentially friendly toward the West and hostile toward the Soviet Union; they considered that if MacArthur's advice were followed, it would strengthen Sino-Russian bonds instead of weakening them.

Finally, MacArthur had at one stroke eradicated the government's long campaign to convince other nations, including Communist China, that American aims in Formosa were, in the President's words, neither selfish nor belligerent, and that the defense of Formosa would end with the restoration of the *status quo* in Korea. MacArthur's implication that the United States must maintain its control over Formosa, and possibly use the island as an American military base, gave credence to Communist charges that the United States harbored designs upon the island, and once more aroused allied suspicions of American intentions [28] — and incidentally, illustrated for the first time in a fairly mild form a phenomenon that was to haunt the Administration in the days following Communist China's intervention: that any American policy which received domestic political support was unacceptable to our allies.[29]

Mr. Truman later revealed that after the General's message had come to his attention, he had given serious consideration to relieving MacArthur of his responsibility as field commander in the Far East, but that after careful deliberation he had decided against it. "It would have been difficult to avoid the appearance of a demotion, and I had no desire to hurt General MacArthur personally." [30] The President also probably had no desire to precipitate a foreign policy conflict at home so soon after the battle had been joined. Instead Mr. Truman sent MacArthur a copy of Ambassador Austin's letter to Secretary-General Trygve Lie, explaining the American government's position on Formosa.[31]

MacArthur, to be sure, has claimed that he was well acquainted with this policy, and that the strategic views stated in his message to the Veterans of Foreign Wars were meant only to demonstrate his full support for the President's policy of keeping Formosa out of hostile hands! [32] But Mr. Truman did not accept that explanation; the tone and timing of MacArthur's message were, in his opinion, quite out of context with his Administration's efforts to preserve a united front against aggression. The Chief Executive might well have reread a column written by James Reston shortly after MacArthur's appointment as United Nations Commander:

General Douglas MacArthur, at 70, is now entering upon the most delicate political mission of his illustrious career . . . he is asked to be not only a great soldier but a great statesman; not only to direct the battle, but to satisfy the Pentagon, the State Department, and the United Nations in the process.

[Unlike General Eisenhower who] had a genius for international teamwork . . . [MacArthur] is a sovereign power in his own right, with stubborn confidence in his own judgment.

Diplomacy and a vast concern for the opinions and sensitivities of others are the political qualities essential to this new assignment, and these are precisely the qualities General MacArthur has been accused of lacking in the past.[33]

Apparently, MacArthur was still lacking them.

General MacArthur had also drawn a conclusion from his conflict with the Administration over Formosa and Chiang Kai-shek, namely, that those who advocated "a policy of defeatism and appeasement in the Pacific" were sheltered primarily in the White House, the State Department, and the Pentagon in Washington, and that one of their cardinal sins was their effort to block his aim of keeping Formosa in friendly hands and securing the Nationalist leader's protection beyond the termination of hostilities in Korea. MacArthur had long thought that "the military fortunes of America lay in the hands of men who understood little about the Pacific and practically nothing about Korea." [34] The controversy over Formosa confirmed him in his opinion; and the arguments which preceded the Inchon landing convinced him not only of the correctness of his view, but opened further the gap which existed between himself and the Administration.

MacArthur first conceived of the landing at Inchon, a west-coast port near the South Korean capital and 150 miles behind the North Korean lines, during his initial visit to the Korean front in late June.[35] Shortly thereafter, on July 7, he informed the Joint Chiefs that he planned to defeat the North Koreans by means of an amphibious strike deep behind their lines. The favorable outcome of such a venture could not, of course, be guaranteed, but MacArthur was convinced that this type of attack was preferable to a frontal assault which, even if successful, would involve heavy casualties. Sixteen days later, he cabled Washington his plan for a two-division landing. MacArthur's choice of Inchon as a landing place is quite apparent: it would present the Communists with a two-front war; it would starve the Communist troops in the south of their supplies; it would cut the best communication line running between the two halves of the country; it would capture the second largest port in Korea; and finally, it would strike a psychological and political blow at the Communists by capturing the South Korean capital.

The timing of the operation provides a rather interesting insight into MacArthur's personality, particularly one of its leading characteristics, self-confidence. Tides limited a landing at Inchon to four dates — September 15, October 11, November 2 or 3. MacArthur chose the first: it would relieve the strain upon his outnumbered and tired troops in the Pusan beachhead and spare them a winter campaign; a period of a month or a month and a half would allow the enemy further time to strengthen his defenses and perhaps make a landing impossible; and only the early liberation of the Republic would enable the South Koreans to harvest the October rice crop for themselves.[36] But the decisive factor for MacArthur's choice was the opposition his plan encountered among his own staff and the Joint Chiefs. Paradoxical as it may seem, it was their objections which convinced MacArthur that Inchon would not fail.

Headquarters planners opposed "the chief" because, in their opinion, the two divisions available for the operation were insufficient to guarantee its success; reinforcements could not be withdrawn from Pusan without jeopardizing the security of the beachhead; stripping Japan of its occupation troops was unwise and perhaps dangerous; the command suffered from a lack of shipping; and the poor landing conditions at Inchon made an amphibious strike there a very risky proposition.[37]

The Joint Chiefs, represented by General Collins and Admiral Sherman, Chief of Naval Operations, presented their case in a meeting at Tokyo on August 23.[38] The navy opened the proceedings. It liked neither the place nor the timing of the landing. The average tide at Inchon was 20.7 feet, one of the highest in the world; on September 15, it would be 30 feet. Within two hours after high tide, the assault craft would be stuck in the mud of Inchon's harbor, easy targets for Communist shore batteries. Only a brief time, therefore, was available for the neutralization of Wolmi-do, the heavily fortified island commanding the harbor and its approaches. And even if this mission were successfully accomplished, the high tide in the afternoon would allow only two and a half hours for securing a beachhead and bringing up sufficient supplies for the troops to hold their ground against counterattacks during the night. Finally, the assault would be right into the city, whose buildings would afford the defenders extra protection and increase their capacity to resist. Admiral Sherman summed up his objections with a curt observation: "If every possible geographic and naval handicap were listed — Inchon has 'em all."

General Collins spoke next. Inchon, he said, lay too far behind the battle lines. Even a successful landing would have no immediate effect on the North Korean army, since the capture of Seoul did not guarantee a link-up with General Walker's forces in the south. MacArthur's strategy would, moreover, require the withdrawal of a Marine brigade from the Pusan beachhead and thus further endanger an already difficult situation. On top of that, the invading troops might meet such powerful resistance near Seoul that they would be defeated. Collins therefore proposed an alternative to Inchon, a landing at Kunsan. This west-coast port possessed few of Inchon's obstacles and had the advantage of being located nearer the beachhead.

In his reply, MacArthur noted the objections of the Joint Chiefs. But, he told them, the "very arguments you have made as to the impracticabilities involved will tend to ensure for me the element of surprise. For the enemy commander will reason that no one would be so brash as to make such an attempt." [39] He recalled that in 1759 the Marquis de Montcalm had believed that he could defend the walled city of Quebec by concentrating his troops on the northern banks of the city, since in the Marquis's opinion no enemy could ever scale the southern river banks. But General Wolfe and his small force had scaled those heights and captured the city; he too had been opposed by his staff but had persisted in his endeavor. History books had recorded the brilliant result of this persistence.

Inchon, MacArthur assured the Joint Chiefs, would be another "impossible victory." He was confident that the navy could overcome the difficulties of tide and terrain. He conceded that a landing at Kunsan would be safer; but it would destroy neither the enemy's lines nor encircle his troops. At best, Kunsan was a flanking attack; at worst, it would be a bloody affair with little certainty of success. Rather than risk the lives of his troops in such a costly venture, he would send them directly to Walker for a frontal assault. This strategy would, however, allow the North Koreans to withdraw along their supply lines. He, MacArthur, would not take the responsibility for such a course.

MacArthur did not, however, confine his analysis to the purely military factors. He ended his presentation with a vigorous political argument, which reflected well his view of the global struggle in which the United States was engaged. The anti-Communist front, he told the Joint Chiefs, did not lie in Berlin, Paris, London, or Washington, but along the Naktong River in South Korea. "It is plainly apparent that here in Asia is where the Communist conspirators have elected to make their play for global conquest." In Europe, the war against Communism was still being fought with words; in Asia, it was already being fought with bullets. He warned that if the Korean War were lost the security of Europe would be seriously endangered. Western prestige demanded more than inertia and passive resistance in Korea. Millions of Asians were watching the outcome of the battle. "I can almost hear the ticking of the second hand of destiny," he concluded. "We must act now or we will die." Inchon would not fail and it would save 100,000 lives. Seven and a half months later, MacArthur repeated this message publicly; the General obviously relished a well-phrased and appealing paragraph.

Within a week, MacArthur received the "go-ahead" from the Joint Chiefs, although they gave their approval only reluctantly; indeed, they never quite overcame their apprehensions, and at the last moment they again questioned the feasibility of MacArthur's "Quebec." [40] Apparently the General shared some of their apprehensions. According to General Whitney, who had accompanied his chief on every amphibious operation since Leyte, MacArthur had never previously betrayed so much last-minute hesitancy. The success of the venture depended upon a single element — surprise. Had its secret been well guarded, or had the enemy learned his plans? Could the obstacles of nature be overcome? Had not the Joint Chiefs or his own staff, perhaps, been correct in their analysis? Would a more cautious course not have been wiser? "No, there was no doubt about the risk. It was a tremendous gamble." In the end, MacArthur of course reassured himself that his project was sound, and that there was indeed no alternative to it — except a bloody frontal assault. And that MacArthur did not consider a plausible alternative.

As MacArthur had predicted, his daringly conceived and skillfully executed maneuver caught the enemy by complete surprise. The Marines landed at Inchon in the early hours of September 15, and by eight o'clock that morning they had secured their beachhead. The landing quickly achieved its aims: it captured the second largest port in Korea; presented the North Koreans with a two-front war; cut off the supplies to their army around Pusan; and struck the regime a near fatal political blow when on September 22 it resulted in the liberation of Seoul.

The next day United Nations forces broke through the Pusan perimeter and began their northward drive. Within ninety-six hours the two armies had successfully closed the pincer and trapped more than half the North Korean army. The rest of the shattered Communist army was in flight. On September 30, allied troops reached the 38th Parallel; after almost three months of bitter rear-guard action, South Korea had been freed from almost complete Communist domination in fifteen days. The history of warfare has recorded few such brilliant operations. MacArthur had gambled "with disaster to achieve an unprecedented victory," and the gamble had paid off handsomely.

But Inchon was more than merely a name for a battle which changed the balance of power in Korea, more than just a great strategic victory; it was also a daring military operation which had a grave impact upon the future relationship between the Administration and General MacArthur, for it was also an intensely personal victory for MacArthur. Inchon had vindicated his judgment. He had — despite all opposition — come, planned, and conquered. He had assumed that the harbor approaches to Inchon would not be heavily guarded or mined; that the difficulties of tide and terrain could be surmounted; that the North Korean reserves stationed near the port would be slender; that the enemy's morale would be quickly broken; and that Japan, stripped of its occupation troops, would remain quiet and orderly. Because he had assumed correctly, he had turned a near-defeat into a glorious success.

It was this very success which augured ill for the future. If an equally difficult situation should arise again, should he, the victorious General, heed the advice of the Joint Chiefs if he again disagreed with it? Or should he prefer his own judgment? Inchon left little doubt of the answer.

Success had reaffirmed MacArthur's conviction that it was wise to adopt the bold course when the military situation appeared to be bleak, and that a "tremendous gamble" was preferable to a purely defensive action — or in triter terms, that "the best defense was an offense." Inchon had been considered as "impossible" as Quebec, and it would have remained so, if he had not been willing to take the risk. The operation had required more than sound planning; it had demanded the kind of daring and self-confidence which the Joint Chiefs — and their civilian superiors — apparently lacked. Victories were not won by "timidity in some office thousands of miles away." This theme was to recur with increasing frequency in the following months.

This difference of spirit which, in the opinion of General MacArthur's headquarters, became a clear-cut difference between a "will to win" on the one hand and "vacillation" and "appeasement" on the other, was reflected in opposing tactical and strategical concepts. The Joint Chiefs had been reluctant to risk their forces, particularly the army, at Inchon; there had been too much at stake. Even MacArthur, in fact, had harbored a few last-minute anxieties; even he had described his operation as a "tremendous gamble." But the successful field commander has strongly implied that the Joint Chiefs' attitude reflected that of their chairman, General Omar N. Bradley. MacArthur certainly seems to have derived a great deal of satisfaction from what he described as his explosion of General Bradley's belief that amphibious warfare had been outdated. Apparently, Bradley had made such a statement to a Senate Committee in 1949, although MacArthur fails to state the context in which it was delivered.[41] In any case, the Commander in Chief, Far East, apparently came to feel that his victory at Inchon had increased General Bradley's hostility toward him. According to MacArthur, he had refused during World War II to accept Bradley as his senior commander for the proposed invasion of Japan, because Bradley's conduct of the Battle of the Bulge had left an unfavorable impression with him. Important here, of course, is not whether Bradley really bore MacArthur any such grudge; what is important is only that MacArthur thought, or said, he did.[42]

MacArthur and his Tokyo staff attributed Washington's lack of wholehearted support not only to the Administration's lack of "spirit" and more cautious military doctrines, but also to a global strategy which the Far Eastern Command claimed failed to recognize the paramount importance of Asia in the scheme of American security. One reason for Inchon's riskiness had been the limited manpower available for the operation — only two divisions. MacArthur later said that on July 7 he had requested Washington to furnish him with reinforcements. These had been refused; among other reasons, he was told that the United States had also to maintain strong defenses in other parts of the world. Here again, MacArthur thought, was the "old faulty principle of 'priorities,' under which the Far East was placed near the bottom, if not at the bottom, of the list" of American interests. Once more Asia was being sacrificed to Europe, even though "it was obvious . . . at the other side of the world that the Soviet military dispositions in eastern Europe were defensive rather than offensive," and that it was in Asia where the Communists had concentrated their efforts to conquer the world.[43]

In retrospect, perhaps, it might be too much to say that Inchon proved a turning-point in the relation between MacArthur and the Administration — after all, MacArthur's self-confidence had never been low, and he had long rated the importance of Asia in the American pattern of security higher than his superiors — but it would be difficult to deny that Inchon did play a significant role in broadening the gap between Washington and Tokyo, although the extent of this gap was not clearly revealed until after MacArthur's offensive of November 24, 1950, and Communist China's full-scale intervention. For the moment, the President and the General exulted in the victory, agreed to chase the enemy across the 38th Parallel, and held their historic meeting at Wake Island. During this short interlude, there was no crisis; their relationship was, on the surface at least, affable and cordial. The North Koreans were almost defeated; and the decision to cross the parallel was taken in the belief that it would quickly end the war. Instead, it was but a prelude to a "hot war" with Communist China, and a "cold war" with the "many-splendored" general who was at one and the same time a devotee of the Orient, a "Republican" soldier, a student of history, and a victorious conqueror.

V

CROSSING THE 38TH PARALLEL:
THE POINT OF NO RETURN

Communist China's diplomacy and propaganda became increasingly active and hostile as North Korea's ability to achieve military victory diminished. According to the United Nations Commander, this chance had passed by July 20. Shortly thereafter, in its first "over-all estimate" of North Korean damage in late July, MacArthur's staff in Tokyo indicated that "270 of a probably 300 tanks . . . [had been] destroyed or damaged and possibly one-third of the troops put out of action." The "headquarters spokesman" said there were no signs that these vital tank losses were being replaced. He noted that whereas columns of twenty-five or thirty Red tanks had been reported on the roads before Inchon, only groups of four or five tanks were now still being sighted; in some cases, Communist infantry units "were operating without any tank support." "It was revealed here for the first time that 'some prisoners' had received only four days' training," while previously "certain types of soldiers had been given far more than a year." Reports of "heavy conscriptions" on both sides of the parallel substantiated reports that estimates of North Korean manpower losses "might be conservative."[1] The Communist air force was described as "depleted." Within two weeks of this estimate, the defense around the Pusan beachhead had been stabilized.[2]

It was at precisely this moment that the Chinese Communists initiated their diplomatic offensive against the United States. On August 20, Foreign Minister Chou En-lai sent telegrams to United Nations Secretary-General Trygve Lie and the Russian chairman of the Security Council, Jacob Malik, accusing the United States of having initiated the Korean War and preventing its peaceful settlement.[3] On August 24, Chou presented the Security Council with a protest against "direct armed aggression" on Chinese territory. He called on the Council to condemn the United States for its "criminal act" of armed invasion of Chinese Communist territory, and to order the withdrawal of the Seventh Fleet from Formosa.[4] Four days later, the People's Government charged that American planes had on the previous days strafed airfield and railway targets in Manchuria just north of the Yalu River. It alleged that three B-29 Superfortresses, five F-51 Mustangs, one Mosquito bomber (British), plus four other unidentified American planes had participated in these attacks.[5] The next day, August 29, Communist China repeated its accusations and charged that the United States was maliciously bent on expanding her "armed aggression." Peking again suggested that the Security Council condemn this country for its act of atrocity and order the immediate withdrawal of America's "aggressive forces" in Korea.[6]

After an investigation of these charges by General MacArthur, the United States, on October 2, acknowledged that on August 27 two Mustang fighters had flown over Chinese territory because of bad weather and poor visibility, but it denied the other violations charged by Peking.[7]

The significance of Peking's accusations lies in the timing. From June until late August, Communist propaganda had vigorously pictured the United States as the inveterate enemy of the peoples of Asia.[8] It had shrewdly confused the issue of North Korean aggression by injecting two other issues: Communist China's representation in the United Nations and the neutralization of Formosa. But after August 24, Communist China and Russia shifted their attention from the Formosa area to the Yalu River frontier.

This political offensive continued during the three weeks between the Inchon landing and the United Nations approval of the crossing of the 38th Parallel. During this time, a note of urgency crept into Peking's warnings. In late September, as allied troops fought their way back into the outskirts of Seoul, Peking suddenly announced that "battle-trained Koreans from Manchuria" had been released from the Chinese People's Army "to defend their motherland"; and Peking added, "We clearly affirm that we will always stand on the side of the Korean people." [9] On September 25, a New China Agency dispatch asserted that an American plane had dropped twelve bombs on Antung just across the Yalu frontier.[10] On the same day, General Nieh Yen-jung, acting Chief of the Chinese Communist General Staff, informed the Indian Ambassador in Peking, K. M. Panikkar, that China would not allow the United States to march up to the Yalu.[11] On

September 31, the day after the United Nations troops reached the 38th Parallel, this warning was repeated publicly. In a major speech, celebrating the first anniversary of the establishment of China's new government, Foreign Minister Chou En-lai praised the "bravery and determination of North Korea," and expressed his confidence that after overcoming "many difficulties," she would gain "final victory." He announced that China was determined to "liberate" Formosa, and condemning the "frenzied and ruthless imperialistic aggression" of the United States, he charged that America was "the most dangerous enemy of the People's Republic of China." China, he concluded, would not "supinely tolerate the destruction of its neighbor by the imperialistic powers." [12] On October 1, Chou made another speech. China, he stressed this time, "will not stand aside" if North Korea is invaded. Although the Chinese people wanted peace, "They will not be afraid to fight aggression in defense of peace. They will not tolerate foreign aggression and will not stand aside should the imperialists wantonly invade the territory of their neighbor." [13] The Chinese Communist government repeated this warning eight days later, two days after the United Nations had indirectly sanctioned the crossing of the parallel by calling for the establishment of a united, democratic, and independent Korea. Peking claimed that the resolution was illegal, and charged that it had been passed "against the will of the overwhelming majority of the world's population." Asserting that "the American war of invasion in Korea has been a serious menace to the security of China from its very start," Peking concluded ominously, "We cannot stand idly by . . . The Chinese people love peace, but, in order to defend peace, they will never be afraid to oppose aggressive war." [14]

According to one interpretation of this diplomatic offensive, Peking was warning the United States not to cross the parallel. The People's Government feared that the United States was treading the path traditionally taken by an expansionist Japan. Red China's leaders were apprehensive lest the United States, like Japan before it, use Korea as the gateway to expansion into Manchuria and Northern China. They doubted that the United States would be "satiated" with a victory in Korea; instead, its appetite whetted, the American government would exploit its military conquest as a prelude to an invasion of Red China herself. The Chinese people, a Chinese Communist spokesman later explained, "know fully well that the United States government has taken this series of aggressive actions with the purpose of realizing its fanatical devotion of dominating Asia and the world. One of the master-planners of Japanese aggression, Tanaka, once said: to conquer the world, one must first conquer Asia; to conquer Asia, one must first conquer China; to conquer China, one must first conquer Korea and Taiwan . . . American imperialism . . . plagiarizes Tanaka's memorandum, and follows the beaten path of Japan's imperialist aggressors!" [15]

This pattern of thought implies that the Chinese Communists thought that American foreign policy consisted of a number of aggressive acts aimed directly at continental China: in Korea, American-led troops were marching up to the Manchurian frontier; in Formosa, Americans were protecting Chiang Kai-shek and training and equipping his troops, presumably for an eventual return to the mainland; in Indochina, America was aiding France with military equipment; and off the coast of Asia, the time was nearing when Japan would rearm and align herself with the United States. John Dille has contended that in a hypothetical situation in which Russian troops were advancing toward the American-Mexican border, the American government would not rely for its security solely on Soviet promises that the Red Army would be halted at the frontier. Yet the Democratic Administration had to go "roaring up to their Rio Grande and [we] stood there virtually thumbing our noses." [16] Or, to state this interpretation of Communist China's warnings and later intervention in terms of the more familiar idiom of Korea as the dagger that points straight at the heart of Japan: a dagger can be turned around and aimed in the opposite direction too. Thus the United States and Communist China intervened in Korea for the same reason: to prevent the enemy from grasping the hilt of the dagger.

But Washington did not consider Peking's warnings seriously. Indeed, the issue of crossing the 38th Parallel seemed somewhat academic. The United Nations navy had sailed beyond the parallel, and its air force had flown over it repeatedly. As Ambassador Austin emphasized in his presentation of the American government's position to the United Nations, the parallel had no basis in either logic or in law.

Today, the forces of the United Nations stand on the threshhold of military victory. The operations authorized by the Security Council have been conducted with vigor and skill. The price paid has been high. The sacrifice in anxiety, sorrow, wounded, and dead must be abundantly requited. A living political, social, and spiritual monument to the achievement of the first enforcement of the United Nations peacemaking function must be erected.

The opportunities for new acts of aggression, of course, should be removed. Faithful adherence to the United Nations objective of restoring international peace and security in the area counsels the taking of appropriate steps to eliminate the power and ability of the North Korean aggressor to launch future attacks. The aggressor's forces should not be permitted to have refuge behind an imaginary line because that would recreate the threat to the peace of Korea and the world.

The political aspect of the problem identified with the 38th parallel becomes a matter of major concern for the United Nations. The question of whether this artificial barrier shall remain removed and whether the country shall be united now must be determined by the United Nations . . .

The artificial barrier which has divided North and South Korea has no basis for existence in law or in reason. Neither the United Nations, its Commission on Korea, nor the Republic of Korea recognizes such a line. Now, the North Koreans, by armed attack upon the Republic of Korea, have denied the reality of any such line.

Whatever ephemeral separation of Korea there was for purposes relating to the surrender of the Japanese was so volatile that nobody recognizes it. Let us not, at this critical hour and on this grave event, erect such a boundary. Rather, let us get up standards and means, principles and policies, according to the Charter, by which all Koreans can hereafter live in peace among themselves and with their neighbors.[17]

On October 7, the United Nations General Assembly approved a resolution recommending that (1) "All appropriate steps be taken to ensure conditions of stability throughout Korea"; (2) "All constituent acts be taken, including the holding of elections, under the auspices of the United Nations for the establishment of a unified independent and democratic government in the sovereign state of Korea"; (3) "All sects and representative bodies of the population of Korea, South, and North, be invited to cooperate with the organs of the United Nations in the restoration of peace, in the holding of elections and in the establishment of a unified government"; and (4) "United Nations forces should not remain in any part of Korea otherwise than so far as necessary for achieving the objectives specified in subparagraphs (a) and (b) above." [18]

The next day United Nations troops crossed the 38th Parallel in force.

Shortly after the outbreak of the war in Korea, Secretary Acheson had stated that the United Nations were fighting in Korea "solely for the purpose of restoring the Republic of Korea to its status prior to the invasion from the north." [19] He had given no hint that a change in the military picture would stimulate a reappraisal of this objective. Indeed, he had inferred that the United Nations members aiding the Republic of Korea were willing to accept a settlement on the parallel as the basis for concluding hostilities. Why then did the United States, the most powerful member of the allied coalition, change its mind after MacArthur's forces had reached the dividing line between the two halves of the country?

One view is that the "sudden military events outran political decision. A decision on whether to unify Korea by force, by crossing the parallel, had to be made, and quickly after Inchon: there was little time to consider all the facets of the problem without losing the military initiative and allowing the North Koreans a breathing spell to regroup. Should the U.N. cross the parallel after such a wait, the cost in lives would mount accordingly." [20] The decision was dictated by tactical necessity; a halt would have surrendered the military initiative to the Communists, and left the American-led forces awaiting a second major offensive when the enemy had nursed his wounds and recovered his strength. In the wake of Inchon's success, such a stop received scant regard. The mood of victory demanded a more positive and daring course: the destruction of North Korea's army in its lair. The opportunity for a second June 25 was to be removed once and for all.

This tactical reason for crossing the 38th Parallel has received powerful support from Secretary Acheson. The June 27, 1950, Security Council resolution "to repel the armed attack and to restore international peace and security in the area," he has maintained, could never have been achieved "if there were people on the other side coming over and fighting you." The crossing of the parallel had not aimed at the military unification of Korea, only a "round-up" of the remnants of the North Korean army. If the Chinese had not intervened, a united Korea would have been established by means of an election whose purpose would have been to choose a government for the whole of Korea. The "long-term political objective of the United Nations in Korea," Acheson stressed, had never been the military objective: "the forces were not put into Korea to do that when they went in in June." [21] General Marshall supported this contention: " . . . at no time have the United Nations forces been given the task of unifying all of Korea by military action." [22] The crossing, then, was merely a tactical move required by the necessity to annihilate the Communist army; if MacArthur had successfully completed his mission without Chinese intervention, Korea would have been united as a kind of political by-product of the campaign!

Senator Cain . . . What, may I ask, were our United forces doing on the shores of the Yalu River last November if it was not in an attempt to crush the aggressor and to unify Korea by force?

Secretary Acheson . . . After the Inchon landing, General MacArthur called on these North Koreans to turn in their arms and cease their efforts; that they refused to do, and they retired into the north, and what General MacArthur's military mission was was to pursue them and round them up . . . and, as I said many times, we had the highest hopes that when you did that the whole of Korea would be united. That did not come to pass, because the Chinese intervened.

Senator Cain. Mr. Secretary, had the Chinese not entered the war, are we not able safely to assume that we were just about to have unified Korea by force?

Secretary Acheson. Our hope was that the rounding-up, or the surrender of the forces which started this aggression, would result in the carrying out of the U.N. resolution of the 7th of October, which was to hold elections in the north, and under the United Nations aegis, try and bring that whole country together.

Senator Cain. If, sir, the Red Chinese had not entered the war, and our allied forces would have rounded up all those who were a party to the aggression in Korea, we would then have unified Korea by force; would we not?

Secretary Acheson . . . Well, force would have been used to round up those people who were putting on the aggression . . . unifying . . . it would be through elections, and that sort of thing.

Force would have played a part by rounding up and defeating those people who attacked the southern part of Korea.[23]

But could a free election have been held in the northern half of the country if it had not first been freed from Communist domination by military force? Did the sequence of the recommendations in the resolution of October 7, 1950, which sanctioned the crossing of the parallel, not indicate a recognition that military unification was a prerequisite for political unification? Did not the clause, "all appropriate steps be taken to ensure conditions of stability throughout Korea" precede the recommendations that "all constituent acts be taken, including the holding of elections . . . for the establishment of a unified, independent and democratic government in the sovereign state of Korea?" These questions the Secretary never answered — because they were self-answering.

Moreover, if the crossing of the parallel had been only a tactical move, why did General MacArthur halt the main body of his troops until October 7? And why was this move submitted for United Nations sanction? No other tactical decisions were referred to the international organization for its approval. Indeed, if the parallel had been crossed solely in order to safeguard South Korea's security and spare it a further attack at some future date, the Administration should by the same logic have favored MacArthur's "tactical" decision to extend the war beyond the Yalu after Communist China's intervention; for the presence of Peking's forces near the 38th Parallel posed an immeasurably greater threat to the existence of South Korea than a rebuilt but once-defeated and battered North Korean army.

In fact, the advance into North Korea reflected a political decision by the United States government to achieve a militarily unified Korea. In the context of the events of late September and early October such a decision should occasion no surprise. It was the logical outcome of the military victory achieved by MacArthur at Inchon and the demand for unconditional surrender issued shortly thereafter. Secretary Acheson could hardly have accepted compliance with this demand. On June 13, 1950, only two weeks before the outbreak of the Korean War, he had himself declared that the "one difference which is just about impossible to negotiate is someone's desire to eliminate your existence altogether." In short, the call for North Korea's unconditional surrender ensured the continuation of hostilities; to paraphrase Sir Winston Churchill, only in theory was this summons based upon the assumption that Kim Il Sung had become Stalin's First Minister in North Korea to supervise the liquidation of part of the Russian dictator's empire.

Another reason for the crossing of the parallel, frequently advanced as *the* reason why the American government believed that the northward advance was safe and would not encounter Chinese Communist troops, was General MacArthur's assurance to President Truman at Wake Island that the chances of Peking's intervention were "very little." The President has subsequently charged that MacArthur misinformed him, and Mr. Truman has strongly implied that he would not have ordered the northward advance if his field commander had correctly estimated Peking's intentions.[24] An evaluation of this charge requires the answers to two questions: what precisely did MacArthur say to the President on Wake Island; and what impact, if any, did this advice have on the President?

In answering the first question, General MacArthur has not denied that he told Mr. Truman that the Chinese Communists would not enter Korea. His belief, MacArthur has said, was based on three considerations. First, allied air power had an overwhelming strength, and "if the Chinese tried to get down to Pyongyang there would be the greatest slaughter." The Communists would lose about half of their troops just trying to get across the Yalu into Korea. Second, the time was past even for Soviet intervention. The Russian air arm in Siberia, though sizable, would prove no match for our own; and the size of the Red Army in the Far East was insufficient for the conduct of a war in addition to its performance of its regular duties. Reinforcements could, of course, be sent, but these could not arrive before the onset of winter. Third, these reasons eliminated a combination of Chinese ground troops supported by the Russian air force. Neither possessed the necessary experience in warfare demanding close air-ground cooperation; even American forces, except for the marines, still had difficulty in skillfully coordinating ground troops with tactical air support.[25]

These appraisals of the possibilities of Chinese intervention were, moreover, based on two more fundamental considerations, which, MacArthur asserts, qualified his prediction of what Peking would do as United Nations troops advanced into North Korea. The General claims that his basic premise was that Red China's intervention would be deterred by the threat of the immediate retaliation against which his hand was later bound. MacArthur says that it never occurred to him to question Mr. Truman whether he would react differently to Chinese Communist aggression than to North Korean aggression — "it would be like asking if we intended to fight the enemy with bows and arrows. Had someone suggested to MacArthur at that stage that we might suffer the Chinese Reds to strike us in full force and retaliate only by warding off the blow as it fell, without striking back on our own, he would not have believed any such preposterous notion." He had been allowed to bomb and blockade North Korea after it had attacked; he expected to receive permission to bomb and blockade Communist China too if she intervened.[26]

MacArthur also claims that his assurance of China's nonintervention was based upon a purely military evaluation, whereas the question of intervention was primarily a political one. His analysis, he had told the President, rested upon his own military intelligence; but since his air reconnaissance was limited to Korea, he had pointed out that his evaluation could not be a fool-proof guarantee. MacArthur at the same time points out that neither the State Department, Defense Department, nor the Central Intelligence Agency had at any time furnished him with any "political intelligence" which indicated that Washington thought that the Chinese Communists would pursue a course contrary to the one he had predicted.[27]

The evidence here favors MacArthur. At one point during the Wake Island conference, for instance, General Bradley asked his colleague whether he could spare one of his divisions for European service by next January; evidently, the chairman of the Joint Chiefs of Staff did not expect the war to continue too long. MacArthur shared this optimism. He expected the war to be over, except for mopping-up operations, by Thanksgiving, and to have the Eighth Army back in Japan by Christmas. Washington and Tokyo were evidently in full agreement that the war was almost over, and that Communist China would not intervene. But MacArthur's qualification that his prediction was only a military estimate is actually no qualification at all; for it is extremely doubtful that the intelligence process can be divided into two neat categories labeled "political" and "military." Moreover, the fact remains that Washington passed all the warnings and indications it had of possible Chinese intervention to MacArthur. The Far Eastern Command and the Administration both knew that the Chinese Communists had massed 300,000 troops in Manchuria; the former had indeed furnished the information. Both were aware that the leaders in Peking possessed the capability to intervene, but did they have the intention to do so? Neither the Administration nor MacArthur answered this question correctly. The Administration admitted later that its estimate had been mistaken. MacArthur never made a similar confession.

Instead, he argued that treason was responsible for his inability to consummate the military unification of the whole of Korea without Communist China's interference. Enemy strategists, according to military logic, must have expected instant and overwhelming counterattack to any such an adventurous move:

If . . . the Chinese entered the Korean war in any force, it would be as logical to bomb their supply bases as it had been to bomb those in North

Korea. All this was of course elementary; why it eluded the President and his military advisers MacArthur will never know.

But it could not have eluded the Chinese generals; of that MacArthur is sure. It naturally follows, then, that there can be only one circumstance under which the Chinese did finally decide to enter the Korean war: someone must have told them.

Someone must have told them what even MacArthur was not informed of before the Chinese intervened in Korea. Someone must have told them that even if the Red Chinese swarmed across the Yalu into North Korea in overwhelming hordes, even if they struck with no more warning than the Japanese had at Pearl Harbor, even if they slaughtered U.N. soldiers (nine out of ten of whom were American) on the battlefields and in the prisoner-of-war camps, the U.S. Government would meekly submit to maintaining the same sanctuary in Manchuria . . .

Only with the knowledge that . . . the United States would continue to protect the enemy's bases and supply lines, would a Communist commander decide to throw the full weight of the Chinese armies into Korea.

MacArthur goes on to suggest that those responsible were "undoubtedly" the two British traitors, Guy Burgess and Donald MacLean. Burgess had served as second secretary at the British Embassy in Washington until a few days before MacArthur's dismissal; and MacLean had been the head of the American section of the British Foreign Office during the same period. "If they did not report to their Kremlin masters fully upon our secrets in the conduct of the war against the Communists in Korea, what then could have been their treasonable purpose? It must be presumed that they did so." Upon this unsubstantiated speculation — which in the convenient absence of Burgess and MacLean in the Soviet Union can be neither proven nor disproven — hangs MacArthur's charge that espionage was responsible for the failure of his Wake Island prediction to be realized.[28]

This accusation does, however, show two things about MacArthur: first, that it apparently never occurred to him that the Chinese Communist government might feel that the presence of American troops on its frontier constituted an intolerable threat to Chinese security, and that Peking was no more willing to allow the United States to grasp the hilt of the Korean dagger than Washington had been willing to allow the Communists to grasp it; and second, that MacArthur must always be 110 per cent right. It could not be that he had failed to appraise the enemy's intentions correctly — an appraisal in which he had the almost unanimous company of all responsible civilian and military American officials (George Kennan was reportedly an exception); the explanation must be that he had been betrayed at home.

MacArthur's claim to perfection betrays a curious state of mind: it is as if the soldier-statesman feared that his magnificent record would be completely wiped out by one mistake; that his deeds would be remembered with pride only if his record remained free of the slightest blemish. He had to remain infallible; failure, MacArthur apparently said with Metternich, had never entered his mind — nor crossed his path. Shortcomings were the result of the incompetence or disloyalty of others. Symptomatic of this state of mind was MacArthur's frequently quoted sentiment: "I have always been able to take care of the enemy in my front — but have never been able to protect myself from the enemy in my rear"! It would probably not be amiss to add that if Burgess and MacLean had never lived, or not fled to Moscow, MacArthur would have had to invent them; there always had to be an "enemy in the rear."

MacArthur's temperamental inability to admit mistakes does not, however, mean that the President can place the responsibility for his decision to cross the 38th Parallel on MacArthur's assurance that the chances of Chinese intervention were "very little." What Mr. Truman and his defenders forget to add when they refer to MacArthur's words is that the General made his statement on October 15, 1950. This was fifteen days after the first South Korean forces had crossed the parallel, and one week after American troops had launched their northward offensive. The President had approved of the extension of military operations north of the parallel on September 11, and the Joint Chiefs had sent MacArthur a directive to this effect on September 15 — that is, one month before the Wake Island conference.[29]

Eleven days later, the Joint Chiefs had informed MacArthur that his "military objective is the destruction of the North Korean armed forces. In attaining this objective you are authorized to conduct military operations north of the 38th parallel." [30] MacArthur had, therefore, tendered his opinion after the Administration had already decided that it was safe to march up to the Yalu River. It is true, of course, that the directive of September 15 had informed MacArthur that he was not to send his troops north of the parallel in case of Soviet or Chinese occupation of North Korea — and his order emphasized that if major Chinese Communist units were sent south of the parallel, the United States "would not permit itself to become engaged in a general war with Communist China": but there are no indications that the Administration gave such intervention serious thought. No evidence exists that President Truman and Secretary Acheson ever entertained the belief that the Chinese Communist leaders might invade Korea because they might really possess a genuine fear of a "reactionary" General and his "imperialistic" armies on the sensitive and strategic Manchurian frontier; at no time apparently did it occur to American officials that Peking might well invoke one of the favorite slogans of American diplomacy, "deeds, not words," and ask for some specific and concrete guarantee against possible United States violations of Chinese territorial integrity. The Administration believed it could militarily unify the whole of Korea without Chinese Communist intervention. The reason: the Chinese Communist government was believed to be so deeply involved in conflict with the Soviet Union that Peking neither would nor could intervene in Korea.

In early 1950 Secretary Acheson had revealed that America's official policy was to exploit the alleged conflict of interest between Communist China and Soviet Russia. The Administration believed that by this means it could minimize the Nationalist government's defeat and turn adversity into opportunity. The American government expected to accomplish this feat and safeguard and promote American interests by disentangling itself from Chiang Kai-shek; this, it hoped, would forestall the growth of anti-American sentiment in China and focus the attention, resentment, and hostility of the Chinese people and regime on the power which was even then encroaching upon China's northern territories — the Soviet Union. The basic assumption behind this policy was that the new Chinese government was more Chinese than Communist, and that it would not, therefore, accept Soviet dictation as had Communist governments and parties in other nations; consequently, Peking would even defend its interests against Moscow.[31]

This policy was to be launched as soon as the United States had cut its last bonds to Chiang; this moment would come when the Chinese Communists had successfully invaded Formosa. The outbreak of the Korean War, however, precipitated a sudden change in American policy toward Formosa. The exigencies of military strategy and domestic politics had made it necessary for the Administration to protect the island by interposing the Seventh Fleet between the island and the Chinese mainland. But the President had immediately emphasized that this act did not constitute a permanent commitment to defend Chiang in his lair; neutralization, he had declared, represented an attempt to localize hostilities in the Pacific during the Korean War. It seems that Secretary Acheson had not expected Peking to be greatly irritated by this temporary change of policy: " . . . the President neutralized it [Formosa] by saying that the Seventh Fleet would prevent any attack upon Formosa, and Formosa should not make any attack upon the mainland. There was a fair proposition . . ." [32]

As soon as the North Korean aggression had been repulsed, the Seventh Fleet was to be withdrawn from the Strait of Formosa. The Chinese Communists could then presumably invade the island, defeat Chiang, and sever the final links binding the Chinese Nationalist leader to the United States. The way would then also be open to the recognition of Communist China. With Formosa in Communist hands and the only barrier to more friendly Sino-American relations removed, incitement of anti-American opinion would no longer be possible. Instead, Chinese attention would focus on Russian imperialism in Manchuria and Northern China; and the resentment caused by this naked display of the Kremlin's motives would manifest itself in hostility toward Russia.

It is significant that the crossing of the 38th Parallel was not considered as an act which would arouse the strong anti-American sentiment that the United States was attempting to minimize. The available material indicates that the American government judged an assurance of goodwill as sufficient guarantee for the men in Peking. The United States harbored no aggressive or malicious intentions toward either them or the Chinese people; its aim was simply to repel aggression and help the Koreans establish a free and united nation. In view of our long history of friendship for the Chinese people and support for their independence, was there any reasonable ground for distrusting our word? Little wonder that Secretary Acheson should later express with some vehemence that "no possible shred of evidence could have existed in the minds of the Chinese Communist authorities about the intentions of the forces of the United Nations. Repeatedly, and from the very beginning of the action, it had been made clear that the sole mission of the United Nations forces was to repel the aggressors and to restore to the people of Korea their independence." This government, the Secretary continued, had repeatedly declared that it wished to localize hostilities in Korea; and it had pledged that we would withdraw our troops from the peninsula shortly after the termination of their mission. The Chinese Communist crossing into Korea was, therefore, "completely unjustified." [33]

Since American declarations of goodwill were estimated as constituting sufficient assurance for China's Communist leaders, the latter's threats of intervention were considered as bluff. The additional warnings relayed to Washington by the Indian Ambassador in Peking caused only ripples on the crest of optimism.[34] The campaign was almost over; the war had already been won. Having refrained from intervention at a time when it might have resulted in an American Dunkirk, the Chinese would surely not be foolish and throw their armies into the battle at this stage. One official in Washington is said to have expressed this attitude in a poignant fashion: "I don't think China wants to be chopped up." [35]

In retrospect, it is surprising that so little attention was paid to the ideological character of China's new leadership. Could anyone who attached some weight to the Marxist-Leninist bias of Peking really have believed that Mr. Acheson's assurances were adequate? Mao Tse-tung more probably considered the Secretary's nice words as a shrewd device to relax his guard and lull him into a false sense of security. For did not Mao know that a system based upon the private ownership of the means of production and factories producing surplus value must harbor evil intentions toward a "democratic" system based upon the collective ownership of property? No amount of American goodwill could have overcome this conviction, since in the Communist lexicon the goodwill of American "ruling circles" and "Wall Street" is by definition nonexistent. Mao probably remembered Karl von Clausewitz' famous sentence, "A conqueror is always a lover of peace," and Lenin's marginal scribble, "Ah, ah, Witty." But even if he had believed Secretary Acheson's benevolent intentions, the Chinese Communist leader would probably have been unwilling to exchange such a volatile commodity as goodwill for a piece of real estate bordering on his strategic frontier. But, in Acheson's opinion, the geopolitical basis of a Sino-Soviet conflict was so fundamental that it could not be overcome by ideological links; in Marxist terms, the geopolitical substructure of the Sino-Soviet Treaty was in "inner contradiction" with its ideological superstructure. Sino-Russian hostility was thus a foregone conclusion; having, in fact, already passed beyond its embryonic stage, only time was needed for its maturation.

These comments do not imply agreement with the fashionable criticism that the American government should have heeded the words from Peking. In the first place, the Indian Ambassador was known to be favorably inclined toward the Chinese Communists. Chou's threats were more probably an attempt to blackmail the United Nations into voting against the resolution sanctioning the crossing of the parallel.[36] Second, warnings are double-edged weapons. They may deter an unwise or foolish act, or they may paralyze the will to act and grant the enemy a victory by default. Important is not so much Washington's neglect of Communist China's threat; after all, not even the Indian government felt sufficiently assured of the truthfulness of Chou's words to vote against the October 7 resolution. India merely abstained. The warning delivered by the Indian representative at the United Nations was hardly unequivocal. "My Government," he said, "fears that the result [of crossing the parallel] may be to prolong North Korean resistance, and even to extend the area of conflict. Our fears may turn out to be wrong, but each government has to judge the situation upon the best information at its disposal and to act accordingly." [37] More important is Secretary Acheson's mistaken analysis of the factors motivating Peking's foreign policy.

Only five days before the Inchon landing, on September 10, the Secretary declared, "I should think it would be sheer madness on the part of the Chinese Communists to do that [intervene] and I see no advantage to them in doing it." He repeated that in Northern China "a great cloud from the north, Russian penetration is operating." And he continued: "Now I give the people in Peiping credit for being intelligent enough to see what is happening to them. Why they should want to further their own dismemberment and destruction by getting at cross purposes with all the free nations of the world who are inherently their friends and have always been friends of the Chinese as against this imperialism coming down from the Soviet Union I cannot see. And since there is nothing in it for them, I don't see why they should yield to what is undoubtedly pressure from the Communist movement to get into the Korean war." [38]

Undoubtedly, Secretary Acheson delivered his statement partly to convince the Chinese Communist regime that the Western powers really were "inherently their friends." But these words also reflect the American government's conviction that the Sino-Soviet conflict would absorb all the energies of the Chinese Communist leaders in the coming months. Consequently, Red China's intervention came as a complete surprise. When one senator later commented, "They really fooled us when it comes right down to it; didn't they?" the Secretary could only reply "Yes, sir." [39]

If in late September and early October the United States government passed the point of no return in the Korean War, it did so with the approval of its allies. It may seem at a first glance that this observation is superfluous, but closer reflection indicates otherwise. It has merely to be remembered that General MacArthur received the Joint Chiefs' approval for his plan of military operations in North Korea on the same day that his troops reached the 38th Parallel, September 30; [40] that South Korean units began their northward advance twenty-four hours later; that the First Committee of the General Assembly did not begin its consideration of the future course of policy it would recommend to the parent body until October 2; and that the General Assembly delayed its deliberations until October 6. Does this sequence not suggest that the United States faced its partners with a *fait accompli?* Once the parallel had been passed, how could they repudiate the action of their leader and principal supporter? [41]

Somewhat surprisingly, support for this charge has come from General MacArthur. The General recalls that on September 30 he wired Secretary of Defense Marshall a directive which he intended to issue to the Eighth Army on October 2. In this message MacArthur explained that under the United Nations Security Council resolution of June 27 recommending assistance for the defense of the Republic of Korea, the field of military operations was limited only by international frontiers and military exigencies. In his reply Secretary Marshall cabled: "We desire that you proceed with your operations without any further explanation or announcement and let action determine the matter. Our government desires to avoid having to make an issue of the 38th parallel until we have accomplished our mission." The implications of this message, General Whitney recalls, made MacArthur "raise his eyebrows . . . MacArthur could appreciate the President's natural inclination to present the other U.N. Governments with a *fait accompli.*" [42]

The manner in which the President avoided a clear answer on the 38th Parallel at his press conference on September 28 also lends some substance to this view. Mr. Truman's attention was called to a State

Department spokesman who had said that "this country's position was that sanction of a pursuit of the Communist forces across the line was contained in the original United Nations Security Council resolution." The President merely replied that "the resolution was very broad." Later, Mr. Truman did remark, however, that "General MacArthur was under direct orders of the President and the Chiefs of Staff and that he would follow those orders." When asked "if these orders implied the authority, Mr. Truman said he could not answer the question." The President was then reminded that "recently he had said that the question of crossing the line was one for the United Nations to decide and he was asked how this squared with his statement that the commander was under his orders. The Chief Executive replied that the United Nations would have to act first and that certainly it would relay any new instructions through him." The *New York Times* correspondent noted, "This reply, suggesting further action at Lake Success, appeared to be in conflict with the position stated by the State Department spokesman and left the world with an enigma." [43]

Actually, there was no enigma. The sequence of events cannot be understood solely in terms of their outward appearance, nor should the Marshall message be read too literally. It is quite true that the General Assembly did not begin its discussion of the crossing of the 38th Parallel until October 6, but it must also be noted that between September 29 and October 6 the Assembly was not in session. Moreover, only South Korean troops were yet across the parallel; if necessary, they could have been recalled by cutting off their logistical and tactical support. One can, of course, question why the President was so vague in his answers to queries of future intent. At the same time, it should be remembered that Ambassador Austin had been quite specific in outlining this government's position. It would surely have been highly improper and undiplomatic for the leading American statesman, who was symbolically also serving as the United Nations' Chief Executive during the war, to announce in advance of the General Assembly deliberations that he had decided to cross the parallel. In form at least, the United States and its allies were conducting the war in Korea under the aegis of the United Nations.

The evidence, then, indicates not that the United States faced its associates in Korea with a unilateral decision but rather that a tacit agreement had been reached by the leading Western powers in late

September. On September 29, just prior to his departure for home, British Foreign Secretary Ernest Bevin declared in New York "that there is no North Korea or South Korea. They [the Korean people] are Koreans and there should be no artificial perpetuation of that division." [44] During the debates in both the First Committee and the General Assembly, the British delegate, Mr. Kenneth Younger, spoke warmly in favor of Korean unification; [45] indeed, it was he who introduced the resolution recommending the indirect authorization for the northward advance. This resolution also received the firm endorsement of other NATO members, such as Canada, France, Norway, and the Netherlands, but the support was by no means limited to these countries. The final Assembly vote of 47 in favor to 5 against (7 abstentions) [46] showed that Mr. Spender of Australia was speaking for the great majority of his colleagues, when he said that it

would be useless if North Korean forces were allowed to remain ready to strike again and threaten South Korea. The only logical interpretation of the Security Council resolution of June 27 was that the North Korean Army, which was the aggressor, must be destroyed as a fighting force; that, by corollary, meant pursuing it across the parallel. Crossing of the 38th parallel would be for the sole object of putting an end to the present struggle and bringing about a unified Korea.[47]

The record, then, is quite clear; Asian and European critics, who later laid Chinese intervention to the foolish American demand for total military victory and unification, have little ground for limiting their criticism and focusing their retrospective eyesight on the United States. There can be no disagreement with Secretary Marshall's comment that "where the foreign governments became very active in this matter [of crossing the parallel], seemingly to disapprove or be fearful of what was to be done, was after there were indications of the Chinese Communists' entry into the fight." [48]

The crossing of the 38th Parallel brought the Administration and MacArthur momentarily closer together. But their agreement upon this action failed to ease the underlying tension between them. Nor could it have done so; their respective attitudes — whether toward the relative importance of Europe and Asia in the global pattern of American defense, or toward Chiang Kai-shek and Mao Tse-tung — were too far apart. Only a miracle, which would have converted MacArthur to the Administration's point of view or the government to the General's outlook, could have resolved their deep differences.

Apparently Harry Truman still believed in miracles; moreover, that he could perform them! On October 10, three days after the United Nations General Assembly had indirectly authorized the military unification of Korea, the President announced that he had decided to meet General MacArthur in person. His objective: to explain his Administration's foreign policy to the General and win a convert. Harry Truman was not only a tough individual; he was an optimistic one.

VI

WAKE ISLAND: THE EAGLE'S
TWO HEADS

"General MacArthur and I are making a quick trip over the coming week-end to meet in the Pacific." With these casual words, the President announced his flight to Wake Island and the dramatic forthcoming meeting with his proconsul in Japan. In what subsequently became a most controversial conference, in which Tokyo and Washington questioned each other's motives and integrity, only the rest of Mr. Truman's words have remained uncontroversial. He would take advantage of his visit, he said, to express to General MacArthur the nation's appreciation and gratitude for the "great service which he is rendering to world peace. He is carrying out his mission with the imagination, courage, and effectiveness which have marked his entire service as one of our greatest military leaders." The President made it quite plain, however, that it was not his intention merely to pay a courtesy call upon his field commander; that he wished to meet MacArthur to "discuss with him the final phase of United Nations action in Korea." [1]

The next day, October 11, the Chief Executive set out on his long journey to the mid-Pacific. He was reported to be well prepared for the mission ahead of him. The President, as one correspondent put it, was traveling as the "completely equipped diplomat," carrying with him a fourth Oak Leaf Cluster for the General's Distinguished Service Medal, a five-pound box of candied plums for Mrs. MacArthur, and a "benign policy" for Asia. Mr. Truman, it would seem, was putting his best foot forward in his attempt to establish an *entente cordiale* between Washington and Tokyo.

The meeting began in an amiable mood. As Mr. Truman's plane came to a stop, MacArthur strode to the foot of the launching ramp, and with hand outstretched greeted the President with every appearance of warmth and friendliness.

"Mr. President," General MacArthur began, seizing Mr. Truman's right arm while pumping his hand.

President Truman smiled and said: "How are you, General? I'm glad you are here. I've been a long time meeting you, General."

"I hope it won't be so long next time, Mr. President," General MacArthur replied.

Observers noted that MacArthur did not salute his Commander in Chief.[2]

After this pleasant exchange, the President and General MacArthur went into immediate conference. The exact nature of their conversation is still unknown. According to MacArthur's confidant, General Whitney, most of their half-hour meeting was devoted to a discussion of the fiscal and economic policies of the Philippine Islands! [3] According to Mr. Truman, the United Nations Commander apologized if his Veterans for Foreign Wars speech had caused the President any embarrassment; predicted the early end of hostilities, and the transfer of one division from Korea to Western Europe by January 1951. In turn, Mr. Truman informed his Far Eastern field commander "something of our plans" for strengthening Europe.[4]

Later, the President and MacArthur held a second meeting. This time, they were joined by Mr. Truman's advisers. These were: from the State Department, Assistant Secretary of State Dean Rusk and Ambassador-at-large Phillip Jessup; from the Defense Department, General Omar Bradley and Secretary of the Army Frank Pace; from the White House staff, Special Assistant to the President, Averell Harriman. For an hour and a half, this group considered a number of different topics: Korean rehabilitation, elections, war-crime trials, the Japanese peace treaty, a Pacific defense pact, and the possibilities of Chinese Communist or Soviet intervention.[5] It was during these ninety minutes that General MacArthur made his famous statement that "if the Chinese tried to get down to Pyongyang there would be the greatest slaughter."

General Bradley later intimated that the agenda for this formal conference had included certain other items, but that these had been deleted from the record released to the public for security reasons. This suggestion was quickly dismissed during the hearings. "I have read the deletions," answered Senator Hickenlooper. "So far as they are concerned, they would add nothing to the serious import of this conference . . . they are only a few lines." [6]

The third and last meeting was a "technical consultation." General MacArthur discussed some of his military problems with Secretary

Pace and General Bradley, while John Muccio, the American Ambassador to the Republic of Korea, consulted the State Department's officials in the President's party.[7]

In the light of this record, General Whitney has asserted that MacArthur was not asked a single question on which Washington did not already possess the General's full views. Any of these matters could in any case have been dealt with satisfactorily through an exchange of messages between Washington and Tokyo. Neither the President nor his advisers had to fly to Wake Island and back to ascertain MacArthur's views on Chinese Communist intervention, Korean rehabilitation, or a Pacific defense pact. Having thus to his own satisfaction dismissed any possible reason for the President's long journey, Whitney charges that the President must have made the visit for other reasons, specifically two: first, to link the Administration to MacArthur's victory just before the mid-term elections; and second, to establish an alibi for the Administration in case Communist China decided to intervene in the war after all. Wake Island was therefore a "sly political ambush." [8]

Whitney's first charge is nonsense which presumes rather naïvely that the Democrats would somehow have been completely disassociated from the successful conduct of the war if Mr. Truman had not decided to visit the victor of Korea to pay his compliments. It is somewhat paradoxical and amusing, to say the least, to hear this charge from a man whose official biography of the "Old Man" argues both implicitly and explicitly that American interests in the Pacific would have been better protected if President Truman had listened more attentively to the oracle from Tokyo. But when the President *did* go and see MacArthur, the Chief Executive's purpose was condemned as the cheap trick of a former haberdasher and small-town politician. Apparently, the President could visit the illustrious General and listen to him only at a time of disaster or grave crisis; judging by the results of the mid-term elections — which certainly confounded General Whitney's judgment about General MacArthur's ability to transfer his alleged political popularity — it would appear that this might have been politically more profitable for Mr. Truman.

In making his second charge, General Whitney is on more solid ground. Mr. Truman has repeatedly asserted that General MacArthur gave him his personal assurance that the Chinese Communists would not intervene in the war, but as we know, this is not the whole story.

It was, of course, natural that at Wake Island the President should ask MacArthur what the chances of Chinese intervention were; perhaps it was also quite natural that the President should later publicize MacArthur's remark and show that his field commander's prognostic powers were not outside the bounds of human frailty. After all, MacArthur is himself not entirely blameless when it comes to shifting the responsibility for certain decisions and events which had unpleasant consequences. Nevertheless, while Mr. Truman has made ample use of MacArthur's "prophecy," there is no reason to believe that he journeyed to Wake Island with the specific purpose in mind of eliciting this assurance and using it politically if the Chinese did decide to come into Korea.

The evidence points precisely in the opposite direction: that Mr. Truman flew out to Wake Island to establish a more cordial and harmonious relationship with his field commander, and thereby deny Peking any reason for intervention. Mao Tse-tung might decide to intervene under one of two conditions: if he had no faith in the integrity of Secretary Acheson's assurances to him — and this Washington did not believe — or if he were afraid that the President and Secretary of Defense could not control MacArthur. Mao knew that MacArthur's thoughts about him were distinctly less than friendly; consequently, he might suspect that MacArthur would extend the war to his country. The Administration was worried.

MacArthur had visited Chiang Kai-shek on Formosa on July 31. Upon the American Commander's return to Tokyo, Chiang had talked of future "Sino-American military cooperation" and "final victory" in the struggle against Communism. What arrangements had the two men made for "Sino-American military cooperation?" What had MacArthur told Chiang that had encouraged the Generalissimo to talk of "final victory"? MacArthur had, to be sure, assured Washington that he had meticulously confined his discussion to problems of the island's military defense, but he had made no secret of his sympathy for Chiang.

In his message to the Veterans of Foreign Wars, he had implied not only that the Chinese Nationalist leader was a loyal ally, but that the United States should aid him in order to prevent the loss of Chiang's unsinkable aircraft carrier and submarine tender; and in private, he had added that the State Department's hostile attitude toward the Chinese Nationalist leader might affect his own mission adversely. Cordial political relations with Chiang were the prerequisite for Formosa's defense. The Administration, however, claimed that such close political alignment might not only estrange the support of America's allies and help alienate the sympathies of most Asian countries, but make it impossible for the United States to exploit the conflict of interests between Moscow and Peking. An unfriendly attitude toward the latter might well bar the possibility of a break between the two principal Communist powers; indeed, it might serve to strengthen anti-American sentiment in Communist China and perhaps incite Peking to intervene in Korea. Therefore, MacArthur must not again issue pronouncements which cast suspicions on our motives and intentions.

MacArthur was also to avoid any provocative actions. Incidents such as the attack on October 9 by MacArthur's planes on a Soviet airbase near Vladivostok had at all costs to be avoided; [9] Moscow and Peking might not believe that such attacks were military mistakes. MacArthur had already been instructed on September 27 that during the course of his operations in North Korea he was not to employ any non–South Korean forces in the provinces neighboring on Soviet Russia and Communist China and that he was under no circumstances to attack any targets in Manchuria or Siberia — even if Peking should defy Secretary Acheson's analysis of the mainsprings of its foreign policy and intervene. The Administration did not want the United States to become engaged in a general war with Communist China. Such a conflict would hamper the military build-up in Europe; and it might bring the Soviet Union into the fray. The United States, with only one spare division at home, had to avoid either contingency. MacArthur must not, therefore, give his orders the same liberal interpretation he had previously given to his directive of June 26, which had ordered him to confine his air force and navy to the area below the 38th Parallel.

On that occasion MacArthur had anticipated Washington's instructions and on his own initiative had instructed his air arm to expand its bombing missions to the whole of Korea; he had reasoned that he could not bring the South Koreans the "effective military assistance" which he had been authorized to do, if North Korea remained "an air sanctuary in which Communist forces could mobilize and maneuver and bring up supplies." Consequently, he had told himself that his directive of June 26 was "permissive, not restrictive, and that implicit in his directive was the discretion normal to field command." [10] MacArthur was not to believe that his orders of September 27 were equally flexible; they definitely were not.

Washington thus felt strongly that if MacArthur did not obey his instructions to the letter, he might precipitate precisely the situation which it wished to avoid; this was to become increasingly obvious as MacArthur advanced northward. In this respect, Mr. Truman was especially concerned by his field commander's expressed belief that Asians respected only aggressive and forceful leadership, and the implication of this remark that Asia's problems could be solved by force; as the President himself put it upon his return from Wake Island, the problem of peace in the Far East was "far more" than a military one. [11] Or as Anthony Leviero of the *New York Times* wrote in his column of October 12, 1950:

Informed sources in Washington said today that Mr. Truman is *desirous* of winning General MacArthur's support for our Far Eastern policy. It is known that the General disagrees in important respects, favoring strong acts backed by military force . . . The basic principle of the policy that the Administration *would like* General MacArthur to support is that communism, especially in China, cannot be overcome by force. Administration advisers see the solution as a long-term one that will come about when the Chinese leaders . . . recognize that their best interests are not served by alliances that keep them subservient to the Soviet Union. [12]

It was therefore essential that at a time when United Nations troops were penetrating deeper into North Korea, the President himself should try to establish a more sympathetic and harmonious relationship between himself and his military executive and make it clear that he did not share the conviction that the problems created by Communism in Asia, and particularly those in continental China, could be overcome merely by the use of force. The war must remain limited and Washington's orders must be obeyed. The United States must not become engaged in a major war in the Far East, and thereby dissipate its strength in a peripheral area; the United States must instead conserve its power and concentrate upon its main task, the build-up of military power in Europe. In his speech at San Francisco, after he had returned from his visit with General MacArthur, Mr. Truman stressed that the United States had not forgotten its commitments to Europe, and he implied that his Administration did not estimate the importance of the Far East in the pattern of American security as

highly as General MacArthur did. The President emphasized that the
Soviet threat was aimed at "both Europe and Asia"; and throughout
his speech, he discussed the Korean War only within the broader context of the Soviet Union's global menace.[13]

It would thus seem that the President did not fly to Wake Island
to reach specific decisions, but rather a precise understanding; that
he did not expect to achieve any concrete conclusions, only a spirit
of cooperation. "I understand that there has been speculation about
why I made this trip," said Mr. Truman. "There really is no mystery
about it. I went because I wanted to see and talk to General Mac-
Arthur. There is no substitute for personal conversation . . ." [14] These
words, however beguiling or platitudinous they might seem at a first
glance, nevertheless sum up the purpose of the conference rather
aptly. Wake Island was not a "sly political ambush," but a "friendly
get-together." A more sympathetic relationship between the President
and the General was not merely desirable; it was imperative during
the present stage of the campaign. And this task could not await the
election returns.

Mr. Truman's means of establishing such a relationship was in
character with his personality: personal diplomacy, direct and simple.
MacArthur had served in the Orient for fourteen years; not once
during that time had he come home, even though several invitations
had been extended to him. Consequently, it was the President's impression that the General's "thoughts were wrapped up in the East,"
and that he had substantially lost his contact with the "home-folks" —
a term, which in Mr. Truman's dictionary, was no doubt synonymous
with that of his Administration. For the President had concluded that
all of his previous efforts to impress General MacArthur with the
global picture, as seen from Washington, "had had little success. I
[Truman] thought he might adjust more easily if he heard it from me
directly." [15]

Nevertheless, one real mystery remains: the choice of that particular weekend for the meeting. It is perhaps significant that in announcing the conference, the President's press secretary said the decision to
meet the General "was not the result of any emergency." According
to a contemporary newspaper account, however, the President had
originally planned to fly that weekend only to St. Louis, where his
sister was to be presented with the title of Worthy Grand Matron by
the Grand Chapter of Missouri, Order of the Eastern Star.[16] Then,

quite suddenly, came the news of the President's longer trip to the mid-Pacific. In his memoirs, Mr. Truman has subsequently written that he chose the weekend of October 15 because he wished to include "a first-hand account" from the United Nations Commander for two speeches scheduled for October 17 and 24.[17] But could the telecom not have served this function equally well? It had for the President's address to Congress on July 19.[18]

Though neither the Truman memoirs nor the official MacArthur biography give any clues for scheduling the conference on October 15, the timing does not seem to be totally unconnected to an attack on October 9 by two United States F-80 Shooting Stars on a Soviet air base in Siberia. This base was not located on the Korean frontier, but sixty-two miles north inside Russian territory and eighteen miles southwest of Vladivostok. The Russians, nevertheless, withheld their fire. Next day, the Soviet government protested this "gross violation" of Russian territorial integrity in a note delivered to our Minister-Counselor in Moscow. Mr. Barbour refused to accept the note, declaring that the fighter planes were operating under the "unified command," and that this incident was therefore a matter for the United Nations.[19] The State Department supported this position in a formal announcement the next day. From American headquarters in Tokyo the reaction was crisp. An official air force spokesman declared that he "knew nothing of the Russian charges." [20] He did not elaborate this statement or clarify whether he meant that the Defense Department had not yet forwarded the Russian protest or whether he knew anything of the attack.

On October 19 the State Department, in a note to the Soviet government, acknowledged the attack and declared that the United States was willing to make restitution for the damage caused to Soviet property. At the same time, Ambassador Austin delivered a report from General MacArthur to the United Nations; in it, MacArthur declared that the attack was due to "navigation error and poor judgment, in that the attack was made without positive identification of the target." The report added that the commander of the air force group had been relieved and the two airmen disciplined.[21]

Was it this attack, so little noted at the time, which was responsible for the President's sudden decision to meet General MacArthur on the weekend of the fifteenth? The attack took place on October 9. The Soviet government protested on October 10. The Presidential flight was announced the same day. The conference resulted on the fifteenth, and the MacArthur note was released four days later. The sequence of these events certainly suggests that this incident might have been an important factor in precipitating the Truman-MacArthur conference. If it was, it underlined the urgency of the President's desire to achieve a better working relationship with MacArthur during this final stage of the campaign. Incidents such as this attack must be avoided lest they provoke an extension of the war; Moscow and Peking might, after all, not believe that MacArthur's pilots had simply made mistakes. The actions — as well as the words — of the United States Supreme Commander in the Pacific must demonstrate that the United States harbored no aggressive desires in Korea or elsewhere in the Pacific.

Evidently, the President thought that his *tête-á-tête* with General MacArthur had achieved this purpose. At the end of their meetings, he described the conference as having been "highly satisfactory," and having achieved a "very complete unanimity of views." Some of Mr. Truman's intimates described him as "buoyant." "Mr. President, how did things shape up?" asked Anthony Leviero of the *New York Times*. "Perfectly . . . I've never had a more satisfactory conference since I've been President." Leviero described the outcome of the Wake Island conference with a classic comment — Mr. Truman, he said, "left Wake highly pleased with the results, like an insurance salesman who had at last signed up an important prospect while the latter appeared dubious over the extent of the coverage." General MacArthur was apparently not in an equally happy frame of mind. When seen by reporters, MacArthur kept looking at his watch; when the conference was over, he refused to stay for lunch. "There are many pressing matters awaiting my return to Tokyo," he told the President, whose business presumably was less voluminous and pressing.²² His post-conference remarks to correspondents were curt: "All the comments will have to come from the publicity man of the President." Perhaps these were merely unfortunately chosen words, but when asked for his impression of Mr. Truman — "now that you have met him for the first time" — the General replied rather irrelevantly that "All the discussions of this meeting are in the hands of Mr. Ross [the White House press secretary]." Later he relented, saying that he had "greatly enjoyed meeting the President." And he added: "The President's visit to the Pacific cannot fail to arouse great enthusiasm throughout the

Far East, where it will be interpreted as symbolizing a firm determination that peace shall be secured in the Pacific, and that Asia shall be free, not slave." [23] These words bear little resemblance to those of General Whitney!

Whether the meeting and the alleged mutual enjoyment had brought about a reconciliation of views or a more pronounced spirit of cooperation between Washington and Tokyo is another matter. The President, to be sure, believed that he and General MacArthur had reached such a better understanding: "When General MacArthur and I discussed the whole problem of peace in the Far East, we recognized that this is far more than a military problem." [24] But he had also thought this after the Harriman-MacArthur meeting. He had been quickly disappointed. MacArthur had felt too deeply about the strategic importance of Formosa and the desirability of wholehearted American support for Chiang Kai-shek. Would history now repeat itself? The further advance into North Korea would tell.

VII

THE "HOME BY CHRISTMAS" OFFENSIVE: PRELUDE TO DISASTER

Although Chinese entry into the war had been dismissed as unlikely at Wake Island, increased concentrations of Chinese Red troops were reported massing along the Chinese frontier between October 15 and 21. According to Hanson Baldwin, the estimate was placed at about 250,000 men near the Korean frontier and 200,000 elsewhere in Manchuria. Reflecting Washington's sentiment that the time has passed for anything but "defensive arrangements," Baldwin continued that "it is considered natural for the Chinese Communists to strengthen their frontier, for Mao may believe that Manchuria is next on the timetable of the American imperialists." The Russians, on "increasing evidence," were pulling out of North Korea "completely." The flow of traffic down the east coast had been halted and the Russian advisers and technicians had turned back to Soviet territory. Baldwin did caution that "the Communists' concept of defense might include an advance south of the Korean frontier for a limited distance to set up a buffer zone between Manchuria and Korea," and he reminded his readers that the "Chinese Communists and perhaps the Russians too may be sensitive about the Yalu River power complex, which supplies not only North Korea but parts of Manchuria, including Port Arthur and Dairen, with power. The grids and distributive system are believed to be on the North Korean side of the frontier." [1]

Baldwin's prognosis was soon reflected in the military communiqués. On October 26, the military communiqué reported: "One regiment of the South Korean Sixth Division ran into a hard-fighting enemy force near Onjong . . . approximately twenty-five miles south of the border." [2] The Communist resistance was characterized as "heavy," a descriptive word which had of late been falling into some disuse. Lieutenant General Walton Walker, commander of the Eighth Army, immediately ordered all forward elements to pull back and rejoin the main body of his troops. Two days later, Lindesay Parrott reported to the *New York Times* from Tokyo that

enemy resistance for the first time in several days included large organized bodies of troops, artillery, and mortar fire . . . The most dangerous situation for the South Korean advance guards developed around the village Onjong, where a regiment of the Sixth Division for a time was surrounded by enemy troops. The Korean Republicans had been thrusting in that area toward the Yalu River's great Supung Dam that provides electric power not only for North Korea but for Mukden and Dairen — a matter of considerable importance to both Manchurian and Soviet industry.

Parrott commented that the fighting "centered along the west coast of North Korea about sixty miles from the Yalu River crossing on the international frontier. The area for centuries has been a traditional route of invasion and counter-invasion of Korea and Manchuria from the days of Genghis Khan . . ." [3]

The South Korean First Division was also reported as "heavily engaged with a vigorously resisting enemy." This time the battle was near Unsan. A United States Eighth Army spokesman, however, "ridiculed" these reports, declaring that "investigation showed that the report was based on the stories of two prisoners of war each of whom told six different stories, adding up to twelve stories, which added up to nothing." However, it was conceded that "nothing" might add up to "a token force of Chinese Communists, perhaps a regiment, [which] may be somewhere in North Korea. [The spokesman at General MacArthur's headquarters] discounts the possibility that any large force from across the border is now in action." [4]

Chinese prisoners of war were, however, captured near Hamhung on October 30. The next day, Tokyo admitted temporarily that Chinese Communists, numbering from one regiment to one division, were in action and had in fact launched a "strong counterattack" which had "cut the communications of advance guards of the Republican Capitol Division, which has been pushing in from the east coast toward the Pujon reservoir." This report, it was acknowledged, was consistent with "repeated assertions" by South Korean officers "that their men for several days had been facing elements of the Chinese Fortieth Corps, which supposedly had been concentrated along the Yalu River." [5]

Striking evidence of large-scale entry into the war now became rapidly apparent. It was reported on November 3 that "some sources" believed that the entire Forty-second Chinese Corps was in Korea, and "there appeared little question that United States and Chinese Communist troops were now in contact." In fact, "Chinese Communist hordes, attacking on horse and on foot to the sound of bugle-calls, cut up Americans and South Koreans at Unsan today in an Indian-style massacre . . ." [6] Twenty-four hours later, a "First Corps spokesman indicated that elements of five Chinese divisions from the 38th and 40th Route Armies had been identified in the hard-pressed western sector . . . where the Republic of Korea Seventh Division had been "pretty badly chewed up." [7] A spokesman for the Tenth Corps on the eastern sector reported that Chinese Communist troops had been encountered "to the strength of one division or more . . ."; but indications "were that the enemy had thrown the bulk of his new power into combat in the west and might expect additional reinforcements there." Pilots flying reconnaissance over the Manchurian frontier reported "considerable movement" north of the line.[8]

Nobody in Tokyo would as yet admit the situation as serious and fraught with disastrous possibilities. It was believed that the so-called Chinese "will prove to be more Manchurian-bred Koreans, like the men of the two Korean divisions of the Chinese Communist Army, which were transferred to the North Korean Red regime after the Chinese Civil War." Headquarters described the situation on October 29 as "not alarming." As "far as verified information was concerned, the United Nations forces were still in contact with the North Korean army. A few allegedly Chinese prisoners were taken near Unsan last week [but] there had been no great influx of Chinese soldiers across the Yalu River." [9] Three days later, on November 1, the Far Eastern Command admitted "frankly that it did not know whether or not actual Chinese Communist units — as such — have been committed to the Korean war . . . [The evidence so far has remained] insufficient to confirm that Chinese Communist forces in Chinese Army organizations under the direction either of China or North Korean general headquarters were taking part in the conflict." The situation was still not critical. The "stubborn opposition indicated that the Communist Army Command had pulled together its remaining troops and weapons for a last stand [and not] that any large-scale reinforcements had been received from Communist China." Michael James, the *New York Times* correspondent, however, reported that same day from Major General Edward M. Almond's headquarters that Almond's troops "were fighting a Chinese Communist Regiment 30 miles north of

Hungnam. This was the first official confirmation that a large force of Chinese as such was fighting against United Nations forces in Korea. Cheerful hopes that the war was virtually over were squelched here this evening." The news, James reported, "came at the end of a day filled with reports that the Chinese had moved into North Korea with heavy guns. One report from an air support unit at Hungnam said two Chinese divisions were moving south on every road! This evening headquarters said this report 'cannot be confirmed or denied.'" [10] The next day, Tokyo confirmed this report, and denied its earlier communiqué which had claimed that most of the resistance came from the remnants of the North Korean army. United Nations forces were now fighting Chinese Communist troops, though this statement was immediately qualified: "We don't know whether they represent the Chinese Government." [11]

The hesitation these communiqués betray in identifying Red China's intervention provide the best indication of MacArthur's uncertain judgment regarding Peking's intentions.

What was the extent of the Chinese Communist commitment, and what was its purpose? Did it aim at the establishment of a buffer zone or allied withdrawal to the 38th Parallel? Was Peking concerned only with the safety of the Yalu River hydroelectric plants or did it wish to drive MacArthur's forces out of Korea altogether? Washington, which during this entire period of Communist Chinese intervention was, according to General Collins, completely dependent for its intelligence upon the Far Eastern Command, did not know. Tokyo headquarters did not know either. In S. L. A. Marshall's apt words, the "Chinese Communist Army was a phantom which cast no shadow. Its main secret — its strength, its position, and its initiative — had been kept to perfection, and thereby it was doubly armed." In the absence of a major clash, MacArthur's intelligence was unable to fathom these facts.

Both the movement and concentration had gone undetected. The enemy columns moved only by night, preserved an absolute camouflage discipline during their daytime tests and remained hidden to view under village rooftops after reaching the chosen ground. Air observation saw nothing of this mass maneuver. Civilian refugees brought no word of it. The remaining chance for its discovery therefore lay in deep patrolling by fairly heavy combat columns, which was not done.

That it was not done does not require excuse. It is easy to cast blame if one has never seen the North Korean countryside or is unmindful of

Eighth Army's strained situation. Within that hill country, a primitive army, lacking in heavy equipment, can be stowed away in less space than a hunt would use for the chasing of foxes. And Eighth Army did not have a sufficient troop strength to probe and prowl every corner of the outland where hostiles might be hiding. In the preceding days, it had been several times clipped for just this kind of enterprise. Detachments had been cut off for striking too deeply while on their own.[12]

While MacArthur was thus unable to estimate properly Chinese strength and evaluate Chinese intentions, he did caution the Joint Chiefs on November 4 against drawing premature conclusions and expressed his belief that the presence of Chinese troops in North Korea did not signify full-scale intervention. Although the latter was a "distinct possibility," there were many fundamental logical reasons against accepting this conclusion. MacArthur suggested three contingencies which he believed more likely: the Chinese forces in Korea were only rendering the North Koreans covert military assistance; these troops did represent "more or less" volunteers whose task it was to aid the North Koreans retain a nominal foothold south of the Yalu; and lastly, the Chinese had committed these soldiers in the belief that non–South Korean forces would be dispatched right up to the Manchurian frontier. "I recommend," MacArthur concluded, "against hasty conclusions which might be premature and believe that a final appraisement should await a more complete accumulation of military facts." [13]

By the next day, however, Chinese participation in the war was sufficient to warrant General MacArthur to issue a special report to the Security Council. In it he stated "that the United Nations are presently in hostile contact with Chinese Communist military units deployed for action against the forces of the Unified Command." Twelve incidents of "hostile contact" were then listed: five concerned anti-aircraft fire from the Manchurian side of Yalu on American bombers flying on the Korean side. Two of these took place before the crossing of the parallel, one on August 22 near the Sui-Ho reservoir and the other on August 24 "in the vicinity of Sinuiju" on the Yalu River. The third incident occurred on October 15, when four F-51's were fired at while flying on the Korean side of the Yalu "near Sinuiju airfield"; one plane was lost by a direct hit. On November 1, anti-aircraft fire from the Manchurian side was directed against a flight of thirteen F-80's, again "in the vicinity of Sinuiju." Another aircraft was lost. Two more incidents took place in the same area. One was on

October 17, when an RB-29 was fired at from the Manchurian side. The last occurred when a flight of thirteen F-80 Saber Jets were attacked by six to nine Communist jets which flew in from across the Yalu River.

The balance of the charges dealt with land forces. These cited that on October 16 a regiment of Chinese troops had crossed the Yalu and proceeded to the Chosen and Fusen dams. Four days later, another force had been deployed to the south of the Sui-Ho Dam. On October 30, two further regiments had been identified "in the vicinity of Changjin," that is, near the reservoir. On November 2 and 3 further units had been identified, but their locations were not named. Again, it is interesting to note that MacArthur did not attempt to evaluate Peking's intentions.[14]

Instead, he followed up his report with a special communiqué the next day. He announced that United Nations troops were fighting "elements of alien Communist forces . . . with adequate supply behind the privileged sanctuary of the adjacent Manchurian border." He denounced the Communists for having "committed one of the most offensive acts of international lawlessness of historic record by moving without any notice of belligerency." He claimed that allied forces had evaded a "possible trap [which] was . . . surreptitiously laid, calculated to encompass the destruction of the United Nations forces . . . This potential danger was avoided . . . [by] the United Nations commander responsible for that sector, who with great perspicacity and skill completely reversed the movement of his forces . . . a new and fresh army now faces us, backed up by a possibility of large alien reserves and adequate supplies within easy reach of the enemy but beyond the limits of our present sphere of military action." MacArthur's concluding words once again show his uncertainty of Communist China's intentions. "Whether and to what extent these reserves will be moved forward," he said, "remains to be seen and is a matter of gravest international significance." [15]

To determine this, MacArthur informed the Joint Chiefs on November 7 that he was planning to resume the initiative "to take accurate measure . . . of enemy strength." [16] On the same day, however, "Chinese and North Korean troops in a surprise manoeuvre broke contact with United Nations forces on the defense line north of Anju this morning . . . 'Vigorous' patrols by United States and South Korean elements this morning failed to find the enemy." Peking's intentions were thus left in a fog, though Tokyo warned that the break was most probably not a withdrawal but a pause for regrouping for "further thrusts." [17] On November 9 an Eighth Army spokesman in Korea said the "Chinese Communist troops might be avoiding a fight in North Korea pending high level diplomatic moves that would affect the course of the Korean war . . . [The Chinese withdrawal] has been gradual over a four-day period [in the northwest]. In the northeast a Tenth Corps spokesman said the Chinese 184th Division was 'in retreat' from the giant Changjin hydroelectric complex." [18] By withdrawing from one of the big reservoirs, the Chinese Communists were strengthening the impression that their intervention had only limited objectives in mind, and that this was perhaps an opportune moment for negotiations.

Assurance after assurance was offered to Peking. On November 7 the Interim Committee on Korea had declared that United Nations troops would "fully support" the Manchurian frontier; [19] three days later a six-power resolution introduced into the Security Council reaffirmed that the United Nations would hold the frontier "inviolate" and "would fully protect Chinese and Korean interests in the frontier zone." [20] Secretary Acheson repeated this pledge the next day when he emphasized that neither the United Nations nor the United States harbored any "ulterior design in Manchuria." If the Chinese continued to misunderstand our motives, a "world-wide tragedy of the most colossal nature was in the making." [21] The President reiterated this theme: "We have never at any time entertained any intention to carry hostilities into China; so far as the United States is concerned, I wish to state unequivocally that because of our deep devotion to the cause of world peace, and our long-standing friendship for the people of China, we will take every honorable step to prevent any extension of the hostilities in the Far East." If Peking misinterpreted our peaceful intentions, "it can only be because they are being deceived by those whose advantage it is to prolong and extend hostilities in the Far East against the interest of all Far Eastern people." James Reston, in commenting on the President's statement, pointed out that the "only criticism heard about Mr. Truman's statement here [Washington] this evening was that it came several weeks late. Some well-informed persons here believe such a statement, if made when the United Nations troops took the North Korean capital, might have prevented the Chinese intervention, particularly if the United States had also offered to allow a United Nations peace commission to take over a buffer zone on the Korean side of the Chinese frontier." [22]

The Chinese rejected these assurances. They denounced MacArthur's report as a "malicious accusation." The true facts, Peking charged, consisted of American aggression against Formosa, violations of the Manchurian boundary by our planes operating from Korea; and in brief, that United States armies in North Korea constituted a threat to Chinese security. "To help Korea in its resistance . . . is to defend our own country. Therefore, the voluntary aid given to Korea is logical and reasonable." The precedent of "volunteer" troops, the Chinese Communists claimed, was initiated by Lafayette during the American Revolution; they cited that both American and British volunteer brigades had served during the Spanish Civil War. The Communists were also repaying the Korean people for their aid in the Chinese revolution of the 1920's. The United States had "smashed her way across the world to Chinese territory and into it [Formosa]." In reassuring the Secretary of State and the President that they had *not* misunderstood our motives, Peking cited a report quoting President Rhee saying, "The war cannot stop at the Yalu River," and Senator Knowland's proposal, "Why not a neutral zone 10 miles north of the Yalu River?" The Administration was using such "lesser lights" to state its real intentions, since "these are the people who can easily be denied by the Government." Reassurances to the contrary were a "mixture of honeymooned words and threats . . . [to] . . . soften up public opinion for an American advance right up the Chinese frontier and eventually across it."

The Chinese Communists brought to attention a series of conflicting press reports issued at various stages of the campaign. On the same day, they showed, it had been reported that United Nations troops would not advance beyond the 38th Parallel, and that they had already crossed it but would halt 150 miles north of the parallel. A later Reuters' dispatch claimed that only Republic of Korea troops would be employed above the "waist," and then United States forces too, only they would not advance farther than twenty miles below the Yalu.[23]

Despite this ominous reaction, there was as yet no indication that the Chinese army was committed to a full-scale offensive. Slowly the allies advanced against decreasing resistance. On November 20 United States troops of the Seventh Division reached the hills overlooking the river at Hyesanya. In other sectors United Nations troops were advancing slowly and cautiously probing for the defense line that the withdrawing Communists were reported to have built somewhere along their main line of communications with Manchuria.[24] The release of twenty-seven prisoners by the Chinese was interpreted hopefully. And on November 24, the day the representative of the Chinese Communist government arrived in New York to participate in the United Nations Security Council debate on MacArthur's special communiqué of November 5, the General launched an offensive that would for "all practical purposes end the war."

He launched it knowing that there were at least 100,000 men facing him in front and 40,000 guerillas behind him. He also knew that the size of his assaulting force was inadequate for a frontal attack; he therefore split his attacking army in two, thereby creating an attractive and fatal vacuum in the middle of his line. As at Inchon, MacArthur was taking a "tremendous gamble," but he believed that he would succeed. Chinese intervention seemed to have only limited aims: Peking itself claimed its troops were only volunteers; these forces had broken off contact after his announcement that he was facing an entirely new war; the allied army had been advancing steadily — the Tenth Corps was continuing its push up the east coast; the Seventeenth Regiment had already reached the Yalu; United Nations prisoners of war had been released. While he had at the same time admitted that full-scale Chinese entry into the war was a possibility, MacArthur's private messages to Washington reflected the contrary opinion. He now expected his boldness to convince Peking that Korea's fate had already been settled, particularly since he had already announced that the "new and nerve-shattering experiences" of a modern army's fire power and low-level strafing had demoralized the Chinese Communist forces and starved them of their supplies. On the very day MacArthur launched his final offensive, his headquarters reported that the air forces have "successfully interdicted enemy lines of support from the north so that further reinforcement therefrom has been sharply curtailed and essential supplies markedly limited."[25] The General was so confident of the offensive's success that he made his military dispositions not upon the assumption of massive Chinese Communist intervention but, in his own words, "upon the basis of the enemy that existed . . . That enemy was the North Korean group, and our forces had practically destroyed them . . . We were limited . . .

by the two conditions: The size of the force I had; and the mission that was given to me. My mission was to clear out all North Korea, to unify it and to liberalize it. The number of troops I had was limited, and those conditions indicated the disposition of the troops I had. As a matter of fact, the disposition of those troops, in my opinion, could not have been improved upon, had I known the Chinese were going to attack." [26]

In his advance toward the Yalu River, MacArthur was guided by two directives. On September 27, the day that Seoul had been liberated, the Joint Chiefs of Staff had directed the Commander in Chief, Far East, that as a "matter of policy" only South Korean troops should advance beyond the "neck" into the northeast provinces bordering the Soviet Union and in the area along the Manchurian border.[27] Three days later MacArthur had received another message, this time from Secretary of Defense Marshall: "We want you to feel unhampered tactically and strategically to proceed north of the 38th parallel." [28] MacArthur considered these words a modification of his preceding directive; sufficient modification, anyway, that it left him the final choice of tactics in the pursuit of the enemy — and he decided it left him the final decision to advance to the international boundary.

When, therefore, on October 23, a spokesman for the United States First Corps announced that all "foreign troops would be halted 40 miles south of the Yalu," it was not surprising that within forty-eight hours "a spokesman for the Eighth Army in Korea and General Douglas MacArthur's headquarters denied . . . that 'foreign' United Nations troops had been ordered to halt their advance 40 miles south of the frontier to minimize the international tension over a Red 'counter-invasion' of the North Korean Communist state." Not only had non–South Korean troops not been told to stop short of the international boundary, there was "no intention of establishing a formal 'buffer territory.'" Headquarters felt that such action would "establish a new 'Thirty-eighth Parallel' . . . It would also offer a North Korean Government a segment of territory where it might freely reorganize for new blows against the Korean Republic." [29]

Headquarters did not explain how an almost totally defeated enemy would rebuild his army for such a strike. But when President Truman at a press conference on October 26 reiterated that "it was his understanding" that only South Koreans would approach the northern frontier of their country, MacArthur quickly squashed this notion: "The mission of the United Nations forces," declared Tokyo, "is to clear Korea." [30]

In any case, on October 24, MacArthur advised his field commanders that he was lifting the restrictions on the employment of non–South Korean troops in the advance toward the Yalu. He authorized the use of all ground forces in the capture of North Korea, though he did caution his commanders to withdraw all non–Republic of Korea troops as soon as feasible. Informed of MacArthur's move, the Joint Chiefs immediately sent him a message stating that his order was not in accord with their instructions of September 27 to employ only South Koreans in the areas bordering on Communist China and the Soviet Union. "The Joint Chiefs of Staff further stated that while they realized CINCFE undoubtedly had sound reasons for the subject instructions, they would like information of these reasons since the action contemplated was a matter of concern to them." [31]

MacArthur in turn notified Washington that the Republic of Korea forces possessed neither the strength nor the leadership to handle the situation. "Military necessity" had made it incumbent for him to disregard the September 27 directive. Referring to the Joint Chiefs' message, MacArthur declared that he understood the basic purpose and intentions of his directive and would take "all precautions." However, he felt that tactical hazard might result from any action other than that which he had directed. He stated that the entire subject had been covered in his conference with the President at Wake Island.[32] MacArthur asserted that his advance would achieve its objective and clear the whole of Korea of enemy troops. Since there was no substitute for victory, there was no alternative. Admittedly, if the Chinese were planning on large-scale intervention, his advance was risky; but in that case, he would spring the Chinese trap before the Communists were ready to launch their own offensive.[33]

A Chinese counterattack seemed a remote danger to the General. He expected that his boldness and determination would cause Peking to abandon the hopeless task of maintaining a rump state in North Korea. On the basis of this confidence, he split his already outnumbered army in two and ordered the advance — all this weeks after he had first proclaimed that he was facing a situation so serious that it threatened the destruction of his command! No general expecting enemy retaliation would have given such an order and left the center of his line unguarded, particularly after his own headquarters had previously reported that 40,000 guerillas behind allied lines had orders to thrust north in Central Korea, where there was but a thin contact between the United States Eighth Army and the Tenth Corps on the east coast.[34] But in his special communiqué of November 24, MacArthur was already talking of the "prompt withdrawal of United Nations military forces" as soon as the offensive was ended.[35]

On that day, the General flew to Korea and personally gave the order for his now famous "home by Christmas" offensive. More often than not MacArthur's remark is condemned as an incredible hoax; but it was China's "massive retaliation" which made it so. MacArthur himself has explained that his remark was prompted by three objectives: it was meant to be an incentive for his weary soldiers, a reminder for General Bradley that troops would soon be available for service in Europe, and an assurance to Peking that the United Nations possessed no ambitions beyond the Yalu.[36] In any case, the reason for MacArthur's confidence on November 24 is quite apparent from his exchange of messages with the Joint Chiefs later in the same day.

In a message awaiting his return from the battlefield, the Joint Chiefs advised MacArthur that there was a growing concern within the United Nations over the possibility of a general conflict if a major clash developed with Chinese Communist troops as a result of his forces' advance against the entire boundary separating Korea and Manchuria. They told him that proposals in the United Nations suggested unwelcome restrictions upon his advance to the north; sentiment among United Nations' members favored establishing a demilitarized zone between his forces and the frontier, in the hope of thereby reducing Chinese Communist fear of United Nations military action against Manchuria. However, the Joint Chiefs informed MacArthur, at a recent meeting of the Secretaries of State and Defense, the Joint Chiefs, and other officials, the political and military consensus was that there should be no change in his mission, though immediate action should be taken to formulate a course of action which would permit the establishment of a unified Korea and at the same time reduce the risk of a more general involvement. Consideration was, therefore, being given to various measures which might reduce tension with the Chinese Communists. These included the following proposals: that after advancing to or near the Yalu, he might hold his forces on the high terrain dominating the approaches of the

Yalu Valley, principally with South Korean troops; that United Nations forces would continue to make every effort to spare the hydroelectric installations in North Korea; and that the United Nations Unification and Rehabilitation Commission would, at the propitious moment, enter into negotiations with appropriate representatives of the Chinese Communist government in order to assure them of an equitable distribution of hydroelectric power.[37]

MacArthur replied immediately. He "believed that the suggested approach would not only fail to achieve the desired results, but would be provocative of the very consequences we seek to avert . . . from a military standpoint my personal reconnaissance of the Yalu River line yesterday demonstrated conclusively that it would be utterly impossible for us to stop upon terrain south of the river as suggested . . ." He continued that it was *his* plan to consolidate positions along the Yalu River as quickly as he could, and then to replace American forces as soon as possible with those of the Republic of Korea. At the same time, *he* would announce plans which would include the withdrawal of all American troops to Japan, the parole of all prisoners of war, and the leaving of all matters concerning the unification of Korea and the restoration of civil government to the Korean people, advised and assisted by the United Nations authorities. "I believe that the prompt implementation of this plan as soon as our military objectives have been reached will effectively appeal to reason in the Chinese mind. If it will not, then the resulting situation is not one which might be influenced by bringing to a halt our military measures short of present commitments. By resolutely meeting those commitments, and accomplishing our military mission as so often publicly delineated, lies the best — indeed the only — hope that Soviet and Chinese aggressive designs may be checked before these countries are committed from which, for political reasons, they cannot withdraw." [38] MacArthur continued his advance.

MacArthur's optimism was borne out by the first communiqués. The attack started well, "against almost no resistance from the North Korean Army reinforced by Chinese Communists estimated to equal the United Nations troops in strength . . . According to all indications the advancing United Nations forces had not yet struck the defense line the enemy was reported to have building farther north to protect the hydroelectric power stations of the Yalu River on the Manchurian side." American marines, however, reported they were "facing" a new

Chinese division near Changjin reservoir, and South Koreans to the southwest reported another.[39]

The allied drive continued on November 26 "to roll closer" to the Manchurian border without encountering even moderate resistance. The next day, however, "strong enemy counter-attacks . . . stalled yesterday the United Nations general offensive," [40] but Tokyo cautioned against any undue pessimism. Not until twenty-four hours later, after allied lines had begun to sag back, did the unified command announce that it was facing "an entirely new war." Enemy cavalry troops had, by November 30, "driven a deep wedge between the United States Eighth Army and the Tenth Corps on the east and might have linked up with strong North Korean guerilla forces northeast of the former Red capital of Pyongyang." [41] The Chinese Communist counteroffensive had begun and MacArthur's hopes lay shattered.

Nowhere were these false hopes and mistaken judgments concerning the "Chinese mind" more clearly revealed than in the special communiqué MacArthur issued on November 28. Peking's intervention, MacArthur began, "has shattered the high hopes we entertained that the intervention of the Chinese was only of a token nature on a volunteer and individual basis as publicly announced, and that therefore the war in Korea could be brought to a rapid close by our movement to the international boundary . . . It now appears to have been the enemy's intent, in breaking off contact with our forces two weeks ago, to secure the time necessary surreptitiously to build up for a later surprise assault upon our lines in overwhelming force, taking advantage of the freezing of all rivers and roadbeds which would have materially reduced the effectiveness of our air interdiction and permitted a greatly accelerated forward movement of enemy reinforcements and supplies. This plan has been disrupted by our offensive action, which forced upon the enemy a premature engagement." [42]

While the last sentence lends to the communiqué an apologetic note, MacArthur's private communications to Washington and his actions between October 24 and November 24 make it clear that this public announcement was not simply a pretentiously worded exculpation for a disastrous turn of events. Only when MacArthur adds that his "home by Christmas" offensive was a reconnaissance in force does his explanation sound stilted: no General launches a reconnaissance in force with his whole army! He holds his main force to the rear as a precautionary move, particularly when the enemy might possibly drive a wedge between the two wings of his army and thereby roll up the flank and rear of either section, or both. As General Collins was later to say: "I don't believe that in the initial phase it was considered as a reconnaissance in force at all, because General MacArthur was bent upon the destruction of the North Korean forces." [43]

In Washington's opinion, it was not General MacArthur's failure to withhold non–South Korean troops from the areas bordering Communist China and Soviet Russia, which led the former to send its troops into Korea. The Chinese had launched their counteroffensive before MacArthur's main body had reached the hills overlooking the Yalu.

> Senator Morse . . . you believe that General MacArthur could have stopped some distance this side of the Yalu and adequately protected his troops?
> General Collins. Yes, sir. But, in fairness to General MacArthur now, I should say that he would have had to have gone farther than he was at the time the Chinese made their mass attack on the 24th of November.[44]

MacArthur's sin was of a far more serious nature. He had violated — in spirit, if not in letter — the policy that Washington had prescribed for him, even though he had invoked Secretary Marshall's message to rationalize his move. Administration policy was to send only South Korean troops into the area along the Manchurian frontier and northeastern provinces bordering the Soviet Union; by this means, the government expected to reassure Peking that the American-led forces would not be used to invade Manchuria. MacArthur condemned this strategy as "appeasement" and ordered his field commanders to use both Korean and non-Korean troops for their advance to the Yalu.

Washington and Tokyo had differed before, but this was the first time that MacArthur had committed a serious infraction of directives. General Collins later testified that the Joint Chiefs had not sent General MacArthur any order denying him the employment of American troops in the border zone because it was impossible to issue so specific a directive to a commander 7,000 miles away.[45] Normal procedures granted an American theater commander a large degree of operational freedom. But this made it essential that the field commander consult his superiors before he varied from the broad policies established for him.

General MacArthur did not consult with us, when he issued his directive [of October 24] . . . and when we called him on it, he came back and said he did it as a matter of military necessity . . . this did represent an instance where a policy clearly enunciated by the Chiefs was not followed . . . In my judgment there was plenty of time during which the Chiefs could have been consulted prior to the issuance of this directive . . . I think this was one indication among many others, which certainly have been clear, that General MacArthur was not in consonance with the basic policies that led us gradually to fear that just as he violated a policy in this case without consulting us, perhaps the thing might be done in some other instance of a more serious nature.

The Army Chief of Staff maintained that after the first South Korean units had failed to clear the "buffer" area, other South Korean troops could have been utilized. Moreover, Collins continued, "I don't agree and did not agree with General MacArthur's reply that it would not be possible to stop upon the high ground overlooking the Yalu." [46] The river could have been controlled by artillery fire from this dominant ground.

The upshot of MacArthur's conduct of the campaign during this period of Chinese intervention was as decisive in the minds of the Joint Chiefs and their civilian superiors as Inchon had been for MacArthur. Later, as MacArthur's opposition to Washington's policy increased, they remembered the weeks before Communist China's massive intervention; and they became concerned lest MacArthur again disobey the policy prescribed for him and thereby precipitate a military incident which might ignite a world war.

But was General Collins, as a Washington bureaucrat, in a position to criticize the field commander's actions? The Army Chief left no doubt that he was: he had made several trips to Korea and with the aid of terrain maps he was in a good position to judge where troops could be halted. Throughout his military career he had placed great emphasis on the study of terrain: "in my judgment General Vandenberg, Admiral Sherman, and I are thoroughly alive to the effect that the terrain in Korea will have on military operations there." [47]

Why then did MacArthur insist upon advancing to the Manchurian frontier with his entire army? Why did he reject the concept of a buffer zone south of the border? First, because the political aim of the war was the establishment of a united Korea. Failure to prosecute the military campaign with the vigor necessary to restore the unity of Korea would be regarded as a betrayal of our word by the Koreans, and as weakness by the Chinese Communists and the other peoples of Asia. The proposition to surrender a portion of North Korea to Communist China's aggression was, he believed, so immoral a proposition that it "would bankrupt our leadership and influence in Asia and render untenable our position, both political and military. It would not curb deterioration of the present situation into the possibility of a general war, but would impose upon us the disadvantage of having inevitably to fight such a war if it occurs, bereft of the support of countless Asiatics who now believe in us and are eager to fight with us." Such a tribute to aggression, MacArthur told the Joint Chiefs, found its most recent precedent in the surrender of Great Britain, France and Italy [!] of the Sudetenland to Germany.[48]

Second, MacArthur was convinced that only resolute action would forestall extensive Chinese intervention. Asians greatly respected aggressive leadership; any hesitation would provoke precisely the result which Washington was trying to avoid. The advance to the Yalu River frontier would "effectively appeal to reason in the Chinese mind." MacArthur, therefore, suggested that the proper course for the United Nations was to condemn the Chinese Communists and call upon Peking to withdraw its troops from Korea; the penalty for noncompliance would be the application of military sanctions.[49] Admittedly, his policy was risky, but was the desire to forestall Chinese intervention not worth a "great gamble," particularly when anything less might well entice the Peking regime into North Korea? MacArthur obviously thought it was.

Third, General MacArthur did not believe that Communist China's political-military strategy hinged upon United Nations' control of North Korea's hydroelectric facilities. The Changjin reservoir, for instance, had been dismantled a full month before the arrival of United Nations troops, but no complaints had been yet heard from Peking or Moscow. What "has been said concerning the hydroelectric facilities in North Korea is for the most part a product of British-American speculation, finding little reflection in any Soviet or Chinese utterances."[50]

Fourth, MacArthur was convinced that an advance to the Yalu was the only feasible military course. He had three alternatives. He could pull his troops back to the shorter and more defensible Pyonyang-Wonsan line. But such a course was unthinkable: it would repudiate our pledge to Korea that the United Nations would unify their wartorn and grief-stricken country, leave the North Korean army defeated but not completely destroyed, and gravely damage American prestige by demonstrating American timidity in the face of Chinese Communist threats. Or he could advance to gauge Peking's intentions and strength. This would be a dangerous course, for if Peking chose to strike, it could hurl allied troops back by sheer force of numbers; no amount of military genius could prevent such a retreat. Or he could hold the line he had reached in early November. But this front was indefensible: the terrain across the "neck" was unsuitable for a line defense, and the United Nations Command did not possess sufficient number of troops for a static line of defense. The Chinese Communists already outnumbered him five to one, and this discrepancy was growing daily. By the end of the year the expected discrepancy would be ten to one and still increasing. Under these circumstances, a "Maginot line of defense" would be out of the question, even fatal. Each division would have to assume responsibility for a front line stretching over twenty miles. Such widespread dispersal would be ineffective against Chinese Communist infiltration tactics. Thus, he could not stand still: politically, because it would have left part of North Korea in Communist hands; militarily, because the terrain and lack of troops made it impossible to hold an unbroken front. The United Nations Command had, therefore, to strike first before the Chinese had infiltrated allied lines and concentrated their own troops in position for their offensive. The only course was to advance. To be sure, this would be the most dangerous of the three alternatives, but to minimize the risk and save the bulk of his army in case of full-scale Chinese intervention, he planned for an immediate and organized withdrawal of the Eighth Army and Tenth Corps.[51]

MacArthur's critics do not accept this last claim. They believe that nothing of this sort was planned before the attack began; they see the "planned withdrawal" as a full-fledged retreat; and they question MacArthur's reasons for his advance. The General had, in early November, himself called attention to the "new war" created by Chinese Communist intervention; he had himself loudly proclaimed that the new forces which faced him threatened his command with destruction. Even after the Chinese Communist armies had broken off their contact with allied forces, MacArthur's communiqués continued to report large numbers of Chinese troops as present in Korea and more waiting to cross the border from Manchuria. For instance, on November 10, while on the battlefield there was "only minor contact with the enemy on either the east or west coasts," Tokyo's report was headlined in the *New York Times* as "60,000 CHINESE REDS IN WAR, MORE READY, MACARTHUR SAYS." The "more ready" numbered another 60,000 with "as many as 500,000 men concentrated in Manchuria" who could march "at will" over the short communication lines "immune from attack on the Manchurian side." [52] A week earlier MacArthur had privately informed Washington that these half a million men were grouped in 56 regular army divisions; in addition, he had reported 370,000 District Security Forces, and other forces still arriving from central China. [53] To launch an offensive under these circumstances was tempting fate in the most foolish manner; in so doing, he was guilty of the worst sin of Greek tragedy, the sin of *hubris.*

The foolishness of this attack, the critics continue, is even more emphasized by the fact that MacArthur had already in early November stated that his command was threatened with destruction. In the meantime, the numerical discrepancy between the enemy forces and his own had grown greatly. Moreover, whereas he had earlier asserted that he could not defend the narrow "neck" in depth with the number of troops available to him, he had finally launched his offensive along a 300-mile front. His critics find the proposition that the long Chinese frontier could have been more adequately defended than the far shorter line across the "neck" peculiarly lacking in logic. To Homer Bigart, the *New York Herald Tribune*'s war correspondent, MacArthur's offensive "made no sense. It was an invitation to disaster." For even if allied troops had reached the frontier, they would have had to be dispersed in small garrisons at isolated points. The Chinese could have infiltrated through the unguarded gaps and exposed the United Nations posts to annihilation — much more easily than at the "neck" where MacArthur claimed he could not stop precisely because he could not avoid such massive infiltration. [54]

Lastly, these critics contend that MacArthur almost ensured his defeat by the manner in which he launched his offensive with a divided command. They dismiss his reasons for doing this, namely, that his lack of troops and the "rugged spinal mountain range" made it necessary to split the Eighth Army and the Tenth Corps. [55] If this area of the front was too "rugged" for an advance by allied troops, and so impenetrable that it was safe to split his forces, how was it possible, they ask, for the Chinese to achieve their breakthrough — particularly since MacArthur had on more than one occasion apparently expected

a battle to occur in precisely this spot? On November 26, Tokyo headquarters had commented that "there were indications that a large-scale
battle — if there was to be one before the end of the war — might
shape up in that snowy mountain sector. With the enemy believed
to have North Korean and Chinese Communist troops numerically
equal to the United Nations forces . . . the absences of major opposition raised the question of what the foe was doing in the wedge-
shaped area of 50 miles deep along part of the Western front . . . A
spokesman at General MacArthur's headquarters said, 'We can only
anticipate that we will run into stiff resistance. We haven't done so
yet.' " [56] Six days earlier, Tokyo had reported "various accounts" as
saying that the 40,000 North Korean guerillas had orders to "break
out to the north in central Korea, where there was only tenuous contact between the United States Eighth Army and the Tenth Corps
on the east coast." [57] And on November 28: "An 'end run' by the enemy
in the central section had long been feared by observers here as a
movement that would threaten to drive a wedge between the two
wings of the United Nations forces and to roll up the flanks and rear
of either." [58]

In view of these communiqués, MacArthur's critics assert that he
should have concentrated on defensive measures, rather than launched
an offensive against a numerically equal, if not superior, North Korean–
Chinese Communist force in front, and 40,000 guerillas behind him;
at the very least, he should not have created such an attractive vacuum
between his forces but prepared defensive positions to which his army
could fall back in case of emergency. His failure to take either of
these actions resulted in a first class American defeat inflicted by an
army only lightly equipped and with practically no air force.

Nevertheless, one question remains: why did the Administration
not exert its control over MacArthur if it was so strongly convinced
that the use of non–South Korean troops in the border region was
dangerous and provocative? Why did it not order MacArthur *not* to
advance further or split his command if it considered these moves
with so much apprehension? General Collins has already testified to
one reason for Washington's reluctance, the traditional freedom of
the field commander to determine his own tactics. But should the man
on the battlefield, in a sensitive limited-war situation, have sole juris-
diction over tactical decisions with such vast strategic and political
implications? Should not the old American attitude that in war mili-

tary considerations have priority over political factors be reversed? Should the political leaders of the government not exert the strictest control over the man who directs the military operations in a particular theater of war? George Kennan once warned that an excessive reverence for tradition could well excuse us into disaster.

The Alsop brothers and James Reston in their contemporary columns report another reason for the Administration's failure to restrain MacArthur. The government's civil and military leaders, wrote the Alsops, were worried by MacArthur's "home by Christmas" offensive, but as General Bradley put it, "he could not fight MacArthur's war for him." The President and the Joint Chiefs and the National Security Council, "no doubt" influenced by MacArthur's previous brilliant success, were concerned lest their counterorder should arouse charges that the Administration was "soft" in its policy toward Communist China and willfully casting away the fruits of MacArthur's efforts.[59] Reston reported in a similar vein that President Truman not only shared MacArthur's belief that the Chinese would not intervene on a full-scale basis, but that, since Inchon, MacArthur's political prestige in the country and on Capitol Hill stood so high that Mr. Truman wished to avoid an open breach with his field commander.[60] Reston might have added that the Administration's political strength at home had, as we shall soon see, suffered a severe decline during the mid-term elections, and that conversely, MacArthur's political support in Congress had risen sharply.[61]

Wake Island's spirit of "complete unanimity" lay shattered; events had shown that this spirit could be preserved only in the absence of emergencies. It could not survive crises, and crisis from now on became the every-day reality.

PART TWO

THE KOREAN WAR
DECEMBER 1950 TO APRIL 1951:
THE PERIOD OF
CHINESE COMMUNIST INTERVENTION

VIII

THE MacARTHUR-TAFT ALLIANCE:
THE GREAT DEBATE

MacArthur sent the Joint Chiefs a grim message on December 3. He painted a somber picture. The effectiveness of the air force in interrupting the enemy's supply system had been "enormously" reduced both by the terrain in North Korea and the limitations of the international frontier at the Yalu. Since the enemy concentrated inland, the effectiveness of the navy had also been greatly diminished. Amphibious operations, MacArthur added, were no longer feasible. The potentials, therefore, of their combined strength were greatly reduced and the comparison had become more and more one of relative combat effectiveness of ground forces. His troops, except for the First Marine Division, were all under strength and "mentally fatigued and physically battered"; and the combat effectiveness of the Republic of Korea forces was negligible.

In contrast, MacArthur pointed out, the Chinese Communists had clearly committed twenty-six divisions to battle, and an additional 200,000 troops were then in the process of being sent into action. They were all "fresh, completely organized, splendidly trained and equipped and apparently in peak condition." Therefore, "unless some positive and immediate action is taken, hope for success cannot be justified and steady attrition leading to final destruction can reasonably be contemplated." (The paraphrase of this message, presented during the Senate hearings, read "the command should be evacuated" unless reinforcements arrived and the "full power" of the United Nations were mounted at once.) [1]

. . . The general evaluation of the situation here must be viewed on the basis of an entirely new war against an entirely new power of great military strength and under entirely new conditions. The directives under which I am operating based upon the North Korean Forces as an enemy are completely outmoded by events. The fact must be clearly understood that our relatively small force now faces the full offensive power of the Chinese

Communist nation augmented by extensive supply of Soviet matériel. The strategic concept suitable for operations against the North Korean Army which was so successful is not susceptible to continued application against such power. This calls for political decisions and strategic plans in implementation thereof, adequate fully to meet the realities involved. In this, time is of the essence as every hour sees the enemy power increase and ours decline.[2]

The implication of MacArthur's message was clear: unless "positive action" were taken, the command should be evacuated. Later, during the Senate hearings, there was much discussion over the question of who had first suggested evacuation, MacArthur or the Joint Chiefs of Staff? MacArthur stoutly denied that he had ever given such a possibility a thought: "The Joint Chiefs of Staff were not sure we could stick in Korea. It was my opinion that we could." [3] The evidence does not support this claim. Evacuation was considered in both Tokyo and Washington; under the circumstances, it would have been surprising — and highly irresponsible — if it had not been given some serious thought at both ends of the chain of command. Admittedly, MacArthur did not mention the word "evacuation" first; the Joint Chiefs did. But the latter only drew forth the implication of MacArthur's messages, particularly the one of December 3. This was made quite clear by Admiral Sherman during his testimony:

Through the month of December there was a great deal of discussion of the probability or the possibility of evacuation becoming necessary, and as I recall it, General MacArthur sent us one message which indicated to me certainly that there must be consideration given to the probability of evacuation.

There was a dispatch on the 3[d] of December in which he discussed the situation and made reference to — this statement appears:

Steady attrition leading to final destruction could reasonably be contemplated.

That had the effect on me of feeling that if it was a case of a military situation involving the final destruction of the forces, that obviously consideration must be given to getting them out . . .[4]

In any case, on December 29, probably in anticipation of the new offensive which the Chinese Communists were expected to launch on New Year's Day, the Joint Chiefs sent MacArthur an important message. They informed him that the estimates at their disposal indicated that Communist China possessed the capacity to compel United Nations forces to evacuate Korea. This could perhaps be prevented by substantially increasing American forces in Korea or by inflicting overwhelming casualties upon the enemy. The Joint Chiefs rejected both courses: the first, because the additional commitment of American troops would seriously jeopardize the security of Japan, and because it was "not practical to obtain significant additional forces for Korea from other members of the United Nations"; the second, because China's intervention might foreshadow a general war, in which event Korea would not be the place to fight a major action. It would, therefore, be unwise to commit our remaining available ground forces to action there.

Accordingly the Joint Chiefs directed MacArthur to defend himself in successive phases, and "subject to the primary consideration of the continued threat to Japan," to make an advanced determination of his last reasonable opportunity for an orderly evacuation. The Joint Chiefs requested MacArthur's views on the conditions which should determine evacuation; they stated that a definite directive on the conditions for its initiation would be provided after his views had been received. "However," the Joint Chiefs added, "a successful resistance to Chinese–North Korean aggression at some position in Korea and a deflation of the military and political prestige of the Chinese Communists would be of great importance to our national interest, if they could be accomplished without incurring serious losses." [5]

To the Administration, this was a clear and unequivocal directive; Chinese intervention might spark major hostilities, which could not perhaps be limited to the Far East. Consequently, wisdom dictated that the United States husband its strength for that contingency; indeed, necessity dictated this course, since a substantial number of fresh troops were not available. Moreover, while it would of course be preferable to hold in Korea, it would be better to withdraw from the peninsula than to endanger the existence of the Eighth Army; even if it possessed the capacity to defend a beachhead over a period of time, it would be subjected to steady attrition by the numerically superior enemy. This would unnecessarily endanger the lives of its men and leave the Japanese islands without any protection on the ground.

To MacArthur, however, the directive was self-contradictory. On the one hand, the Joint Chiefs stated that successful resistance at "some position in Korea" would be highly desirable, and at the same time they declared that Korea was not the place to fight a major war. In MacArthur's opinion, this objective remained unattainable while he was operating under the restrictions imposed upon him by Washington. Deflation of Communist China's prestige could be achieved only if the risk of a major war were taken. In his message of December 30, therefore, MacArthur asked the Joint Chiefs to clarify his instructions.

It was quite clear, he said, that the entire military resources of Communist China, logistically supported by the Soviet Union, were committed to a maximum effort against the command. In implementing this commitment, the Chinese would leave themselves vulnerable in areas from which troops for Korea had been withdrawn. In the meantime, his air and naval power was being only partially utilized and the "great potential" of Chinese Nationalist forces on Formosa and guerilla action on the mainland were being ignored.

MacArthur then outlined retaliatory measures which, in his opinion, would render evacuation unnecessary and secure victory: a naval blockade of the Chinese coast; air bombardment of China's industrial complex, communication network, supply depots, and troop assembly points; the reinforcement of his forces by Nationalist Chinese troops; and "diversionary action possibly leading to counter-invasion" by Chiang Kai-shek against vulnerable mainland areas. These measures, he assured the Joint Chiefs, would "severely cripple and largely neutralize China's capability to wage aggressive war" and thereby ensure not only a victory in Korea, but also "save Asia from the engulfment otherwise facing it."

MacArthur continued that China had committed itself "fully and unequivocally." Nothing the United States would do could further aggravate the situation. MacArthur expressed his belief that the Soviet Union would not intervene in the struggle, since such a decision would depend upon the "Soviet's own estimate of relative strengths and capabilities with little regard to other factors." His strategic program was, in other words, relatively safe, involving only, as he said later, the risks which are inherent in all international relations.

If, on the other hand, Washington should reject his proposals, and should instead accept the evacuation of Korea without any retaliatory action against Communist China, it would incur grave political and military consequences. First, its inaction would alienate the peoples of Asia, including the Japanese. Second, it would demand "a material reinforcement of the forces now in this theater . . . if we are to hold the literal defense chain against determined assault." Third, "the evacuation of our forces from Korea under any circumstances would at once release the bulk of the Chinese forces now absorbed by that

*campaign for action elsewhere — quite probably in areas of far greater
importance than Korea itself . . ."*

MacArthur pointed out that he thoroughly understood the demand
for European security and he concurred in doing everything possible
in that sector, but not if this meant accepting defeat anywhere else —
an acceptance which could not but fail to ensure a later defeat in
Europe itself. He dismissed the argument that American troops should
not become tied down in Korea, since they must also be used to
bolster and supplement Europe's defenses. He said that the most optimistic estimates did not believe that Europe would be defensible for
another two years; the use of American forces in the present emergency in the Far East could not, therefore, prejudice these preparations in any way. Quite the contrary: their employment would ensure
that the troops which were to be stationed in Europe would be thoroughly seasoned — not that MacArthur any longer expected, as he did
on December 3, to employ ground forces of the "greatest magnitude."

MacArthur concluded that if his military recommendations were
not carried out, the "tactical plan of successively contracting defense
line south to the Pusan beachhead is believed the only possible way
[in] which the evacuation could be accomplished." In such an eventual-
ity, it would not be necessary for the Joint Chiefs to make an antici-
patory decision for evacuation until the troops were forced into a
beachhead.[6]

The Joint Chiefs rejected the immediate implementation of these
recommendations on January 9, 1951. A naval blockade would require
British consent, since their trade with Communist China passed
through the Crown Colony of Hong Kong; naval and air attacks on
objectives in Communist China would probably be authorized only
when and if the Chinese Communists attacked United States forces
outside the Korean area; Chinese Nationalist forces could be employed
more usefully elsewhere — presumably in the defense of Formosa —
and they would in any case have no decisive effect on the Korean
campaign, because their "battle-worthiness," as Sir Winston Churchill
used to phrase it, was not of a high order. The Joint Chiefs, therefore,
repeated that, subject to his primary mission of protecting the security
of Japan and the safety of his troops, MacArthur should defend himself in Korea until it became evident "in your judgment that evacuation is essential to avoid severe losses of men and material . . ." Then
he should withdraw his troops to Japan.[7]

MacArthur remained dissatisfied; he felt that the Joint Chiefs were not giving him a clear answer or directive. They had evaded his central question: how did they reconcile the deflation of Communist China's political and military prestige with the evacuation of Korea? Consequently, on January 10, he sent the Joint Chiefs another message; this time he stressed the need for clarification in "view of the self-evident fact that my command as presently constituted is of insufficient strength to hold a position in Korea and simultaneously to protect Japan against external assault . . . " He continued:

There is no doubt but that a beachhead line can be held by our existing forces for a limited time in Korea, but this could not be accomplished without losses. Whether such losses were regarded as 'severe' or not would to a certain extent depend upon the connotation one gives the term . . .

The issue really boils down to the question whether or not the United States intends to evacuate Korea, and involves a decision of highest national and international importance, far above the competence of a theater commander . . .

MacArthur pointed out that this decision should not however "be left to the initiative of enemy action, which in effect would be the determining criteria under a reasonable interpretation of your message." His query, therefore, was whether the present objective of the United States was to maintain a position in Korea indefinitely, for a limited time, or whether it was to minimize losses by immediate evacuation. This question, he emphasized, "must be based upon the over-riding political policy establishing the relativity of American interests in the Far East." [8]

In response to MacArthur's "rather gloomy" message with its clear implication that under the "extraordinary limitations and conditions imposed upon the command in Korea" allied troops would have to be evacuated or face "complete destruction," the Administration took three actions. First, the Joint Chiefs of Staff on January 12 drew up a memorandum enumerating a sixteen-point program of action which might be put into effect if Korea had to be evacuated; this dire possibility was "the primary assumption" for the implementation of this program, which included the four proposals MacArthur had recommended on December 30.[9] The Joint Chiefs submitted their study to the Secretary of Defense on the same day; they also sent MacArthur a copy.

Second, the President on January 13 sent MacArthur a long letter explaining "our basic national and international purposes in continuing the resistance to aggression in Korea." Successful resistance in Korea, Mr. Truman told MacArthur, would serve the following aims:

(a) To demonstrate that aggression will not be accepted by us or by the United Nations and to provide a rallying point around which the spirits and energies of the free world can be mobilized to meet the world-wide threat which the Soviet Union now poses.

(b) To deflate the dangerously exaggerated political and military prestige of Communist China which now threatens to undermine the resistance of non-Communist Asia and to consolidate the hold of Communism on China itself.

(c) To afford more time and to give direct assistance to the organization of non-Communist resistance in Asia, both outside and inside China.

(d) To carry out our commitments of honor to the South Koreans and to demonstrate to the world that the friendship of the United States is of inestimable value in time of adversity.

(e) To make possible a far more satisfactory peace settlement for Japan and to contribute greatly to the post-treaty security position of Japan in relation to the continent.

(f) To lend resolution to many countries not only in Asia but also in Europe and the Middle East who are now living within the shadow of Communist power and to let them know that they need not now rush to come to terms with Communism on whatever terms they can get, meaning complete submission.

(g) To inspire those who may be called upon to fight against great odds if subjected to a sudden onslaught by the Soviet Union or by Communist China.

(h) To lend point and urgency to the rapid build-up of the defenses of the Western world.

(i) To bring the United Nations through its first great effort on collective security and to produce a free-world coalition of incalculable value to the national security interests of the United States.

(j) To alert the peoples behind the Iron Curtain that their masters are bent upon wars of aggression and that this crime will be resisted by the free world.

The President continued that if it became impracticable to hold a position in Korea, MacArthur should if it were practicable and advisable, continue his resistance from the off-shore islands of Korea. But if it became necessary to evacuate, it must "be clear to the world that the course is forced upon us by military necessity and that we shall not accept the result politically or militarily until the aggression has been rectified." [10]

Lastly, the Administration dispatched Generals Collins and Vandenberg to Korea to check the military situation for themselves. This visit and the President's message with its emphasis on the importance of continuing the fight *in* Korea both betray an Administration belief that MacArthur had perhaps deliberately exaggerated the desperateness of the military situation in order to win approval of his own strategic program. Each time the Administration had asked him whether he could retain his grip on Korea under the restraints imposed upon him, MacArthur had simply answered "no": he could do so only if his forces were "unleashed." At no time had he told Washington what it desperately needed to know; instead, he had replied only that he could hold if the Administration adopted his strategic proposals. What he seemed in fact to be saying was that he would cooperate with the Administration only on *his* terms; and his greatest aid in pressuring the government to extend the war across the Yalu was the Administration's lack of knowledge of what the real conditions on the battlefield were. Washington did not know whether MacArthur's prophecy of the "final destruction" of his forces reflected an objective analysis of the actual military situation, or whether it was primarily a means to force the government to sanction an all-out war against China.

The result was that Generals Collins and Vandenberg flew out of Washington the evening of January 12, after completing their study of possible courses of action if the allies had to pull their troops out of Korea. Five days later, on January 17, they reported from Tokyo that they had just returned from Korea where they had found the allied forces in good shape. There was no need for an evacuation; nor was there a need, therefore, to implement all of the measures outlined in the Joint Chiefs' study. These had been planned for the most extreme contingency; that contingency had now passed.[11]

MacArthur apparently saw the Joint Chiefs' memorandum of January 12 to the Secretary of Defense in a different light. To him, it meant that the gap between the objectives which the President had listed as the principal aims of the war and the means which were necessary for their achievement would soon be closed. MacArthur, as General Whitney has related, "was gratified to learn that in Washington the Joint Chiefs of Staff had finally overcome their illusions that fighting back against China would bring on global war," and that they had recommended:

That we were to continue and intensify *now* economic blockade of trade with China.
That we were to prepare to impose a naval blockade of China and place

it into effect *as soon as our position in Korea is stabilized or when we have evacuated Korea,* and depending upon circumstances then obtaining.

Remove *now* the restrictions on air reconnaissances of Chinese coastal areas and of Manchuria.

Remove *now* the restrictions on operations of the Chinese Nationalist forces and give such logistical support to those forces as will contribute to effective operations against the Communists.

MacArthur interpreted the repetitive use of the words "now" and the phrase "as soon as our position in Korea is stabilized or when we have evacuated Korea," as indicating the almost immediate implementation of these recommendations.[12] He has maintained that the language of the study did not indicate that an evacuation was the prerequisite for the implementation of the new strategy. Indeed, he failed to see the logic or the merit in the Administration's alleged position that it would be safer to execute this program after the United States had been forced out of Korea than beforehand, since the impact upon Peking and Moscow would be the same.[13]

Asked later why he believed the new strategy had not been implemented despite the purported agreement between himself and the Joint Chiefs, MacArthur replied that it must have encountered "a veto somewhere along the line," probably in the office of the Secretary of Defense.[14] It is difficult not to conclude that MacArthur thought this because he was reading into the President's message and the Joint Chiefs' study what he wanted to read into it; or, more probably, that he was saying his military colleagues agreed with him in order to fortify his own position. For it seems incredible that General Collins, during his stay in Tokyo, did not clarify to MacArthur the exact meaning of the January 12 study and the precise circumstances under which it was to have been put into effect.[15] Moreover, MacArthur knew that the January 12 program was not a directive, and would not become one until after it had received the approval of the Secretary of Defense, the Secretary of State, and the President.

The President's message of January 13 had left little reason to believe that such approval would soon be forthcoming, even if the Joint Chiefs had been in disagreement with their superiors [16] — for which, MacArthur notwithstanding, there is no evidence.

Our course of action at this time [Mr. Truman had informed MacArthur] should be such as to consolidate the great majority of the United Nations. This majority is not merely part of the organization but is also the nations whom we would desperately need to count on as allies in the event the

Soviet Union moves against us. Further, pending the build-up of our national strength, we must act with great prudence insofar as extending the area of hostilities is concerned. Steps which might in themselves be fully justified and which might lend some assistance to the campaign in Korea would not be beneficial if they thereby involved Japan or Western Europe in large-scale hostilities . . .

In reaching a final decision about Korea, I shall have to give constant thought to the main threat from the Soviet Union and to the need for a rapid expansion of our armed forces to meet this great danger.

In other words, no military sanctions would be applied to China *in* China. This in effect meant that the Administration had reversed its post-Inchon policy of militarily unifying Korea. From the moment of China's intervention, it had once more accepted its original objective: the restoration of the *status quo* which had existed prior to North Korea's aggression. Korean unification was now to be achieved once more only by "peaceful means"; the United Nations resolution of October 7, indirectly sanctioning the unification of Korea by force, lay abandoned. Since MacArthur's dark forebodings of evacuation had remained stillborn, a division of Korea was inevitable. MacArthur was never able to reconcile himself to this situation.

The General made sure the American people knew that he opposed such a settlement and that he favored a quick and clean-cut victory; also, that he was not responsible for Chinese intervention. MacArthur was apparently deeply wounded by the criticisms voiced at home of his "home by Christmas" offensive, and he felt compelled to answer publicly and outside regular channels the "defamations made against him by irresponsible correspondents at the front, aided and abetted by other such unpatriotic elements at home." [17] The adjective "irresponsible" seems a strong condemnation for some of the veteran war correspondents who preferred to exercise independent judgment rather than always to accept headquarters releases and explanations as the gospel; and the adjective "unpatriotic" is less a reflection on the patriotism of those who criticized MacArthur's strategy and tactics in North Korea than it is one more demonstration of the General's well-known inability to admit human error.

To be sure, in the daze of defeat, many Americans and Europeans were searching for a scapegoat; the calamity of Chinese Communist intervention had to be explained somehow. It was more comfortable to rest in the illusion that the West had no "real" quarrel with Peking and easier to condemn MacArthur for allegedly precipitating Communist China's entry into the war than to face China's enmity and what MacArthur called the "new war." The consequence, however, was that the man who had been cheered as a military genius after Inchon was now widely criticized as a military incompetent, who, in the editorial words of the *New York Herald Tribune,* was responsible for "one of the greatest military reverses in the history of American arms" because he had "compounded blunder by confusion of facts and intelligence." [18] The fact was of course that although MacArthur had committed a serious error in North Korea and had hardly lived up to his reputation as the infallible oracle for Mars, he was still the great military commander he had been before the November offensive; but undoubtedly a very strong element, even if not the main element, of his vehement advocacy of bombing and blockading Communist China was his desire to recoup his reputation among the public.

And yet, it must be added, the strong, at times biting, criticism which MacArthur suffered during these weeks was not totally undeserved. For years MacArthur's staff had been presenting the public a picture of the "old man" as not merely a military genius but an *infallible* military genius. George Kenney, MacArthur's friend and World War II Air Force Chief of Staff — who has the sole distinction among former MacArthur staff members of having written the only book which portrays MacArthur as a very human figure, as a man capable of great warmth and charm — recalled that the General's

public-relations officers invariably adored MacArthur almost to the point of idolatory. To them unless a news release painted the General with a halo and seated him on the highest pedestal in the universe, it should be killed. No news except favorable news, reflecting complete credit on an infallible MacArthur, had much chance getting past the censors. They [and one might add all members of his staff] seemed to believe that they had a sacred mission, which was to "sell" the General to the world, and they didn't trust the newsmen to interpret MacArthur properly. They never seemed to realize that they didn't have to sell Douglas MacArthur. The General was a brilliant, colorful, likeable personality, who could sell himself much better without any help. He was not a demigod, he was human.[19]

John Gunther heard members of MacArthur's staff compare him to Alexander the Great — naturally to Alexander's disadavantage — and describe him as the greatest man who ever lived. Now MacArthur — who, unfortunately, had always actively aided his own "selling" campaign — fell victim to his own legend. Undoubtedly, he was a very vain man with much to be vain about; but he was not infallible. By

CHARLIE MACARTHUR

his campaign in North Korea, MacArthur had himself broken the legend of the invincible general and victorious conqueror. In these circumstances, MacArthur should have expected criticism — indeed, criticism of the sharpest sort; and a man with his magnificent record should have been able to take it in his stride. But MacArthur had always been determined to keep his record perfect; the result was that his hypersensitivity to criticism led him to equate criticism with disloyalty and to allay responsibility for his predicaments and failures upon his civilian and military superiors in Washington.

It was against the latter that MacArthur, in late November and early December, released his verbal barrage. On November 28 he issued a special communiqué and sent a cablegram to Ray Henle of the Three Star Extra newsbroadcast; on November 30 he sent a reply to a message he had received on the previous day from Arthur Krock of the *New York Times;* on December 1 he gave an interview to the editors of *U.S. News and World Report* and sent a lengthy message to Hugh Baillie, president of the United Press. Other interviews and messages were given or sent to Ward Price of the London *Daily Mail;* to Barry Faris, managing editor of the International News Service; and to the Tokyo Press Corps.[20] In these public pronouncements, MacArthur advanced a number of themes.

First, he re-emphasized that his "end of the war" offensive had prematurely forced the enemy's hand and forestalled the implementation of his strategic plan which envisaged the concentration, under cover of concealment, of an army so powerful that it would be able to achieve the complete destruction of the United Nations Command and the conquest of Korea "in one invincible movement."

Second, he vigorously denied that his conduct of the campaign in North Korea was responsible for Communist China's intervention. "It is historically inaccurate to attribute any degree of responsibility for the onslaught of the Chinese Communist armies to the strategic course of the campaign itself." Repeating that his every strategic and tactical moves had been "in complete accordance" with the resolutions passed by the United Nations, MacArthur repudiated the "misleading anonymous gossip" that he had ever received from "any authoritative source that in the execution of his mission the Command should stop at the Thirty-eighth Parallel or Pyongyang, or at any other line short of the international boundary." (The Joint Chiefs were not apparently an "authoritative source.") In any case, the "decision by the Chinese Communist leaders to wage war against the United Nations could only have been a basic one, long premeditated and carried into execution as a direct result of the defeat of their satellite North Korean armies . . ."

Third, MacArthur objected to the description of his "planned withdrawal" from North Korea as a full-fledged retreat. This impression, he charged, was due to "ignorant" correspondents who confused the speedy withdrawal, planned prior to the launching of the November 24 offensive just in case the Chinese Communists should intervene, with an army "running in full flight." The fact was that the "withdrawal" was made with consummate skill; indeed, it was one of the best operations he had ever conducted, perhaps his best! [21] He was willing to grant that the Chinese Communists had achieved "some tactical successes," but they had attained these solely because of their numerical superiority. As it was, they had won these only "at staggering personnel loss."

Finally, MacArthur asserted that his inability to defeat the Chinese "volunteers" was due to the limitations imposed upon him by Washington. These restrictions, "without precedent in history," were an enormous handicap to the effective conduct of military operations. His inability to use his air power to attack the Chinese supply lines in Manchuria was an especially severe handicap; for south of the Yalu, the rugged terrain made it possible for the Chinese Communists to move their troops and supplies under cover of night without air detection and bombardment.

Mr. Truman was quite upset by MacArthur's series of statements, because he felt that MacArthur was trying to allay responsibility for the failure of his "home by Christmas" offensive by saying "that he would have won the war except for the fact that we [the Administration in Washington] would not let him have his way . . . I should have relieved General MacArthur then and there. The reason I did not was that I did not wish to have it appear as if he were being relieved because the offensive failed. I have never believed in going back on people when luck is against them . . . " But MacArthur had to be told that the kind of public statements he had been issuing were out of order.[22]

MacArthur, therefore, received two directives on December 6; although these were addressed to all executive officials, they were specifically meant for him. The first ordered that speeches, press releases, or other statements concerning foreign policy and military policy should not be released until they had received clearance from the State or Defense departments. The purpose of this order, it was explained, was "to insure that the information made public is accurate and fully in accord with the policies of the United States Government." The second directive stated that "Officials overseas, including military commanders and diplomatic representatives, should be ordered to exercise extreme caution in public statements, to clear all but routine statements with their departments, and to refrain from direct communication on military or foreign policy with newspapers, magazines or other publicity media in the United States." [23] For a while Douglas MacArthur remained silent; but his battle-cry was now taken up by another group powerfully entrenched in the United States Senate — the Taft wing of the Republican party, recently revitalized by its successes in the mid-term election.

The Administration suffered a further reverse in the November election, which reduced the Democratic majority in the Senate from twelve to two, and cut it by two-thirds in the House.[24] In Illinois, Iowa, Utah, California, and Maryland, Democratic candidates, who had defended the Administration's foreign policy, had lost to Republicans who had made foreign policy one of their principal issues. Three of the Administration's strongest supporters, Senator Scott Lucas, the Democratic Majority Leader; Senator Millard Tydings, the chairman of the Armed Services Committee; and Senator Francis Meyers, the majority whip, were defeated; on the other hand, Senators Robert Taft, Bourke Hickenlooper, Eugene Milliken, Homer Capehart, Alexander Wiley (Republicans), and Senator Patrick McCarran (Democrat) were returned. The election of several other pro–Nationalist Chinese and pro-McCarthy supporters, such as Senators Everett Dirksen, John Butler, and Richard Nixon, strengthened the Administration's critics.[25] These returns, at a time of grave international crisis, showed that the electorate had apparently listened attentively to those who attributed the "loss" of China and other gains of Communism to a conspiracy within the American government and voted for candidates who advocated a more vigorous anti-Mao policy, a reduction of economic aid, less deference to our allies in Western Europe, and a thorough "house-cleaning" of the State Department, beginning of course with the Secretary of State. Richard Stebbins later observed that although the Administration's policies in Europe and Asia had already been subject to severe criticisms for quite some time, it had never been clear whether these criticisms had really represented a major segment of national opinion. But "after November 7 there could no longer be any doubt that large numbers of Americans were out of sympathy with the Administration's methods and dubious about its objectives." [26]

This mid-term election was the first election held since the collapse of bipartisan cooperation in foreign affairs, the fall of Nationalist China, the extensive suspicion of incompetence and disloyalty in the Administration, the end of America's atomic monopoly, and the Korean War, which had all of a sudden threatened to turn into a major war with China, if not indeed into World War III. Certain domestic factors aggravated the frustrations and disillusionment with a containment policy which in many respects seemed to have failed to contain and had increased American insecurity; and these factors, added to all the other reasons, account for the dominant influence of foreign affairs in the 1950 election. According to Samuel Lubell, the Korean War broke out at a time when the national debt had already been swollen by twenty years of deficit spending: first to lift the country out of the depth of depression and vast unemployment; later to fight and beat the Germans, Italians, and Japanese; and then to reconstruct the economy of Europe and save it from Communism. Taxes were high and the mass of the population was not eager to add to them through additional foreign commitments. Moreover, businessmen, for instance, wished to avoid further inflation and possible governmental controls; nor did veterans relish the thought of fighting once again. The Korean War, Lubell concluded, was fought during a period when it was difficult "to balance the interests of business, farmers, and workers with one another and with those of the unorganized public." [27] Arthur Krock, another veteran observer of the American political scene, seems to have been right when he succinctly summed up the mid-term election results the day after the votes had been accounted: the State Department, he said tersely, had been the loser in the election.[28]

Senator Taft, now the unchallenged leader of the Republican party on Capitol Hill and the most likely presidential candidate for 1952, endorsed these opinions and elaborated upon them. He interpreted the victory of his party, particularly his own smashing victory in Ohio, in two specific ways.[29] First, they indicated that opposition *per se* was good politics, and that only by vigorous criticism of all Administration proposals could the orthodox faction of the Republican party — the only "true" Republican party — increase its membership and influence in Congress and win the presidency in 1952. In 1948 Dewey and his heretical "internationalists" had lost the election because they had conducted a mild "me-too" campaign; [30] in 1950 the Republicans had increased their congressional representation because they had fought a hard "me-opposed" campaign. On the basis of this conclusion, Taft

believed that for a Republican of his type to be elected President —
and who of this orthodox type was more qualified than he to run
for President? — he need only wage the type of hard-hitting campaign
he had successfully fought in Ohio. According to his sympathetic
biographer, William S. White, Taft was convinced that his re-election
to the Senate meant that Ohio greatly preferred him *and* all that he
represented. It would need only his "smashing, rock-breaking sort of
campaign full of nothing but attack, to put him, or any other really
solid Republican, over anywhere." White adds that it never occurred
to Taft that thousands voted for him in Ohio "in complete disapproval
of his legislative record but in the instinctive feeling that would be
something historically incongrous in refusing to return to the Senate
an Ohioan who was its most powerful member, a man of national and
even worldly distinction"; or because his opponent, Joseph Ferguson,
was almost unknown and held little prestige; or because some labor
people resented being told so fiercely for whom to vote.[31]

Second, the election results confirmed Taft's pre-election estimate
that Republican attacks upon the Administration should not be confined to domestic politics — since Taft was well aware that on this
issue the Republicans were unlikely to capture a majority of seats in
Congress; [32] they should instead continue and intensify their assaults
upon the Administration's foreign policy. Here was a fertile field for
the exploitation of votes — Teheran, Yalta, and Potsdam; [33] Alger Hiss
and more recent cases of espionage; the war in Korea; and above all,
the collapse of China. Nor was political expediency — particularly
Taft's own desire for election in what would be his third and final attempt to win the presidency — his only reason for selecting foreign
affairs as a major target for partisan criticisms. It was also a matter of
deep conviction. The opposition party's function was to oppose; its
function was to hold the party in power responsible for its conduct of
foreign policy, not to allow it to cover up its blunders and failures to
safeguard American security under the label of bipartisanship.

The Republicans quickly set out to make their record of vigorous
opposition and to lay before the public their alternative policies.
Their strategy was divided into two closely related types of attack.
First, they attacked Secretary of State Acheson and demanded his
dismissal, despite his solid anti-Soviet record. Acheson had been one
of the first after the war to warn of Russia's imperialistic ambitions.
He had taken the leadership in the formulation of the Truman Doc-

trine, which saved Greece and Turkey and forestalled a Russian break-through into the Middle East, South Asia, and North Africa; the Marshall Plan, which had rebuilt Europe and kept this decisive weight to the global balance of power in the American scale; the North Atlantic Treaty Organization, which had linked the United States and Europe militarily and had enlisted German power on the side of the Western powers; and he had been the first to recommend that the United States accept the Communist challenge in Korea. This record might well sup-port Elmer Davis' prediction that historians will one day rate Acheson as the third greatest American Secretary of State, directly behind John Quincy Adams and William Seward.[34]

Nevertheless, Acheson as Secretary of State was the symbol of Amer-ica's global involvement and the target upon whom most of the ac-companying fears and disappointments focused. Fifty years before the attacks upon Acheson, that discerning observer Henry Adams had recognized that the public's frustrations, which derive from living in a world in which the United States cannot always determine all events in all parts of the globe in its own favor, seek their outlet through Congress in vigorous criticisms of the Secretary of State. "The Secre-tary of State has always stood as much alone as the historian. Required to look far ahead and around him, he measures forces unknown to party managers, and has found Congress more or less hostile ever since Con-gress first sat. The Secretary of State exists only to recognize the exist-ence of a world which Congress would rather ignore . . . Since the first day the Senate existed, it has always intrigued against the Secre-tary of State whenever the Secretary has been obliged to extend his functions beyond the appointment of Consuls." This is understand-able: Congress does not like to face the voters and ask them to let their sons serve in the forces, to sanction an increase in taxation for more military spending and continued economic aid to friends and allies. This is an unpleasant and politically hazardous task, particularly since the politicians can give the voters no guarantee that the prob-lems of the world can be quickly solved, if indeed they can be solved at all. In foreign affairs, congressmen can give their constituents no promises that their burden will shortly be relieved and their sacrifices soon ended; they can give no promises of a foreign policy which would have the supreme distinction of rendering any further foreign policy unnecessary.

Secretary Acheson was, therefore, not only a tempting target, he was an easy target. His position on the Hill had never been a strong one: he had never possessed a personal following in the Democratic party; nor had he ever exercised much influence within Democratic circles. He had depended for his support upon three other sources: the backing of the White House, the success of his policies, and the skill of his advocacy. But the President's popularity in Congress had never been high; the collapse of Chiang Kai-shek's government and the Secretary's remark that he would not turn his back on a friend after Alger Hiss's conviction on perjury left Acheson suspect with many people; and his habit of leaving "an adversary to swallow the dust of the dispute" [35] annoyed a large number of congressmen, many of whom were upset anyway by the Secretary's aloofness and dapper "British" appearance — elegant moustache, well-cut clothes, and black homburg. In short, Acheson had won few friends in the legislative halls.[36] The result of the election rendered him even more vulnerable. For the significance of the election was not simply that the Democrats had lost key seats in the Senate and House, but that few Democrats would in the future relish the task of defending Dean Acheson against any criticisms, however unscrupulous they might be.[37]

Combined with these attacks upon the Secretary of State and the calls for his resignation, the Taft wing launched a frontal assault upon the entire range of the Administration's foreign policy, particularly its European policy. On November 13, Senator Taft proposed that the United States "re-examine" the scope, methods, and character of its economic and military aid to Europe [38] — which, in its turn, prompted Acheson to characterize Taft as "a farmer [who] goes out every morning and pulls up all his crops to see how they have done during the night." [39] Nevertheless, shortly thereafter, the Senator gained his wish. The Administration, fearing that the Soviet Union might follow Communist China's example — but on the other side of the world — sent four divisions to bolster European defense and appointed General Eisenhower as Supreme Commander of all NATO forces. Senator Taft immediately challenged the President's constitutional right to send these troops without congressional authorization. Taft argued, "We had better commit no American troops to the European continent at this time . . . There is no legal obligation to send American troops to Europe." [40] Two days later, Senator Wherry, Republican floor leader, introduced a resolution onto the floor of the Senate: "Resolved, That it is the sense of the Senate that no ground forces of the United

States should be assigned to duty in the European area for the purposes of the North Atlantic Treaty pending the formulation of a policy with respect thereto by the Congress." [41]

The foreign policy debate which followed lasted several months; known as the Great Debate, it focused on three questions: should American ground forces, beyond those serving as the army of occupation in Germany, be sent to Europe at all; if so, how many divisions and men was the United States obligated to station in Europe under the North Atlantic Treaty; and could the President make such a commitment of troops without congressional authorization? These questions were debated in an atmosphere hardly conducive to the calm deliberation needed for the careful consideration of different strategies of survival. Communist China's full-scale intervention in Korea on the eve of allied victory in late November, the resulting defeat and long withdrawal of United Nations forces below the 38th Parallel, the Administration's restraints upon MacArthur which the General claimed forbade him from winning the war, the increasing casualty list, and the apparent willingness of our closest allies to conciliate Communist China in order to end the fighting — all had intensified the American people's disillusionment with the cold war. Their bitterness against both the Administration and America's European allies found their emotional outlet in the violent Republican attacks against the Administration's European policy; in their rebellion against the pains of constant and intense global involvement and "entangling alliances," and their simultaneous desire to strike out against the President and Secretary of State, against Britain and France, and against Communist China, they discovered a spokesman in Senator Taft. In expressing the public's ambivalent isolationist-aggressive state of emotion, Taft was more than "Mr. Republican"; he became "Mr. America" — and he remained so until General MacArthur, a more dramatic and apocalyptic figure, returned from the field.

For four months, from December 1950 to April 1951, Taft and his supporters within Congress, as well as some outside such as ex-President Herbert Hoover, indicted the Administration's political and military policy on three counts. First, it strained America's economic strength; indeed, if it were continued over a long period of time it would cause the collapse of the entire economy. Taft expressed a strong fear that owing to the Joint Chiefs' "tremendous emphasis . . . on the conducting of a land war in Europe," the United States may have to commit "far more" than six divisions to the European continent. "If we commit ourselves without limitation to the European project we will be faced with the constant effort to increase the Army and the tremendous expense involved in that effort. There is practically no limit to the size or expense of the type of army which ultimately would undertake to win a war against Russia on the continent of Europe and in Russia itself." As it was, the President's present program which envisaged only twenty-five divisions — "obviously insufficient to control the land in Europe and Asia" — was already "at the very limit of or beyond our economic capacity." [42]

Second, it committed the United States to "Operation Land War" in Europe. This strategy was ill-conceived. It would in all likelihood incite Russia "to a war which it might not otherwise undertake." The Administration might argue that NATO was only a defensive alliance, but the United States "cannot have an adequate armament for defense which cannot be converted overnight into a weapon of offense"; Russia might well fear that the large-scale rearmament of NATO and particularly the addition of American divisions might threaten its safety. "If they do not have the intention of starting a third world war, then I believe there is only one incitement on our part which might lead them to change their minds and begin such a war. That would be the creation of a condition in which Russia feared the actual invasion of Russia or invasion of some satellite country sufficiently close as to threaten the future invasion of Russia." Besides being provocative, the Administration's ground strategy would fight the Communists on their own terms and risk the loss of any future war. American forces could easily be isolated in Europe; the Russians could quickly atom bomb the harbors through which our troops could be reinforced and receive their supplies. Under these circumstances, an American Dunkirk would be an impossibility. In short, Democratic strategy spelled the graveyards of millions of American soldiers; and it would sap the vitality of all of Western civilization. NATO with its sixty divisions could not succeed where Napoleon with his Grande Armée and the Germans with their 240 divisions had failed. The United States must therefore rely on its air and naval superiority to control the Atlantic and Pacific Oceans and forbid any invasion of the Western hemisphere. [43]

Third, this almost total reliance on sea and air power against an antagonist who was the largest land power in history left Europe an expendable area. "In my opinion," Taft said, "we are completely able

to defend the United States itself." Even without Europe, Herbert
Hoover asserted, "Americans have no reason for hysteria or loss of
confidence in our security or our future." All that was necessary was
the preservation of this "Gibraltar of the Western Civilization." Taft
and his supporters thus denied the Administration's fundamental assumptions: namely, that Europe was vital to American security; and
that the continent and Great Britain, sickened by war, destruction, and
famine, had first to be nursed back to good health and strength under
the protective wing of American power. They claimed that Europe
was an essentially healthy society which, if it possessed the requisite
determination, could take all or almost all the measures necessary for
its own defense; the failure to establish such a structure of defense
was symptomatic of certain characteristics which orthodox Republicans had long considered traditional European characteristics: lazi-
ness, unreliability, and untrustworthiness. The European nations had
sufficient manpower, natural resources and industries to establish
strong forces of their own; what they lacked was will-power. The
primary obligation for European defense must rest upon the European
nations themselves. In Taft's words, "The initiative should be theirs
and not ours." He was unwilling to commit American troops to Europe
unless there was a "reasonable chance for success"; since he had, however, voiced strong doubts that such success was achievable, Taft was
actually saying that the United States should not send any divisions
to help Europe in its defense until Europe had become so strong that
she would no longer need any American help. Perhaps because he was
no longer running for political office, Herbert Hoover was more forthright when he stated that the precondition of further economic and
military aid must be "organized and equipped combat divisions of
such huge numbers as would erect a sure dam against the red flood." [44]

These criticisms, besides betraying a strong nationalist and traditional anti-European bias, again demonstrate how strongly the
conservative Republicans were attached to their ideal, the nineteenth-
century American political and economic system. It dictated their
whole stand on foreign policy. For it committed them against Big
Government and a strong executive, which they feared would result
in dictatorship and end all political and civil freedoms; against large-
scale expenditures, which would hand the government the opportunity
of·exerting its "Socialist" domination over the economy by imposing
controls to prevent wages and prices from spiraling upward; against

high taxation, which stifled the initiative of private enterprise. Yet the conduct of foreign policy, even more than the New Deal, required all these things: a Big Government, which could handle our relations with foreign nations; a powerful President, who could act decisively and vigorously; vast appropriations to sustain a sizable military establishment as well as economic and military aid. In short, according to orthodox Republican philosophy, active participation in world affairs was incompatible with the preservation of the political democracy and free enterprise which they conceived of as being the foundation stones of the American system; not only war, but even the balanced forces which the Joint Chiefs regarded as necessary to deter war, could destroy these foundation stones. To preserve the domestic system, conservative Republicans had to assume external security and American self-sufficiency. They could not first assess the international situation and then decide whether the situation demanded more money for economic aid or for larger armed forces, or whether the President had the constitutional right to commit American forces to Korea or Europe. They assumed that such measures undermined the American democratic system; consequently, they were against them. They could never face the other side of the picture and ask themselves whether American democracy could in fact afford *not* to extend presidential power or raise the budget in order to survive. To have done so would have meant giving up their fundamental faith that domestic policy held an absolute priority over foreign affairs.

The resulting foreign policy of the Taft Republicans was thus primarily concerned with defending the oceans surrounding the American Gibraltar. Their primary concern was the depth and width of the oceans, not the capabilities and intentions of the enemy eyeing the American bastion across bodies of water reduced by modern technology to the dimensions of small lakes, or the multitude of forces with which the Administration had to contend to assure the American people a reasonable sense of security. Their only aim was to sit in Fortress America waiting for the fate the Communists had prepared; their only faith that America was economically and militarily self-sufficient; their only program that America should "go it alone" — except, of course, for Chiang Kai-shek and Franco. This was not the isolationism of the 1930's; its strategy was different. But the basic attitude was familiar.

These attacks upon American foreign policy had their impact on both the Administration's European and Far Eastern policies. Republican insistence that the President had no right to send American troops to Europe without congressional authorization was written into the compromise McClellan resolution introduced on April 4, 1951. This resolution incorporated the Administration's plan to commit American divisions to European defense, and it approved the selection of General Eisenhower as Supreme Commander of all NATO forces, but the resolution also embodied all the Republican demands: that Congress support this assignment of American troops; that it support the assignment of any additional troops sent abroad in the future; and that the Europeans make the major contribution to the NATO command. To emphasize the latter point, the resolution requested the President to report to Congress every six months on the status of European defense. Yet the damage had been done.[45]

The four months' debate had demonstrated that many Americans were uncertain about or hostile to the Administration's basic supposition that Europe was America's "first line of defense." For although Congress had finally approved the President's decision to send four divisions to Europe, the victory had been won by those who mistrusted the Administration's European policy and hoped to limit American support to the nations of Europe, if not stifle it altogether. A French correspondent summed up Europe's impression of the Great Debate: Congress, especially the Senate, seemed to be the most unstable and unpredictable legislative body in the world. It made the President hesitate to act firmly against MacArthur's verbal offensive against his Administration, and it questioned the very fundamentals upon which American policy was based. Europe, the correspondent said, no longer identified the United States with the President, but with the Senate, whose distrust Europe repaid measure for measure. "If a basis for confidence is not provided soon, the political effects will be marked and they will be serious. Meanwhile, the moral and political foundations on which the Atlantic Alliance is built are crumbling in mistrust." [46]

The Republican assaults upon the Administration's European policy and allies also had their impact upon its Far Eastern policy: they strengthened MacArthur's political support and increased the pressure upon the government to adopt his policy; at the same time, they made it impossible for the Administration to comply with the wishes of its allies that the United States negotiate an end to the Korean War on the basis of Communist China's demands that it be brought into the

United Nations and that the United States withdraw its fleet from Formosa. If, in order to maintain allied unity, the government granted these concessions to Peking, the Republicans threatened the Administration's commitments in Europe. The Republicans claimed that they only wanted the United States to apply the same policy in the Far East that it already followed in Europe. "Broadly speaking," Senator Taft said, "my quarrel is with those who wish to go all-out in Europe, even beyond our capacity, and who at the same time refuse to apply our general program and strategy to the Far East . . . [Yet in Korea] the Administration refused to fight that war with all the means at its command, on the theory that we might incite Russia to start a third world war. But in Europe we have not hesitated to risk a third world war over and over again. When we moved into Greece to support the Government the Russians might have moved in to support the Communists. The building up of a Turkish Army and Air Force within easy reach of Moscow is far more of a threat to Russia than the bombing of Chinese supply lines in Manchuria." [47] The Taft Republicans demanded an equally tough policy in Asia.

Taft conveniently ignored the contradictions in his point of view. In June 1950 he had seen North Korea's aggression as inspired by the Soviet Union, and he had feared that this aggression "might lead to war with Soviet Russia. It is entirely possible that Soviet Russia might move in to help the North Koreans and that the present limited field of conflict might cover the entire civilized world." [48] After Communist China's intervention, he drew a distinction between the Russian and Chinese Communist threats and aggressions; he now found no evidence that Russia itself had any intention of attacking. "I cannot see that any bombing of China without invasion can be regarded by Russia as an aggressive move against Russia itself, or reason for war." [49] He therefore fully supported MacArthur's recommendations to bomb beyond the Yalu, impose an economic and naval blockade upon Communist China, and "unleash" Chiang Kai-shek to invade or pose a threat of invasion "to keep south China in an uproar." In Asia, he was not greatly concerned lest a "tougher" American policy would turn the Korean War into a global holocaust; he cheerfully accepted this risk. But in Europe, he was afraid that the "tougher" policy he claimed he wished to see applied in Asia, would provoke the Soviet Union. One of the reasons he had voted against the ratification of the North Atlantic Treaty and the sending of American troops to Europe during the

Great Debate was that he felt that the Russians might feel the security of their homeland or satellites threatened and attack.

Consistent with Taft's distinction between the earlier Soviet menace and the lack of it after Communist China's entry into the war was his distinction between the national war which the United States had fought against the North Koreans and the "Democratic" or "Truman" war which the Administration was now fighting against the Chinese Communists. After the outbreak of hostilities, he had approved President Truman's decision to fight in Korea — although constitutionally the President's decision was illegal — as evidence that the Administration had finally applied the containment policy to the Far East and not limited it any longer to Europe; he had welcomed the President's move toward the far more determined anti-Communist policy he and his colleagues had been urging upon the Administration for over six months. North Korea's attack was symptomatic of Soviet expansionist aims; the Communist aggression was, therefore, a threat to American security. The Administration's decision to fight was consequently a national action consistent with American national interest. After Communist China's intervention, Taft changed his mind. The Korean war had never been in the national interest. The United States had been "sucked" into something which was more than it could undertake by the United Nations which was "a weak reed." [50] The President had "rashly sent to Korea any American soldier who was available"; in doing so, Mr. Truman had "completely usurped power where he had no constitutional right." Moreover, after it had become "apparent that the policy of punishing aggression could not be carried through," that America's allies were deserting the United States in order to "appease" Peking, and that a war against Communist China "was a wholly impossible operation," Taft alternated between two positions: a United States withdrawal from Korea to more defendable positions in Japan, Okinawa, and Formosa, and MacArthur's more aggressive policy. In this too, Taft was being inconsistent.[51]

Nevertheless, whatever Taft's inconsistencies, the total impact of his criticisms upon American policy was to deprive the Administration of any degree of diplomatic freedom and maneuverability. This increasing inflexibility had, of course, been apparent since the beginning of 1950. It had first manifested itself in the decision in late June to protect Formosa — although the President had at the same time added that the presence of the Seventh Fleet did not constitute a permanent commitment to defend Chiang, and that once peace had been re-established the "most complex questions are susceptible of solution." Presumably, this had meant that the Administration could at such a time finally unravel and initiate its new China policy and allow the Chinese Communists to invade the island. Yet, between June and late November 1950, when the Chinese first intervened in full force, the American government had gradually been forced to inch closer to Chiang. On July 28 the State Department had announced that it had assigned a chargé d'affaires to Taipei, the capital of Formosa. On July 31, General MacArthur had visited the island, and four days later, General MacArthur's deputy, Major General Fox, had arrived in Taipei to begin a study of Chinese Nationalist forces for the Joint Chiefs of Staff.[52]

After Peking's entry into the war, the United States edged even closer to the Nationalist leader. During the first three months of 1951, the Joint Chiefs recommended a military aid program amounting to $300 million, and the establishment of a sizable military assistance advisory group and training mission.[53] Defense Department spokesmen announced that arms shipments to Formosa were receiving "equal priority" to those going to Europe. At the same time, the Administration verbally endorsed the Republican stand on Formosa and Communist Chinese admission into the United Nations. The United States would "never" allow Formosa to fall under Communist domination; and it would continue to vote against the seating of Peking in the international organization. The question had already come up seventy-seven times in the forty-six bodies of the international organization; only once had the vote been in favor of admitting Communist China, and that had been in the Universal Postal Union, in which the vote had shortly thereafter been reversed. The United States did not, however, expect to use the veto to maintain its position: "it would accomplish very little if . . . the Chinese Communists were in 45 parts of the UN and not in one part." If the United States ever found itself to be in a minority, it would seek a ruling from the International Court of Justice; nevertheless, this country did not expect to find itself in a minority. The important thing was to persuade the majority of the soundness of the American view that "a claimant for seating cannot shoot his way into the UN and cannot get in by defying the UN and fighting its forces." [54]

Conversely, the Administration's tone against Communist China took on a new note of firmness. Indeed, it became so firm that the words of Assistant Secretary of State Dean Rusk on May 18, 1951, sounded very much like a call for revolution within Communist China and unqualified American support for the Nationalist government:

. . . the United States will not acquiesce in the degradation which is being forced upon them [our friends in China]. We do not recognize the authorities in Peiping for what they pretend to be. The Peiping regime may be a colonial Russian government . . . It is not the Government of China. It does not pass the first test. It is not Chinese . . .

We recognize the National Government of the Republic of China, even though the territory under its control is severely restricted. We believe it more authentically represents the views of the great body of the people of China, particularly their historic demand for independence from foreign control. That government will continue to receive important aid and assistance from the United States . . . [55]

The Administration had once more embraced — reluctantly, to be sure — Chiang Kai-shek. This move was symptomatic of the twofold effect of American domestic politics upon the conduct of the nation's diplomacy: it had increased the pressure upon the Administration to extend the war to China, unilaterally if necessary; and it had simultaneously foreclosed a settlement of the war through negotiations with Communist China, as our European allies urged.

IX

THE ALLIES SEEK PEACE: MR. ATTLEE AND MAO TSE-TITO

Nowhere was the proposal to attack continental China received with greater anxiety than in Western Europe. Britain, France, and America's other continental allies had only recently suffered the scourge of war and occupation; they were still engaged in the process of recuperation. In these circumstances, any other reaction but opposition to an extension of the war would have been unnatural. For an American attack upon the mainland of China could result, in their opinion, only in one of two consequences: it could lead to major hostilities, which, although they could perhaps be confined to the Far East, would divert American power to Asia and thereby leave Europe without any substantial defense; or, if the war could not be so limited because the bombing of China and Manchuria would precipitate Soviet intervention, Europe would quickly be overrun by the Red Army. Neither prospect was to the Europeans a particularly welcome one.

The increase of Republican influence in the mid-term election, and the support MacArthur's strategic program had received within Congress and among the public, lent both eventualities an unpleasant air of reality. The mood of Congress during the winter of 1950–51 seemed to be bellicose. On January 19, the House of Representatives adopted a resolution demanding that the "United Nations should act and immediately declare the Chinese Communist authorities as aggressor in Korea"; and the Senate adopted a similar resolution demanding Communist China's condemnation four days later. It appeared as if the United States were willing to go to war at the drop of Mac-Arthur's hat. The Atlantic allies were frightened by the picture of an American public which to them seemed only too willing to accept the new Communist challenge, no matter what the consequences.

The real danger of this possibility was vividly brought home to the Europeans on November 30, 1950, when at a press conference, Mr. Truman remarked that the use of the atomic bomb was under "active consideration," and implied that its employment was entirely within the discretion of General MacArthur. The President's subsequent statement that "by law, only the President can authorize the use of the atom bomb, and no such authorization has been given" did little to assuage the fears of an atomic holocaust which the President's original words had aroused; [1] for Mr. Truman had implied that the employment of the bomb was solely a matter for the United States to decide, whereas our allies believed that "a decision of such grave import could not be taken on behalf of the United Nations without the fullest prior consultation with those member states who are at present participating in international police action in Korea" [2] — or, in the modern version of a famous American revolutionary slogan, "no annihilation without representation."

Ninety-six hours after the President had uttered his famous remark, Prime Minister Attlee landed in the United States for a four-day conference with American officials. During these talks, the Prime Minister represented not merely his own country. The meetings, to be sure, were bilateral in form, but the issues the two men discussed were of vital concern to all NATO members. This had been signified by the conference which Attlee had held prior to his departure from London with the French Premier and Foreign Minister; according to the communiqué the French and British leaders had issued after their meeting, they had "established a general identity of objectives of the two Governments in the present international situation." [3] Attlee in a very real sense thus arrived in Washington as leader of America's most powerful ally and as spokesman for all of Western Europe.[4] His mission: to ensure joint consultation and agreement on all major policy decisions in Korea and thereby prevent the United States from becoming too deeply involved in the Korean-Chinese theater.

The basic reason for the Prime Minister's concern was elementary indeed: strategic.[5] An American decision to fight a major war with Communist China, would, in his view, subtract from American power available for Europe, curtail American economic and military assistance before the task of rebuilding Europe was complete, and possibly force the Administration — as much by circumstance, as by Republican pressure — to relegate Europe to a position of secondary interest. NATO, the bulwark of Britain's and Western Europe's defense, would thus be deprived of its military strength, economic health, and political vitality, and be reduced to so many pretty words on a piece of parchment. Admittedly, it would still commit America to fight if the Russians launched an attack across the Elbe; but it would be impossible to halt such an offensive, certainly not before it reached the English Channel. Another D-Day might eventually come; but the Americans would be invading a continent devastated by atomic warfare. They would, in short, be liberating a corpse.

The first task of defense, therefore, remained the marshaling of sufficient military capacity to deter a Russian attack, or to hold it if it came. This fundamental reason for British and European reluctance to take the risk of a third world war in Korea or to overcommit NATO's still rather limited strength to a "war of attrition" on a distant Asian peninsula would have been shared as strongly by a Conservative government led by Sir Winston Churchill — a man few could accuse of "appeasement" or lack of sympathy for the United States. One need merely recall his words spoken at the time in his capacity as Leader of the Opposition:

... the [Soviet] plan would evidently be to get the United States and the United Nations, so far as they contribute, involved as deeply as possible in China, and thus to prevent the reinforcement of Europe and the building up of our defensive strength there to the point where it would be an effectual deterrent. It is one of the most well-known — almost hackneyed — strategical and tactical methods, to draw your opponent's resources to one part of the field and then, at the right moment, to strike in another ... Surely ... the United Nations should avoid by every means in their power becoming entangled inextricably in a war with China ...
... the sooner the Far Eastern diversion — because, vast as it is, it is but a diversion — can be brought into something like a static condition and stabilised, the better it will be ... For it is in Europe that the world cause will be decided ... it is here that the mortal danger lies. Perhaps we are biased by the fact that we live there or thereabouts. But none the less, one cannot conceive that our natural bias has in any way distorted the actual facts.[6]

This statement by Sir Winston admirably sums up the British and European case; nothing need be added to it.

If Britain's concern for the safety of Europe — the principal approach, after all, to the home islands — was her basic reason for advocating American restraint in the Far East, it was reinforced by a number of other almost equally vital considerations. Perhaps the most important of these was the British view of the future of Sino-Soviet relations. On the whole, the British regarded these rather optimistically, since they assumed that the character of Mao Tse-tung's government was somehow different from that of other Communist countries.

This faith was based only partly on the presumption, held by members of the Labor party's left-wing that the Chinese Communists were essentially nineteenth-century English radicals whose aim it was to bring China political, social, and economic reforms along Western democratic lines. Nor was the attitude of this group unimportant in British domestic politics; even if the Attlee government had been willing to adopt MacArthur's strategy, the impact would probably have split the Labor party, and the government, which held power by a small majority, would have fallen. If Harry Truman could not ignore the clamor of those in the opposition who condemned his policy for being "too weak" toward Communist China, Clement Attlee could not be deaf to those in his own party who accused his policy of being "too strong" toward Communist China.

Primarily, however, this faith was based upon the expectation that China could not be regarded as a Soviet satellite. The Chinese Communists were an indigenous party; they had come to power through their superior organization and morale, as well as their greater sense of unity and purpose. The British were convinced that if the new China were given proper encouragement and friendly contacts with the West, its government could be weaned away from Moscow and be used to counterbalance Soviet power in the Far East. The British were equally convinced that America's hostile attitude toward Peking, manifested by its continued support of Chiang Kai-shek, only drove the Soviet Union and Communist China closer together; British policy was meant to offer an alternative course and encourage the Chinese Communist leader to change his name from Mao Tse-tung to Mao Tse-tito.[7] British policy was apparently greatly influenced by the analogy of Western hostility toward the new Russia after 1917. According to Foreign Secretary Bevin's interpretation, Russia's enmity toward the Western powers was largely the result of their intervention in Russia after the collapse of the tsarist empire, their postwar attempts to isolate the new Soviet regime, and their refusal to treat it as an equal. These Western actions had reinforced the ideological predisposition of the new Soviet government to be hostile toward the capitalistic nations; Western friendship and trust might have been able to overcome this ideological suspicion. The United States and Great Britain must not again treat a newly emerged Communist regime as a social outcast; they must gain its trust and confidence, not incur its hostility.

The Chinese masses had rejected the Chiang government, which they had identified with the United States. If the Truman Administration now utilized Chiang's anti-Communism to reimpose his feudalistic regime, the United States would alienate the friendship of the Chinese people. One of the main social pillars of the Nationalist government had been the landlord class; the result was that the Nationalists could not satisfy the basic land hunger of the Chinese peasants. No regime likes to commit suicide. The Chinese Communists, however, had won much popular support by their promises of land reform. The United States–backed Chiang government had been thoroughly discredited as socially reactionary; by contrast, Mao had become identified with social progress and national independence and self-respect.

The British government believed that the United States, despite its general anticolonial tradition, did not recognize either the popular base of the Chinese Communist revolution or its anti-Western character. Under the circumstances, American hostility would only consolidate popular support behind Mao and ensure the hostility of both the Chinese people and their new government; American enmity toward Mao and continued support for Chiang would rally both Chinese nationalism and peasant fears of losing their promised acres of land to the Communist regime. Western friendship and support for the new China would, on the other hand, demonstrate that the Western powers, above all the United States, were not hostile to the nationalist and social aspirations of the Chinese masses; the United States and Great Britain would instead become identified with national independence and social progress, rather than with colonial and social reaction. The British government claimed that it had avoided alienating India and kept her on the side of the free world by recognizing the desires of the Indian people for self-government and a higher standard of living and life. Only by treating the desires of Mao's China in a similar manner could the United States hope to preserve the friendship of the Chinese people and gain the trust of their new government; not to recognize these aspirations was the way in which to drive Mao into Stalin's arms.

Indeed, Western acceptance or rejection of China's new nationalism was being watched by all of Asia's non-Communist peoples. Would
the Western powers, especially the United States, recognize or overthrow the Chinese Communist government by force? Would they
identify themselves with the revolutionary aspirations of the Asian
masses or with counterrevolution? China was in Asia's eyes the test
case of Western understanding and sympathy for the new trends in
Asia. The answers to these questions were of paramount importance
to the British government: they would largely determine the future
balance of power in the world, as well as the Indian government's
decision whether to stay within the British Commonwealth. India was
its largest member.

The British government suggested two principal means that the
Western powers could employ to achieve Mao's conversion and win
the sympathies of the Asian nations, particularly India. The first of
these was to grant Mao's regime recognition as the *de facto* government of continental China, and to establish diplomatic relations with
it.[8] Britain itself had extended *de jure* recognition. The different
ideological nature of the Chinese Communist government did not sway
her: Mao seemed to be in effective control of the mainland; moreover,
Britain had for centuries had diplomatic relations and dealings with
nations of whose form of government she disapproved — Russia, for
instance. To be sure, full diplomatic relations with Communist China
had still to be attained, but one British representative in Peking was
better than none at all.[9] The second means was to admit Communist
China into the United Nations. This followed logically from the recognition that the new regime was in effective control of the mainland
and the overwhelming majority of the Chinese people. Neither the
question of recognition nor admission into the United Nations was a
question of morals and good behavior; both were issues of fact. If
Mao's government had been admitted into the United Nations immediately after Chiang had withdrawn from the mainland to Formosa,
Western relations with Communist China might now be more cordial.
As Foreign Secretary Bevin explained during a foreign policy debate
in the House of Commons on November 29, 1950, "Some of the difficulties with which we are now faced in the Far East would have been
avoided if there had been those opportunities for mutual discussion of
problems which membership of international bodies affords": [10] or, if
such membership would perhaps not have avoided them, it would

certainly now aid in solving them — for, in Attlee's words, "it did not pay to pretend that the 'nasty fellow' on the other side was not there." A settlement in Korea should come through the United Nations, and "I'm inclined to think myself that we would get less loss of face than if we were dealing with someone outside"! Once the Chinese Communists were seated in the United Nations, "it would be possible to use the arguments of the principles of the United Nations in dealing with them. It was not possible to do this so long as they stayed outside." [11] Here again was the British belief that Mao Tse-tung's regime differed somehow from those of other Communist nations, for these words of advice implied that once they had been admitted into the international forum, the Chinese Communists would, quite unlike their Soviet comrades, interpret the words of the Charter more in line with the Western democracies.

A third factor which must be remembered in understanding the British position is that the English saw the war in Korea, and particularly Chinese intervention, in quite a different perspective from the Americans. Britain's interest in Korea was largely symbolic; the importance of the American decision to fight in Korea lay in its promise to respond in a similar manner to any Soviet moves in Europe. As the *Economist* expressed it shortly after the beginning of the war, "those who wondered whether the United States really would come to the assistance of any victim of aggression, the answer is now on record." [12] At the same time, however, the British were unwilling to become deeply involved in a peninsula which was not of primary concern to them.

This reluctance to commit too much of their own, as well as American, strength in Korea, was reinforced by the belief that Chinese intervention was at least partly the result of unwise American policy. One member of Parliament expressed this widely held British belief when he stated that in his opinion the United Nations had provoked Communist China's intervention by their northward advance and refusal to heed Peking's warnings. "The Chinese action in Korea was no better and no worse than the actions of any other great Power in history in similar circumstances . . . We have gone to war on more than one occasion to prevent hostile armies occuping the Low Countries or the Channel ports of France. Therefore, we have to realize, after all, in this matter, there is a Chinese argument that we ought to understand, and we ought not to show ourselves too much in an attitude of self-complacency and high moral rectitude about the superiority of our own international politics." [13] This position was also advanced, although more tactfully, by as staunch a friend of the United States as Sir Winston Churchill. He had hoped, he said, that General MacArthur's advance would stop at the neck or waist of the Korean peninsula, and leave a no man's land which could then be dominated by allied air power.

To pierce a properly fortified line not only would masses of artillery have to be accumulated, but there would also have to be very heavy concentrations of armour. Those would present admirable targets to overwhelming air power. It certainly seems that the Chinese armies, if they had attacked such a line, might well have renewed on an even larger scale the painful experiences which we ourselves so often suffered on the Somme and Passchendaele and in other bloody battlefields of the First World War. I cannot help feeling that it would have been well if all these matters had been talked over at the right moment and in good time in Washington by the highest authorities in both countries. [14]

While Sir Winston diplomatically refrained from any criticism of General MacArthur, left-wing members of the Labor party were less unwilling to offend American sensibilities. "I should have thought," said one of its members referring to the Chinese break in contact on November 7, "that if the Chinese fell back a long way without being pushed, and deliberately left this great no-man's land, and then proceeded to release some prisoners, they were ready to sit down and talk to somebody. Instead of anybody going along and sitting down and talking with them, General MacArthur chose that moment to launch an enormous attack bang in the middle of a first-class blizzard." [15] It was, in short, General MacArthur who had provoked the Chinese into Korea, and who had brought the world to the precipice of atomic warfare.

This distrust of General MacArthur ranged far beyond Labor's left wing. [16] Few Britons liked or approved of the General's imperious attitude and forceful manner of expression, or his overwhelming self-confidence and his impatience for results. This hostility toward Mac-Arthur was partly a reflection of the normal democratic distrust of generals who seem too eager to formulate policy and incur an extension of hostilities; and this distrust was strengthened by contrast to the modesty, friendliness, and cooperative and conciliatory approach of the highly respected and likable General Eisenhower. Partly, also, MacArthur was the whipping-boy of all those — and this constituted almost the entire British population — who preferred to believe that the West had no basic conflict with the new China; that Peking would not have intervened in Korea if the United States had not crossed the 38th Parallel and MacArthur not launched his "home by Christmas" offensive to thwart the establishment of a buffer zone in North Korea; and that even then the war and all outstanding Far Eastern problems could be solved if General MacArthur and his pro-Nationalist congressional supporters were not, out of sheer anger over Chiang's defeat, deliberately obstructing the Administration from adopting Britain's "wiser" and more conciliatory approach to Peking.

But Britons also saw in MacArthur's alleged arrogance, irresponsibility, impetuousness, and rashness dangerous traits typical of their new and inexperienced overseas "cousin," who wished to assert her immense and youthful power on the global scene in happy disregard of consequences. They resented that Great Britain, a politically "mature" power, a nation of long-standing international responsibilities and diplomatic experience, should play second string to a headstrong America. If only British brains could be combined with American brawn.

The British thus feared that if the Administration now failed to withstand the pressure General MacArthur and the Taft wing of the Republican party were exercising upon it, the world would in all probability soon find itself engaged in its third world war — the second in eleven years. Since most Englishmen were in any case unsympathetic toward American policy in the Far East, MacArthur became the symbol of a policy which was almost universally regarded as dangerous and provocative of war because of its intransigeance and uncompromising hostility toward Communist China.

General MacArthur, in his turn, believed that Britain's conciliatory attitude was dictated largely by the security of the Crown Colony of Hong Kong and a profitable trade with Communist China. Upon his homecoming, MacArthur testified that "the port of Hong Kong is now a means by which great quantities of materials, strategic and otherwise, pour through into Red China." A report from the American consul general in Hong Kong showed that $210 million (or $40 million American) of material on the American strategic list had passed through the port during the last two weeks of February and the first week of March 1951. MacArthur read part of the "very compendious list": "many chemicals . . . instruments and accessories . . . radio parts . . . machinery and fuels . . . minerals . . . medicines of various sorts . . . metals . . . laboratory equipment . . . petroleums." When Senator Knowland asked him whether these imports would have been of substantial assistance to the Chinese Communists, MacArthur replied, "There is no question about it . . . It is the very essence of the movement of an army and armed troops." [17]

The British denied that either the security of Hong Kong or Chinese trade played a significant role in determining British policy toward Peking. Even before the Korean War, Britain had totally prohibited the shipment of arms and ammunition, and restricted materials and products that might be of strategic value to the normal peacetime consumption of Communist countries. Since the outbreak of hostilities in Korea, these restrictions had become much more stringent. As Sir Hartley Shawcross, the President of the Board of Trade, asserted in May 1951, nothing was being exported from Britain or her colonies which built up Chinese military potential. "It is very understandable that in other countries which are less dependent on exports to pay their way in the world a stricter line should be taken, but, as a matter of fact, it is to be observed that our policy in this matter has been more restrictive than that of any other country, apart from the United States themselves." It was "complete nonsense" to suggest that Britain was flooding Hong Kong with exports which would increase China's war-making capacity. "That is quite untrue; there is not the slightest foundation in it."

In evidence, Sir Hartley cited Britain's exports of rubber to Communist China. The economics of Malaya and Singapore were largely dependent on the income of rubber sales, but the Chinese Communists were not dependent upon these sources of supply. Nevertheless, the United Kingdom had felt that the quantities of rubber being imported into China during the first half of 1951 were in excess of civilian requirement and that they would fully satisfy China's civilian needs for the whole year; consequently, it had asked the government of Malaya to take the necessary steps to ensure no further exports of rubber during the current year. The British government would buy the rubber Malaya and Singapore had already contracted; this would be in addition to the regular British purchases. None of the other rubber-producing countries, Sir Hartley pointed out, had yet followed Britain's example.

Most of the remaining trade did go through Hong Kong, but Hong

Kong was an international port: American as well as British exports passed through it on the way to Communist China. This trade, and the local industries which imported the raw materials and then exported the finished products, were the lifeblood of Hong Kong; without trade, in short, the two and a half million inhabitants would not be able to support themselves. In addition, the island was dependent upon China for its food supply and water. Thus severe restrictions upon Hong Kong's trade would cause serious food shortages and would give rise to economic and political conditions which would breed Communism. Yet, despite Hong Kong's high degree of dependence on the China trade, the Hong Kong government had restricted over 200 industrial items besides the total prohibition of arms, aircraft, and ammunitions.

Britain's concern that Communist China should receive nothing of strategic value was clearly shown by the list which MacArthur had cited. This list, to start with, had not been compiled by the United States consul general, as MacArthur had stated, but the Hong Kong government; it had been furnished to United States authorities as part of the system of keeping careful watch and statistical check upon exports to Communist China. MacArthur was quite correct in referring to the strategic items it enumerated, such as diesel and fuel oils, gasoline, kerosene, and lubricants.

Certainly they were on the list . . . what he does not seem to have pointed out . . . is that the list showed nil quantities as being exported to China. In fact all exports of that kind had been prohibited as long ago as July, 1950 . . . Others again, although on the list, are not ordinarily regarded as being of strategic importance, such, for instance, as fertilizers, hand tools and insecticides . . . Of the remaining items to which he specially referred, many were not . . . being exported in quantities which can be regarded as strategically significant. I do not want to reduce the thing to an absurdity — but in the list for the period 19th February to 4th March from which the General was apparently quoting, he chose to select cameras. The list showed one camera exported to China over that period.

Sir Hartley concluded by pointing out that the considerations which had led the Hong Kong government not to place a total embargo on exports to Communist China were "exactly the kind" which had undoubtedly led General MacArthur to allow Japan's exports to Communist China in 1950 to increase substantially during the last quarter of the year, that is, after Peking's intervention in Korea. Total Japanese exports to China in 1950 had amounted to $19.5 million worth of materials, of which $17 million was in iron and steel, machine tools, and such items as precision instruments. What was necessary for the livelihood of Japan, Sir Hartley implied, was necessary for the liveli-hood of Hong Kong; the same rules applied to both.[18]

Sir Hartley might have added that what MacArthur thought was necessary for the nation he ruled, the British government believed of equally vital importance for Britain. For England, like Japan, was an island-nation living on the money it earned by exports; without suf-ficient exports, England's standard of living would have to be lowered and her armed forces diminished. The result would be twofold: it would swell the support for the left-wing of the Labor party; and Britain would no longer be able to fulfill her military commitments in Western and Central Europe, the Middle and Far East. Britain could not, therefore, afford to lose any market; Britons often pointed out that their country would prefer to increase its sales in the American market, but was prevented from doing so by the American tariff wall. The Chinese market, although severely restricted, helped Britain earn her living, and made it possible for Britain to get along with less economic aid from the United States. What was "moral" for Japan was not "immoral" for England.

The impact of these considerations — particularly the priority of Europe in the pattern of British defense, the British view of Mao Tse-tung as a potential Tito to balance Russian power in the Far East, and the intense distrust of General MacArthur — determined the British and European stand against an extension of the war to Com-munist China. Moreover, these factors shifted allied emphasis from "punishing aggression" to conciliation and mediation. This change in attitude was not the result of any alleged European "immorality," "cowardice," or desire to "appease," as Americans often thought; it was the product of different and conflicting interpretations of national interests.

While the war in Korea had been limited to fighting the North Koreans, European-American differences over the Far East had re-mained submerged; but once Peking became involved in the hostilities, these differences over the nature and character of the Chinese Com-munist regime came to the fore. The Europeans were convinced that Peking's demands were not wholly unjustified, that as the *de facto* government of continental China, it had a "legitimate" right to be represented in the United Nations and the satisfaction of the allies' wartime promises to return Formosa to "China"; that a more friendly

American attitude toward the new Chinese regime in the past might have forestalled her intervention; and that the continuation of the present inflexible American policy could only spark the already grave and potentially explosive situation, which would probably envelop all Europe in its flames.

The allied view that restraint of the United States was more important than restraint of Communist China received powerful support from the "neutral" Arab-Asian bloc led by India. Indeed, the drama of the following weeks, during which the allies brought pressure to bear upon the American government to conciliate Peking in order to end the war, had already been enacted once before, although on a smaller scale, by India and the United States. India had from the beginning of the war wanted the United States to grant Peking its "legitimate" rights in order to avert the possibility of a war. For India, like Britain and France after Communist China's intervention, had been motivated from the outbreak of the Korean War by the overwhelming fear of major hostilities. Although she had voted for the June 25 resolution and "accepted" the June 27 resolution because she opposed the settlement of international conflict by resort to aggression, India had made it clear that the "acceptance" of the second Security Council resolution did not involve any modification of her foreign policy. "This policy is based on the promotion of world peace and the development of friendly relations with all nations. It remains an independent policy which will continue to be determined solely by India's ideals and objectives. The Government of India earnestly hopes that even at this stage it may be possible to put an end to the fighting and to settle the dispute by mediation." [19]

India's desire to end the fighting by mediation before it expanded into a major war enveloping all of Asia, was based on considerations to which responsible Western statesmen, particularly leading British officials, paid close attention. First, as an ex-colonial nation, India was extremely sensitive to any suggestion of Western influence and domination. Prime Minister Nehru was strongly convinced that the Western powers, especially the United States, continued to take decisions affecting vast areas of Asia without understanding the needs and spirits of its people. American failure to recognize the new government of China, American determination to continue the support of Chiang's corrupt and feudalistic regime, which had been rejected by the

Chinese people, fell into this category of decision. Through its support of the Nationalist regime and denial of self-determination to the Chinese people, the United States was placing itself at the head of counterrevolution and social reaction. Peking represented the will of the Chinese people, and nonrecognition constituted intervention in China's domestic affairs. Old forms of imperialism may be dead, Nehru told the Indian Parliament on August 3, 1950, but new forms of colonialism were arising. "We Asians," he continued, "are in a better position to know what the people of other Asian countries, such as Korea, China and Indochina really want." Yet, Western statesmen were still determining the future of Asia. It was time that they treated the new Asian nations as equals and listened to their views. Thus, to India and her leader, both greatly influenced by past Western domination, any war against Communist China spelled a military crusade against the Chinese revolution which they saw primarily as part of the popular and nationalistic ferment stirring almost all the underdeveloped and colonial areas in Asia and the Middle East.[20]

India's desire to prevent the extension of the Korean War was also influenced by domestic considerations akin to those which had influenced the United States a century and a half before when this country had placed priority on economic development rather than foreign policy. Independence itself was not enough to India, as it had not been to the United States at an earlier age; independence had to be given social and economic meaning by creating a better life for its people. Nehru was above all else determined to lift his country by its own sandal straps, so that its people, after centuries of poverty, ill health, lack of sanitation and education, could begin to enjoy a higher standard of living and life. To achieve this, India needed a long period of peace. She could not afford to become involved in the cold war by joining one or the other side; "foreign entanglements" would have meant the diversion of needed funds for economic development to an arms build-up, and the division of her people.

It was for these reasons that India had, immediately after the outbreak of the Korean War, set out to try and extinguish the Korean blaze before it would engulf the whole globe or all of Asia. The Soviet Union's full-fledged support of North Korea made an accommodation among the great powers seem imperative. Russia had, however, withdrawn from the Security Council in protest against the continued representation of China in that body by the Nationalist government.

Thus the first step toward a speedy settlement of the Korean War was to bring Russia back into the Security Council. This could be achieved by granting Communist China her "legitimate" seat on the Council; this was just not only because Peking was the *de facto* government of China, but also because she was Korea's powerful neighbor. No stable and lasting peace settlement was possible without Peking's presence and participation at the negotiating table deciding the future of the strategic peninsula which the Japanese had traditionally used as a springboard for the invasion of Manchuria.

Prime Minister Nehru had, therefore, sent personal messages on July 13, 1950, to both Secretary Acheson and Premier Stalin. "India's purposes," he declared, "is to localize the conflict and to facilitate an early peaceful settlement by breaking the present deadlock in the Security Council so that representatives of the People's Government of China can take a seat in the Council, the U.S.S.R. can return to it, and, whether within or through informal contacts outside the Council, the U.S.A., the U.S.S.R., and China, with the help and cooperation of other peace-loving nations, can find a basis for terminating the conflict and for a permanent solution of the Korean problem." [21]

Stalin quickly agreed, but added: "I believe that for a speedy settlement of the Korean question it would be expedient to hear in the Security Council representatives of the Korean people." [22] Since the North Korean Communists were by definition the only true representatives of the Korean people, and since Pyonyang was at the time in control of most of the country, Stalin's addition in effect meant that the Soviet Union was not willing to agree to the restoration of the 38th Parallel as the dividing line between North and South Korea. Stalin, in short, was using Nehru's sincere desire for peace as a lever to pressure not only Communist China's admission into the United Nations, but also to gain peacefully the goal he was then seeking to attain by force, a unified Korea. Stalin was not willing to return to the *status quo* as demanded by the United Nations resolutions of June 25 and 27, 1950. Nonetheless, Nehru found Stalin's reply "encouraging"; his fear of a major war was so strong that Stalin seemed to him to be in a conciliatory and responsive mood.

The United States, by contrast, seemed to him to be opposed to a speedy settlement of the war. The American position, as explained to him by Secretary Acheson — who was to repeat this position many times to our allies after Communist China's intervention — was that

"We do not believe that the termination of aggression from northern Korea can be contingent upon the determination of other questions which are currently before the United Nations . . . In our opinion, the decision between the competing claimant governments for China's seat in the United Nations is one which must be reached by the United Nations on its merits . . . I know you will agree that the decision should not be dictated by an unlawful aggression or any other conduct which would subject the United Nations to coercion and duress." [23] Thus, to India, the United States was, even before Peking's intervention, in large measure responsible for the continuation and possible expansion of hostilities: Korea's problems could not be settled in the absence of its large and powerful neighbor; yet the United States refused to recognize the new China's "legitimate" status in the United Nations and right to Formosa. The first step toward a termination of the Korean War was to remedy these two issues.

America's European allies supported this Indian position wholeheartedly after Communist China's intervention threatened to expand the Korean War to a vast area of Asia, if not to Europe as well. The result was that the European powers led by Britain and the Arab-Asian bloc led by India joined forces in two attempts to end the war by conciliating Communist China.

The Arab-Asian bloc sponsored the first effort. On December 12, they introduced a resolution which aimed at two objectives: one, a cease-fire, and two, a conference on the Far East. The resolution was adopted on December 14 by a 51–5 Soviet bloc majority; [24] it charged a three-man group, composed of Assembly President Nasrollah Entezam, Canada's Minister for External Affairs Lester Pearson, and India's Sir Benegal Rau, with the responsibility of consulting the two high commands or their representatives, and reporting back to the General Assembly the basis for a cease-fire conference. In its effort, the group spared itself little humiliation. It appealed to Peking to allow its representative, present at Lake Success for the debate on Communist charges of American aggression against China, to stay; it assured the Chinese Communist government that in its view, and that of the twelve sponsoring Asian governments, negotiations between the United States, United Kingdom, Soviet Union, and Communist China to settle outstanding Far Eastern issues pacifically would "at once" follow a cease-fire; the group even offered to come to Peking! All these efforts were in vain.

Peking considered United Nations resolutions dealing with major problems, particularly on Far Eastern matters, as illegal and null and void if it had not participated and concurred in their adoption. Consequently, the People's Government would not establish any contact with the illegal "three-man committee." The sponsoring Arab-Asian nations were undoubtedly motivated by a desire for peace, but they had "failed to see through the whole intrigue of the United States Government in supporting the proposal for a cease-fire and negotiations afterwards, and therefore they had not seriously considered the basic proposals of the Chinese Government concerning the peaceful settlement of the Korean problem." Foreign Minister Chou En-lai, pressing home the advantage of Communist China's military victory, declared

that as a basis for negotiating a peaceful settlement of the Korean problem, all foreign troops must be withdrawn from Korea, and Korea's domestic affairs must be settled by the Korean people themselves. The American aggression must be withdrawn from Taiwan. And the Representatives of the People's Republic of China must obtain a legitimate status in the United Nations. These demands are not only the justified demands of the Chinese people and the Korean people; they are also the urgent desire of all progressive public opinion throughout the world. To put aside these points would make it impossible to settle peacefully the Korean problem and the important problems of Asia.[25]

Despite this firm rejection, sentiment in the United Nations remained in favor of one more effort. Communist China's intervention had brought the world to the brink of war, and American tempers had risen to the point where it was unsafe to assume that the United States would not accept the challenge. In London, the prime ministers of the British Commonwealth urged the Great Powers to seat themselves around a conference table and negotiate their differences and avoid war. We must not despair, they said, of reaching "the overwhelming majority of the people of all lands who want peace . . . We should, in the name of a common humanity, make a supreme effort to see clearly into each other's hearts and minds." [26] The Norwegian delegate to the United Nations expressed it in a slightly different way: hostilities were "attended by death and destruction affecting combatants and non-combatants alike. Under those circumstances, it was imperative that the United Nations, like any single government involved in a war, should make every effort to arrive at an honorable and peaceful settlement. Such an effort should not be regarded as appeasement." [27]

The new resolution, presented by the three-man cease-fire group and co-authored by the Commonwealth prime ministers,[28] was introduced into the General Assembly's Political Committee on January 11 by Lester Pearson, and passed by a vote of fifty to seven (with one abstention) two days later. It embraced "Five Principles":

1. In order to prevent needless destruction of life and property, and while other steps are being taken to restore peace a cease-fire should be immediately arranged. Such an arrangement should contain adequate safeguards to assure that it will not be used as a screen for mounting a new offensive.
2. If and when a cease-fire occurs in Korea, either as a result of a formal arrangement or, indeed, as a result of a lull in hostilities pending some such arrangement, advantage should be taken of it to pursue consideration of further steps to be taken for the restoration of peace.
3. To permit the carrying out of the General Assembly resolution that Korea should be a unified, independent, democratic, sovereign state with a constitution and a government based on free popular election, all non-Korean armed forces will be withdrawn, by appropriate stages, from Korea, and appropriate arrangements, in accordance with United Nations principles, will be made for the Korean people to express their own free will in respect of their future government.
4. Pending the completion of the steps referred to in the preceding paragraph, appropriate interim arrangements, in accordance with United Nations principles, will be made for the administration of Korea and the maintenance of peace and security there.
5. As soon as agreement has been reached on a cease-fire, the General Assembly shall set up an appropriate body which shall include representatives of the Governments of the United Kingdom, the United States of America, the Union of Soviet Socialist Republics, and the People's Republic of China with a view to the achievement of a settlement, in conformity with existing international obligations and the provisions of the United Nations Charter, of far eastern problems, including, among others, those of Formosa (Taiwan) and of representation of China in the United Nations.[29]

Peking rejected these "Five Principles" for the same reason it had dismissed the earlier United Nations attempt to achieve a cease-fire: it was unwilling to agree to a cease-fire before negotiations. It therefore submitted four counterproposals:

A. Negotiations should be held among the countries concerned on a basis of agreement to withdrawal of all foreign troops from Korea and the settlement of the Korean domestic affairs by the Korean People themselves, in order to put an end to the hostilities in Korea at an early date.
B. The subject-matter of the negotiations must include the withdrawal of United States Armed Forces from Taiwan and the Taiwan Straits and Far Eastern related problems;
C. The countries to participate in the negotiations should be the following seven countries: the People's Republic of China, the Soviet Union,

the United Kingdom, the United States of America, France, India and Egypt, and the rightful place of the Central People's Government of the People's Republic of China in the United Nations should be established as from the beginning of the Seven-Nation Conference;

D. The Seven-Nation Conference should be held in China, at a place to be selected.[30]

The United States considered these counterproposals a complete rejection. Secretary Acheson, in his statement to the press on January 17, accused Peking of a "contemptuous disregard of a world-wide demand for peace." Once again, the Chinese Communists had shown "a total lack of interest in a peaceful settlement of the Korean question." There could no longer be any doubt that the United Nations had explored every possibility of finding a peaceful settlement in Korea. "Now, we must squarely and soberly face the fact that the Chinese Communists have no intention of ceasing their defiance of the United Nations." [31]

Members of the First Committee who met to consider Communist China's reply were less sure that the United Nations had explored every possibility of finding a peaceful settlement of the war; and they continued to fear what to them seemed the growing number of indications that the United States was drifting toward a full-scale war with Communist China. Sir Benegal Rau, speaking on behalf of the Indian government, did not see Peking's counterproposals as an outright dismissal, "but as partly acceptance, partly nonacceptance, partly as a request for elucidation and partly a set of counterproposals." Then, turning to Secretary Acheson's statement that Peking had no intention to cease its defiance of the United Nations, Sir Benegal said that further negotiations would not, as implied, damage the authority and prestige of the United Nations, or constitute appeasement. In this connection, one had to ask "the reason for Chinese intervention in Korea. Though no one could tell for certain what that reason was, one possibility was that the intervention was not the result of a desire for expansion of Chinese territory or influence, but of a fear for China's own territorial integrity. Reasons of history, a generation of continual war of one kind or another, and the isolation resulting from non-representation in the United Nations and other causes had tended to create various fears and suspicions in the Chinese mind." Sir Benegal insisted that the "United Nations knew that these fears and suspicions were without justification; but it was not enough for the United Nations to know that fact. The Organization must do all it could to remove all groundless fears from the minds of others as well. To remove misunderstandings or misfounded suspicions which were likely to lead to war was not an unworthy task, and negotiations to that end could not possibly be described as appeasement." To brand Communist China as an aggressor, therefore, would serve "no useful purpose. If such a step were taken, it would hardly increase the prestige of the United Nations unless it were intended to be followed by other steps. Since the feasibility of further steps had not yet been examined the only result of such a resolution would be not only to leave all Far Eastern problems unsolved, but also to make them insoluble . . ." [32]

Two days later, on January 22, Sir Benegal announced that the Indian government had requested the Chinese Communists to elucidate certain points. The reply which New Delhi had received from Peking read:

I. If the principle that all foreign troops should be withdrawn from Korea has been accepted and is being put into practice, the Central People's Government of the People's Republic of China would assume the responsibility of advising the Chinese volunteers to return to China.

II. Measures for the conclusion of the war in Korea and the peaceful settlement of the Korean problem could be carried out in two stages:

First: A cease-fire for a limited time period can be agreed upon at the first meeting of the Seven-Nation Conference and put into effect so that negotiations could proceed further.

Second: In order that the war in Korea might be brought to an end completely and peace in East Asia assured, all conditions for the conclusion of hostilities would have to be discussed in connexion with the political problems, in order to reach agreement on the following points:

Steps and measures for the withdrawal of all foreign troops from Korea; proposals to the Korean people on the steps and measures to effect the settlement of the internal affairs of Korea by the Korean people themselves; withdrawal of the United States armed forces from Taiwan and the Straits of Taiwan in accordance with the Cairo and Potsdam Declarations; other Far Eastern problems.

III. The definite affirmation of the legitimate status of the People's Republic of China in the United Nations had to be ensured.[33]

The United States found nothing in this "elucidation" to suggest any essential modification of Peking's position. The Chinese Communists still rejected the one condition which the United States insisted was the absolute prerequisite for an end of the shooting: a cease-fire *before* political negotiations. Communist China, the United States charged, had once again slammed the door on negotiations. India disagreed. So did Great Britain. Sir Gladwyn Jebb, the British representative at the United Nations, found Peking's "elucidation" sufficiently hopeful to suggest further clarification before the United Nations took any other action. Peking, he said, had "not entirely rejected the principle of a cease-fire before negotiations." The Chinese reply mentioned a cease-fire for a limited period as a first step. The length of this period could at least be discussed; obviously, it would make a considerable difference whether Peking meant one week or six weeks. It was also evident that the principles on which the internal affairs of Korea were to be settled by the Korean people would be a matter for the post–cease-fire conference to settle; Peking's previous intention had been to leave this question entirely in the hands of the Koreans themselves. On the issue of Communist China's expectation of a United Nations seat prior to negotiations, Sir Gladwyn thought that it "would make a considerable difference if that question was looked at in its proper perspective since . . . the only question arising would be not whether the Peking government should have to justify its admission but whether it had the right to be represented as the Government of China . . . that was not a question of morals or behaviour but a question of facts. If that simple truth could generally be accepted, a great deal of our unnecessary controversy might be avoided." Lastly, Sir Gladwyn did not feel that Peking's "advice" to the volunteers need arouse any great concern over what would happen if they refused to accept the "advice"; Peking should not be expected to eat all its former words all at once. It had to save face.[34]

Allied and neutral concern that Peking, which had just won a major military victory, should save face is evidence both of their fear of a major war and of their sympathy for China's desire to obtain admission into the United Nations and control Formosa. Our Allies and their Arab-Asian supporters recognized that their demands upon the United States would involve a fundamental change of American policy toward Communist China; but since they disapproved of the American position in the first place, they welcomed this prospect. They regarded such a modification of existing American policy as a step forward, not as a diplomatic retreat; but even if the latter were the case, they regarded this contingency with less alarm than the possibility of a major war. Korea was simply not "worth" that price.

Neither was it "worth" that price to the American government. Nevertheless, while the American government, like its allies, was ready to conclude a cease-fire on the basis of the prewar division of Korea, it was, unlike its allies, determined to avoid surrendering Formosa or allowing Peking "to shoot its way into the United Nations." This refusal on the part of the United States to conciliate Communist China threatened to disintegrate NATO; holding the alliance together thus became one of the Administration's major preoccupations in the weeks following China's intervention.

X

CHINA'S CONDEMNATION
AND MacARTHUR'S DISMISSAL:
HARRY TRUMAN, MIDDLE-MAN

During December 1950 and January 1951, the United States government found itself caught between the viewpoints and pressures of General MacArthur and his political supporters on the one hand, and the allies on the other. Moreover, their conflicting attitudes were so far apart that it was impossible to bridge them. MacArthur pointed to Communist China as an inveterate enemy of the West and a great threat to the future of Asia; the remedy was a vigorous military course. The allies were convinced — or, more accurately, hopeful — that Moscow could not control Peking, and that Communist China would develop an independent policy if the Western powers left the door to the free world open; in short, they saw Peking as a potential friend and counterbalance to Russia in Asia. The General saw the failure to liberate all of Korea as a betrayal of a promise made to the Korean people by the United States and the United Nations; the Europeans acknowledged no such pledge. The Commander in Chief, Far East, was convinced that the struggle between the United Nations and Red China would not demand substantially more forces, only the lifting of current restrictions on his air and naval arms and the "unleashing" of Chiang Kai-shek. The allies feared that an extended war in the Far East would divert considerable American strength from Europe and leave the West defenseless. One doubted that Soviet Russia would openly participate in the war, and therefore stigmatized the desire to negotiate an end to the war as a symptom of weakness which would provoke rather than deter Russian intervention; the other thought that the Kremlin would fight and thereby precipitate a total war for which they were not yet prepared.

The two sides shared only one common characteristic: they thought of each other in blackest terms. MacArthur thought the Europeans held an unrealistic picture of the world and condemned them as too prone to "appeasement." The Europeans in their turn, were distrustful of MacArthur: they disliked his impatience for results, his preoccupation with political matters that allegedly were no concern of his, and they were always fearful lest Washington fail to control him.

These contradictory viewpoints and pressures presented the American government with a real dilemma. Whose advice ought it to take? Should it listen to General MacArthur and risk the possibility of a world war and the alienation of its allies? Or should it accept the counsel of its NATO partners and thereby precipitate a cold war at home, particularly between itself and Congress? The choice was not an easy one. For notwithstanding popular mythology, the Administration did not totally reject the argument presented by its field commander; nor did it wholeheartedly welcome the views of its allies. With the former it agreed that no concessions ought to be made to the Chinese Communists; with the latter it agreed that the war must not be expanded.

The Administration's firm opposition to admitting Communist China into the United Nations or granting her a free hand in the Strait of Formosa was not based upon recognition of the facts of domestic political life; its argument against these concessions rested upon their harmful effects upon America's international status and prestige. An accommodating spirit might encourage the Communists to commit further acts of aggression; it would probably lead them to raise their demands; and even if it did not increase their appetite, a settlement at the price of the United Nations admittance and Formosa would undermine Asian confidence in the United States, particularly in Japan and the Philippines. Rewarding Peking's aggression would be tantamount to admitting that the Communists "had won the game and could now collect the stakes." The American people, Acheson told Attlee during his visit, could not at the same time be expected to support a vigorous foreign policy in Europe and accept aggression in the Far East, or at least the aggression of a large power — "It would be a very confusing thing . . . " Should Communist China's entry into Korea, moreover, foreshadow the possibility of Russia's intervention in Korea or elsewhere, it would be a grievous error to try and buy her off. "My own guess" declared Acheson, "is that it wouldn't work. All we might get would be time, but never enough to do any good. Just enough time to divide our people bitterly. Just enough time to lose our moral strength." It was better to be forced out of Korea than to negotiate at the point of a gun.[1]

Apparently, then, Communist China's intervention had changed the Secretary's views, for the time being at least, on Sino-Soviet relations and the possibility of a Chinese-Russian struggle for power in Northern China. On November 29, in the same speech in which he had said that "no possible shred of evidence could have existed in the minds of the Chinese Communist authorities about the intentions of the United Nations" in North Korea, Acheson denounced Peking's intervention as an "act of brazen aggression . . . the second such action in five months . . . This is not merely another phase of the Korean campaign. This is a fresh and unprovoked action, even more immoral than the first." [2] And when the British Prime Minister suggested that the Western powers should pursue a policy which would turn Communist China against Russia — a policy which before China's intervention Acheson had himself hoped to implement upon the fall of Formosa — Acheson answered that "we could not buy the friendship of the Chinese Communists . . . and we ought not try to prove that we were more friendly to them than the Russians. After what they had done to us, it seemed to him that the Chinese would have to prove that they were *our* friends." [3]

While the Administration thus agreed with General MacArthur that the acceptance of Communist China's demands would be politically disastrous, it did not share his enthusiasm for more vigorous military action. President Truman and his advisers agreed with the allies that air and naval bombardment of Communist China would probably result in a world war. Red China was the Soviet Union's largest and most powerful ally or satellite. Consequently, Russian self-interest and prestige in the Far East, embodied in the Sino-Soviet treaty, would make it difficult for her to ignore a direct attack upon the Chinese mainland.[4]

Indeed, even without American bombardment of Communist China, the Administration believed that it stood on the brink of war. The imminence with which it expected the Soviets to launch their attack is suggested by a story in Mr. Truman's memoirs. On the morning of December 16, 1950, Under Secretary of Defense Lovett called the White House and reported that radar screens in the Far North were reporting large formations of unidentified planes. Fighter planes were immediately sent up to reconnoiter and alert signals flashed to air centers throughout New England. For a time apparently, it was believed that these planes were Soviet bombers on their way to drop their deadly cargo on American cities. Later, Lovett informed the President that the report had been in error, and that the mistake had been due to the effects of some unusual atmospheric disturbance upon the radar equipment.[5]

China's aggression, in short, seems to have given American policy-makers a jolt. The containment policy had been based upon the assumption that the Soviet Union would not accept the risk of a major war until 1952–1954; but North Korea's aggression, and now Communist China's intervention, suggested that the Soviet timetable might be much shorter than had originally been anticipated. The Kremlin, in other words, might not be talking of a world war simply to frighten the Western powers and weaken their powers of resistance; it might actually have decided that the time was ripe for war with the United States and its allies. Soviet military preparations and propaganda indicated the possibility of moves in Berlin, West Germany, Indochina, Yugoslavia, and Iran.[6]

In each of these areas, a minor incident could easily give the Russians an excuse for open intervention. Such incidents were to be avoided if possible, because neither the United States nor its allies were ready to fight a global war; their most serious weakness was a lack of ground troops. The United States at the time possessed only one division at home ready for action. The Korean War had, to be sure, initiated a large-scale rearmament program in both the United States and in Western Europe — including the proposal to rearm West Germany — but this was only just getting under way, as evidenced by General Eisenhower's recent appointment as Supreme Commander, Allied Forces in Europe. The United States did, of course, possess a relatively strong air force equipped with atomic bombs, but the Russians were believed to be strong enough to capture the Strategic Air Command's European bases; and without these bases, the command's effectiveness would be reduced by as much as 75 to 80 per cent. The United States possessed few intercontinental jet bombers; certainly not the numbers necessary to sustain continuous operations during a major war, in which a high rate of attrition of planes and crews could be expected.

Even if the Soviet Union should not intervene in Korea, however — and here again the Administration found itself in agreement with its allies — the United States must limit its commitment on this distant Asian peninsula and conserve its strength for any possible future contingencies in other areas of the world.[7] A long war in Korea would make it impossible to build a strong military defense in Europe, whose priority in the scheme of American defense had been reaffirmed by President Truman and Prime Minister Attlee during their recent conference.[8] Indeed, the absorption and attrition of American power in the Far East might not only leave Europe exposed to the Red Army; it might even attract an attack. This risk could not be taken, since Europe, with its strategic location, skilled manpower, natural resources, industrial strength, and air bases was of vital security to the United States and a key factor in the global balance of power.

Twice in this century, the Europeans had suffered from war; it was natural that they wished if possible to avoid another world war, particularly one which would be fought with atomic weapons. This is not to say that they would not fight if the Soviets left them no choice; they were reluctant, however, to let American impatience draw them into a catastrophe while more honorable and less destructive alternatives still existed. Korea, in their opinion, was not worth the risk of a global conflict.[9]

If in these circumstances the Administration disregarded their point of view and implemented MacArthur's program, the United States would undermine the confidence and mutual trust which were essential for NATO's preservation; it might even alienate its allies and lose them. Such a course was unthinkable, particularly since the Administration was not sure that it might not soon be fighting the Soviet Union. As the President put it:

The Kremlin is trying, and has been trying for a long time, to drive a wedge between us and the other nations. It wants to see us isolated. It wants to see us distrusted. It wants to see us feared and hated by our allies. Our allies agree with us in the course we are following. They do not believe that we should take the initiative to widen the conflict in the Far East. If the United States were to widen the conflict, we might well have to go it alone.

If we go it alone in Asia, we may destroy the unity of the free nations against aggression. Our European allies are nearer to Russia than we are. They are in far greater danger. If we act without regard to the danger that faces them, they may act without regard to the dangers that we face. Going it alone brought the world to the disaster of World War II. *We cannot go it alone in Asia and go it with company in Europe* . . .

I do not propose to strip this country of its allies in the face of Soviet danger. The path of collective security is our only sure defense against the dangers that threaten us.[10]

"Going it alone" was not.

The Administration's differences with both its allies and its field commander faced it with two extremely difficult policy problems. First, how could it pursue a policy in Korea which at the same time would retain the support of its allies, withstand their pressure for concessions to Peking, and yet preserve their unity in the area most vital to American security — Western Europe? Second, how could it reject MacArthur's demands for an extension of the war without increasing domestic disharmony and political partisanship to the point where its entire foreign policy might be endangered for want of the support it had generally received in the past?

American determination not to yield to the demands of the Communists or to the pressures of the allied and neutral nations divided the free world, isolated its leading power, and supported the Communist contention that it was the United States which stood as the obstacle to peace by depriving Communist China of her "rights" to be represented in the United Nations and govern Formosa. In fact, all the Communists seemed to have to do was to bide their time. They knew that the Administration was unwilling to negotiate from its position of weakness in Korea; on top of that, they were well aware that even if the American government had been so inclined, domestic politics would have prevented such negotiations. Indeed, the MacArthur-Republican pressure served the Communists well in their campaign to alienate the United States from its allies. By keeping alive the threat of a major war, this pressure made the allies anxious to end the hostilities by conciliating Peking! By hinting that they would agree to a cease-fire in exchange for admission to the United Nations and control of Formosa, the Communists presented their demands in terms which the allies regarded as legitimate. The firmer the Communist demand for satisfaction, the more strongly did the Republicans oppose such "appeasement": and the more loudly that the Republicans called for an extension of the war, the greater the allied pressure upon the Administration to concede China its "due." The Administration seemed powerless to act; it was caught in the middle. The Communists watched with glee.

Yet if the United States wished to forestall a possibly fatal split of the NATO alliance, further alienate India and other members of the Arab-Asian bloc, and place the responsibility for the continuation of the war on Peking, it had to support the United Nations attempts to end hostilities. And this is precisely what the Administration did, although this decision was very unpopular in the United States itself. Cries of "appeasement" were heard everywhere. But as Secretary Acheson said at the time, both resolutions were supported by an overwhelming majority of United Nations members who believed that the Chinese Communists might still be prevailed upon to cease their aggression. The United States did not share this opinion, but it did recognize that this opinion was sincerely held and that any American abstention or opposition would destroy any possibility of their success. Moreover, acceptance of these resolutions did not indicate acceptance of Peking's demands; it simply meant that the United States was prepared to discuss outstanding Far Eastern issues after a cease-fire had been arranged and effected. "The whole basis of the United Nations Charter is that we settle questions by peaceful means. We are required to go before the United Nations Organization and discuss questions. We are not called upon to agree. We are not called upon to give up our position or anything that we regard as some basic interest." The United States did not regard the seating of Communist China or Formosa as part of a Korean settlement; these issues could only be discussed after Communist China had halted her aggression! [11]

The United States, therefore, supported the two United Nations attempts to end hostilities; *but* at the same time it included in both proposals terms which would be unacceptable to Peking. In short, in accepting both United Nations resolutions, particularly the one of January 12, Washington was playing a shrewd game: *It was accepting the form of negotiations while denying the substance of concessions.* This gave the impression, on the one hand, that the United States was willing to cooperate with its allies in seeking a speedy termination of hostilities and earnestly attempting to remove the most likely causes of any future Far Eastern explosions; and on the other hand, the inclusion of terms which the Administration knew Peking would reject made sure that the post–cease-fire conference would never take place. Secretary Acheson vehemently opposed "saying to the Communists that they had won the game and could now collect the stakes; it would be like offering a reward for aggression. For that reason, if for no other, Acheson preferred that there be no negotiations at all, even if the Communists won and forced us out of Korea." Similarly, the Assistant Secretary of State for Far Eastern Affairs, Dean Rusk, "could see no reason why we should have to prove our good will [to the Chinese Communists] by agreeing to the seating of the Chinese Reds in the U.N. in order to get a settlement. . . . If we agreed to admit the Chinese Communists now just so we could talk with them, we would have to make a major concession. We had over and over again shown our willingness to talk and should not be asked now to make concessions before we were allowed to talk." [12]

To prevent such talks from taking place, Washington insisted that both United Nations resolutions include the same conditions for an end to the fighting. The first one demanded that a cease-fire should precede negotiations. Since this would freeze the front and allow the United Nations troops time to recover from the blows they had suffered from the enemy, Communist China's rejection was a certainty. In rejecting the Arab-Asian proposal on December 22, Chou En-lai asked rhetorically why the United States suddenly favored an immediate cease-fire? He cited that when the Americans had landed at Inchon, and had advanced across the 38th Parallel toward the Yalu River, they had not shown much enthusiasm for a cease-fire or willingness to negotiate with the North Koreans. Only now that they had themselves suffered a defeat, Chou said, had the Americans reversed their position. Their proposal, however, was nothing but a tactical maneuver to gain time, a "breathing space" to prepare for another attack. Chou made it clear that Peking would follow the American example; when United States troops had "arrogantly" crossed the parallel in October, they had "thoroughly destroyed and hence obliterated forever the demarcation line of political geography." [13]

The second condition upon which the United States insisted was that prior to any negotiations, the Chinese Communists renounce the use of force. To put it simply, the United States was willing to talk about Communist China's right to a seat in the United Nations and right to administer the affairs of Formosa, but it was also determined to maintain the *status quo*. The Chinese Communists, unlike American senators, were well aware that the American priority would destroy its opportunity for attaining its objectives; only the use of force would call the West's immediate attention and serious consideration to what Peking claimed were its legitimate grievances. Once the employment of force was abandoned, it could no longer exert effective and sufficient pressure to achieve its purposes, and its demands would no longer receive the necessary urgent deliberation. Talk would resolve nothing, except give the United States forces time to recover from the losses inflicted upon them. Communist China was, therefore, unwilling to accept a cease-fire until after the "negotiations" had satisfied its ambitions; consequently, it rejected both resolutions.

Washington's skillful tactics thus ensured that Peking incurred the responsibility for blocking settlement of the war. By achieving this, the Administration had held together the Western alliance and placed itself in a position to demand the condemnation of Communist China as an aggressor. Peking's negative attitude made it, in fact, impossible for the other nations to vote against this American move. The United States government, despite an extremely difficult position at home, had gone along with the general demand to try two approaches to Peking to end the war. Ambassador Austin therefore pressed ahead with his resolution condemning Peking as an aggressor. The General Assembly now disallowed the Indian claim that if Communist China were condemned as an aggressor, Peking would not even listen to further proposals to settle the conflict. Instead, the Assembly now accepted the Israeli Ambassador's incisive remark that Peking's lack of hesitation to call certain members of the United Nations aggressors had not prevented it from inviting those very members to a conference in Peking. This seemed to suggest that the Chinese Communist government implicitly rejected the view that name-calling ruled out subsequent negotiation and agreement. In following the United Nations debates, Peking must long ago already have reached the conclusion that a majority of the members of the United Nations disapproved most strongly of its military intervention in Korea. An official finding would thus only confirm a concensus of opinion already expressed over several weeks.[14]

On February 1, the Assembly by a vote of forty-four to seven (the Communist bloc, India and Burma) and nine abstentions (the eight Arab-Asian bloc members, Sweden, and Yugoslavia) found Communist China guilty of aggression, because by giving direct aid and assistance to those who were already committing aggression in Korea, it had itself engaged in hostilities against United Nations forces. The resolution called upon Peking to cease its hostilities and withdraw its forces from Korea. If China did not desist, the United Nations was determined "to continue its action in Korea to meet the aggression," and it called upon "all states and authorities to continue to lend every assistance to the United Nations action in Korea." The resolution also provided for the establishment of two bodies: first, a Collective Measures Committee to consider "as a matter of urgency" the "additional measures to be employed to meet this aggression": and second, a Good Offices Committee, whose function it would be "to bring about a cessation of hostilities in Korea and the Achievement of United Nations objectives in Korea by peaceful means." [15]

It was the American government's view that the first of these bodies was the more important, since it would consider the application of sanctions, such as an economic embargo. Quick or meaningful action, even on nonmilitary sanctions, was, however, unlikely. The inclination to take a favorable view of Communist China's "legitimate" demands could not be erased overnight by a formal resolution, pressed upon the Assembly by the United States, and passed only because Peking had twice shown itself to be uncompromising; as Mr. Attlee declared on January 23 in the House of Commons, "For our part we have not lost hope of a negotiated settlement of the Korean war, nor have we lost hope that China may yet be ready to play her traditional part in world affairs and live on friendly terms with other members of the world community." [16] Nor could the fear that the United States was tugging at the leash of a major war be dampened quickly; the Administration might be moderate, but General MacArthur and his congressional supporters were not in favor of the same self-restraint. Could President Truman and Secretary Acheson continue to withstand the mood of the country, as apparently expressed in the House and Senate resolutions calling for the branding of Red China as an aggressor by the United Nations? And if so, how long? The expectation that sanctions would, moreover, result in Communist retaliation and precipitate full-scale hostilities in the Far East — if not throughout the whole world — remained strong; since ineffective sanctions would, on the one hand, only damage the prestige of the United Nations and the Western powers, it was better to apply no sanctions; consequently, there was in fact no alternative to a negotiated peace.

Before approving the resolution condemning Communist China, therefore, Britain and France had received an assurance from Ambassador Austin that the work of the Good Offices Committee would hold priority over that of the Collective Measures Committee.[17] "We attach primary importance to the work of the Good Offices Committee," said Sir Gladwyn Jebb. "My Government has the utmost confidence that the President will lose no time in appointing the other two members of the group, so that it may be able to start work forthwith . . . the consideration of sanctions (which would be 'dangerous, double-edged or merely useless') should not even be started by the General Assembly for a long time yet, so as not to prejudice any hope of an agreed solution that may remain . . ." [18]

The Administration had succeeded in preserving the form of allied unity; but it had done so at the cost of the substance of action. It was precisely this unwillingness to follow up the condemnation of Communist China with effective military sanctions that set the stage for MacArthur's final challenge.

MacArthur was unwilling to reconcile himself to the limitation of the war to the Korean peninsula, particularly after the failure of the Chinese Communists to drive his troops into the sea had indicated that their armies were not, despite their larger numbers and the privilege of a Manchurian sanctuary, immune to defeat. If only he were allowed to take advantage of his superior fire-power on land and his greater mobility in the air and on the sea, he could drive the enemy out of Korea, and inflict a heavy military, as well as political, defeat upon Peking. This course was, according to his mind, absolutely necessary; after the dark days of December and early January, he was convinced "even more deeply than before" that the question facing Washington and Lake Success was not how many Red Chinese soldiers could be killed in Korea, but how to forestall *future* Chinese Communist aggression. [19] Slaughtering Chinese troops could not achieve this aim; new troops could be found and trained. The index of modern war was not manpower, but matériel; and the only way to halt Peking's future military expansion was by destroying its power to wage war *now*. The immediate military alternative, given China's numerical superiority, potential for reinforcement and supply, and "unprecedented military advantages of sanctuary protection for his military potential," was a military stalemate at or near the parallel. This MacArthur made quite clear in his two statements of February 13 and March 7.

Talk of again crossing the parallel and advancing into North Korea, he said, was "purely academic" and an "illusion," for as our battle lines shift north the supply position of the enemy will progressively improve, just as inversely the effectiveness of our air potential will progressively diminish, thus in turn causing his numerical ground superiority to become of increasing battlefield significance . . . [Under] existing limitations upon our freedom of counter-offensive action, and no major additions to our organizational strength, the battle lines cannot fail in time to reach a point of theoretical military stalemate. Thereafter our further advance would militarily benefit the enemy more than it would ourselves . . . [Therefore] vital decisions have yet to be made — decisions far beyond the scope of the authority vested in me as the military commander, decisions which are neither solely political nor solely military, but which must provide on the highest international level an answer to the obscurities which now becloud the unsolved problems raised by Red China's undeclared war in Korea.[20]

The hint was clear.

According to General Whitney, to be sure, MacArthur had by February 11 already completed a new plan to defeat the Chinese Communists without extending the war into Communist China itself. First, he would regain the Seoul line as the base of future operations. Then, as an alternative to attacking Manchuria and China, he would block the enemy's major supply and communication lines by "sowing" a "defensive field of radioactive wastes" across Northern Korea. The objective of this operation was to render the southern bank of the Yalu impassable. Simultaneously, he would launch amphibious and airborne landings at the upper end of both coasts of North Korea — possibly reinforcing his own troops with those of Chiang Kai-shek — to close the "gigantic trap." "It would be Inchon all over again, except on a far larger scale." [21]

No evidence was given at the Senate hearings that such a plan existed. This is not to say that it did not exist either in MacArthur's mind or on Tokyo's planning boards. But MacArthur has always denied that he at any time recommended the employment of atomic weapons or bombs in the Korean war.[22] Moreover, his statements after March 7 make it quite clear that he still expected to unify Korea and defeat Communist China the way he had planned since she had first intervened: by carrying the war to her.

The Administration's failure to sanction this course led MacArthur to an outright challenge of his superiors — at least, his civilian superiors, since he apparently subscribed to the false belief that his views coincided with those of the Joint Chiefs. Thus he entered the final fray in the opinion that he could count not only on powerful support in Congress but also on the backing of four men with more prestige than any corresponding group in the United States government — although it seems only fair to add that MacArthur's convictions on the military unification of Korea and destruction of Communist China's war potential were so strong that he would not have kept silent even if he had possessed no faith in the Joint Chief's support.

In any case, the clash came over the question of crossing the 38th Parallel. The attempt had been made before and failed. Should it therefore be tried again? Unlike the Commander in Chief, Far East, the Administration felt itself to be under no obligation to unify Korea by military force — at least, not a second time; certainly, it did not share his belief that the war could be extended without grave risks. The Chinese had suffered heavy casualties and most of South Korea had by now been liberated. Consequently, Washington felt that a proposal to end the war and restore the *status quo*, delivered without any threats or recriminations, might well receive a favorable reception in Peking. The Department of State drafted a statement designed to meet this purpose and, on March 19, discussed it with the Joint Chiefs and the Secretary of Defense.[23]

On March 20, General MacArthur was informed that the President would shortly announce that he was willing to discuss suitable terms in an effort to end the bloodshed. MacArthur was also asked whether, during the next few weeks while the United States would be engaged in negotiating this new approach with allied governments, he would need any particular authority to permit his troops the freedom of action they would require to provide for their security and maintain contact with the enemy. In his reply, the United Nations Commander recommended that no further restrictions be imposed upon his command. He again pointed out that with the forces at his command and operating under limitations, it was "completely impracticable" to attempt to clear North Korea, or even to make any appreciable effort toward that objective. His current directives, therefore, covered the situation quite well.[24]

Upon receipt of this message, the Administration submitted the forthcoming presidential statement to the allied nations which had troops in Korea. The text emphasized that the Chinese had been driven back to approximately the vicinity from which the Communists had originally attacked "and that, therefore, the principal objective of repelling North Korean and Chinese Communist aggression against the South Korean Republic had been achieved." The statement then called upon the Chinese Communists to cease their fire and added that "a prompt settlement of the Korean problem would greatly reduce international tension in the Far East and open the way for the consideration of other problems in that area by the processes of peaceful settlement envisaged in the Charter of the United Nations." At the same time, it warned Peking that if it refused to negotiate, the United Nations would continue the conflict.[25]

Three days later, on March 24, MacArthur issued what he later called a "military appraisal" of the situation. He too called attention to the liberation of South Korea, but the content and tone of the rest of his statement were the opposite to that which the Administration had envisaged. Red China, he declared, had demonstrated, "its complete inability to accomplish by force of arms the conquest of Korea," even though the inhibitions which had been imposed upon his forces had extended Peking a military advantage. The "human wave tactics" were no substitute for the industrial potential to conduct modern warfare. He pointed out that

. . . numbers alone do not offset the vulnerability inherent in such deficiencies. Control of the seas and the air, which in turn means control over supplies, communications, and transportation, are no less essential and decisive now than in the past. When this control exists as in our case, and is coupled with an inferiority of ground fire power as in the enemy's case, the resulting disparity is such that it cannot be overcome by bravery, however fanatical, or the most gross indifference to human loss.

The United Nations tactical successes and China's inability to furnish its troops adequately with many of the critical items necessary for the conduct of modern war, had demonstrated that Red China was not "the exaggerated and vaunted military power" which had at times been assumed.

"These basic facts being established, there should be no insuperable difficulty arriving at decisions on the Korean problem if the issues are resolved on their own merits without being burdened by extraneous matters not directly related to Korea, such as Formosa and China's seat in the United Nations." MacArthur then offered his readiness to confer with the enemy commander in chief at any time to "find any military means" to prevent further bloodshed and achieve the United Nations' objectives, "to which no nation may justly take exception." MacArthur suggested that if the Chinese would not accept his terms, the United Nations might carry the war to China herself. The enemy "must by now be painfully aware that a decision of the United Nations to depart from its tolerant effort to contain the war to the area of Korea, through expansion of our military operations to his coastal areas and interior bases would doom Red China to the risk of imminent military collapse." [26]

Whether this statement can simply be called a "military appraisal," as MacArthur designated it, is questionable; whether it can be dismissed as a weapon of psychological warfare, as MacArthur also did, is doubtful.[27] A third explanation by MacArthur seems more relevant in explaining the substance and timing of MacArthur's statement. He had, he believed, forestalled one of the most "disgraceful plots" in American history: the appeasement of Chinese aggression by the surrender of Formosa and the cession of Nationalist China's seat in the United Nations in return for peace in Korea; he had "unquestionable wrecked [this] secret plan." [28]

That such a "secret plan" existed has never been substantiated. Indeed, the curt sentence that a settlement of the Korean War could open the way for the peaceful settlement of other problems as envisaged in the United Nations Charter merely reaffirmed the position the United States had taken earlier in December and January; a cease-fire before negotiations, and a conference which would settle all problems "peacefully." This time, moreover, the Western powers had omitted any specific arrangements for a post–cease-fire conference; this diminished not only the possibility of an immediate conference following the cessation of hostilities, but possibly a cease-fire itself.[29]

A more likely explanation of MacArthur's move must, therefore, be found in his desire to extend the war to China; [30] for in MacArthur's judgment, such action was required by the highest interests of the United States. Only if Communist China's potential to wage war were destroyed could her future expansion to other areas of Asia be halted. Negotiations would leave China's war potential intact, to be strengthened for future engagements; such negotiations had, therefore, to be prevented.

MacArthur could have found no more appropriate manner in which to achieve this than by his delivery of a virtual ultimatum; for he was asking Peking to admit that it had lost the battle. The claim that the allies were actually the victors, and that all that Peking had to do was to recognize this simple and overwhelming fact, made certain that

Peking would not lay down its arms. A victory could have been achieved only if the United States had been willing to extend the war to Communist China and risk a global war or a major investment of resources in the Far East. In face of the Administration's unwillingness to do either, a cease-fire could be arranged only in the absence of any claims of victory by either side. Great nations do not generally broadcast their defeat or appearance of defeat. To call upon Communist China to confess its defeat, therefore, was to ensure its rejection and the continuation of the war.

This, it would seem, was the real purpose of MacArthur's statement of March 24, and in that respect it was successful. The consequences of forestalling a settlement of the war, MacArthur knew, would be the military stalemate to which he had earlier called attention. But how long could the Administration afford to lose manpower by simply holding a line, and how long would such a course be politically possible in the face of strong congressional opposition and a public so frustrated that it would demand "strong" retaliatory measures? Such thoughts certainly did not escape the British; according to the diplomatic correspondent of *The Observer*, Whitehall had "some doubt" that President Truman and Secretary Acheson could indefinitely continue to resist the change in policy which MacArthur and his congressional supporters demanded.[31] This anxiety was widespread in other allied nations, and was not overlooked in the United States either.

MacArthur's challenge of the Administration was climaxed when, on April 5, the Republican Minority Leader in the House, Joseph Martin, released a letter MacArthur had written to him on March 19. In it the General again expressed his dissatisfaction with the limitation of the war to Korea. The restrictions imposed upon him were not in accord with "the conventional pattern of meeting force with maximum counter-force" which "we have never failed to do in the past." Martin's view that the United States should allow Chiang Kai-shek to establish a second front on the Chinese mainland in order to relieve Peking's pressure in Korea was, MacArthur said, "in conflict with neither logic nor tradition." MacArthur also repeated publicly what he had told General Collins and Admiral Sherman just before Inchon. The battle in Asia must be met with determination and not half-measures, for it was "here in Asia . . . where the Communist conspirators have elected to make their play for global conquest, and that we have joined the issue thus raised on the battlefield." Thus Asia, and not Europe, held priority on the Kremlin's list of objectives for absorption; and "if we lost the war to Communism in Asia the fall of Europe is inevitable, win it and Europe most probably would avoid war and yet preserve freedom." [32] In plain language, the Administration's strategy to limit the war in Korea because it was reluctant to divert American military power to Asia and weaken American strength in Europe was wrong; because, as he had said on several earlier occasions, only resolute reaction would deter the Soviets and Chinese from further expansion.

MacArthur later characterized his letter to Martin as "merely [a] routine communication as I turn out by the hundreds." [33] But there is only one minority leader in the House of Representatives, and MacArthur must have known when he wrote to Martin that this very partisan critic of the Administration would not keep his letter confidential. A senior commander does not, as Secretary Marshall put it during the hearings, tell an opposition leader "that he as the Commander is in total disagreement with his own people." [34] To be sure, Martin had requested the General's opinion "on a confidential basis or otherwise," but MacArthur's reply had not specified that he wished his opinion to be kept from the public's ears.

MacArthur's letter to Representative Martin was his last public challenge. The March 24 statement had convinced the Commander in Chief that he could no longer ignore MacArthur's threat to his constitutional authority in the field of foreign affairs and civilian control of the military; MacArthur's letter merely confirmed him in this opinion. The conflict between the President and his field commander could no longer be tolerated. "If I [Truman] allowed him [MacArthur] to defy the civilian authorities in this manner, I myself would be violating my oath to uphold and defend the Constitution . . . MacArthur left me no choice — I could no longer tolerate his insubordination." [35] MacArthur had forced the President to choose: to submit to him or to relieve him. Mr. Truman believed that he had been patient long enough; for almost a year he had tried to win MacArthur over to his policy — or at least to bring the General to understand the nature of that policy so that he would implement it with tolerance rather than challenge it at almost every turn. The President was convinced that he had shown his wish to get along with his proconsul in Japan: he had praised and decorated him for his military achievements; he had sent emissaries to explain Administration policy; he had even flown to Wake Island himself to establish an *entente cordiale* with his General.

IT HAD TO HAPPEN

None of his efforts had been rewarded. MacArthur persisted in challenging the prerogatives of his office, prerogatives of which he was very jealous; he was no more likely to abide MacArthur's intrusion on his authority as the nation's Commander in Chief and chief diplomat than he had the Senate's attempt to share what he believed was his right to send American troops anywhere in the world to protect American interests. Harry Truman would under these circumstances not delay; the authority of the Presidency of the United States was at stake.

The Truman-MacArthur conflict had finally, therefore, to be resolved; it was. On April 10, President Truman, with the courage for forthright action that never seemed to fail him in a crisis, dismissed General MacArthur from all of his commands — as United Nations Commander; United States Commander in Chief, Far East; Supreme Commander for the Allied Powers in Japan; and Commanding General, United States Army, Far East. A great soldier-statesman's service to his country had come to an end. That he should have insisted on challenging his country's civilian and military leadership, rather than quietly carrying out its orders, was, as the *Economist* remarked, a true measure of MacArthur's self-assurance and self-confidence. If these characteristics were responsible for some of MacArthur's more reprehensible qualities, such as his hypersensitivity to criticism, his need to be always in the right, and his disposition to blame his failures and shortcomings upon others, they were also the virtues which heartened and benefited the free world in the dark days of July and August 1950. If this self-same optimism blinded him to the possibilities of Chinese intervention in North Korea — a judgment in which almost everyone in the American government concurred — it did appraise correctly the impact of the brilliant amphibious operation at Inchon upon the course of the war. If his certainty that he was correct in advocating an extension of the war to China itself after Peking's intervention led him to challenge the President's conduct of foreign policy, it was by no means certain that he had been wrong in believing that Korea was the free world's test whether it could deter future aggression by punishing the aggressor now. "His last claim was that he could achieve complete victory if he were given the means and the authority to open a second front in China; but his instructions were to fight a war of limited liability. Because the Communists feared he might be right they called him a warmonger; because most Europeans and many Americans feared he might be wrong, they called him dangerous and irresponsible." [36]

MacArthur was actually dismissed for three reasons. First, he had failed to submit his statements for clearance in accordance with the President's directives of December 6 ordering all military and civilian officials overseas to "exercise extreme caution in public statements," and to "clear all but routine statements" with the Defense or State Departments respectively. The government had reminded him of these orders after the episode of March 24.

Second, MacArthur had challenged the President's role as the nation's spokesman on foreign policy.[37] This could not be tolerated. It is the President who bears the principal responsibility for the nation's most vital task, its self-preservation. He must therefore retain the supreme direction of its most significant function: the conduct of its diplomatic and military strategy. He is primarily responsible for the formulation and execution of the country's foreign affairs and he is the embodiment of the democratic belief that the civilian authority is and must remain in control of its military arm. The United States could not allow itself to speak with two voices in the international arena, particularly when one was civilian and the other military.

MacArthur's challenge of the President's authority greatly embarrassed the Administration, confused its allies, and thereby hampered its leadership of the free world. After the statement of March 24, allied governments had anxiously inquired in Washington whether the United States had changed its policy and was about to extend the war to China. Secretary Acheson could only reply that MacArthur's statement had been both unexpected and unauthorized; these words did little, however, to reassure them that the "irresponsible statements," which British Minister of State Kenneth Younger said "came out at frequent intervals from highly placed quarters, without the authority of the United Nations or indeed of any member Government," [38] would not generate such powerful political and popular support that the Administration would not be able to maintain its political position unless it adopted its critics' policy.

Confusing and complicating the relations between the United States and its allies was not the only effect of MacArthur's pronouncements; the statement of March 24 had in addition prevented the execution of presidential policy. The General's explanations that his pronouncements merely constituted an appraisal of the "military situation" and a weapon of psychological warfare meant to induce the destruction of the enemy's morale were regarded as quite unsatisfactory in Washington. The General had openly challenged the President's constitutional authority to direct the nation's foreign policy. In Secretary Acheson's words, "it was quite impossible for the President to make a statement after that one had been made; in other words, the field had been occupied, a statement had been made, and if the President had made one, then everybody puts together the statement of General MacArthur, which he made, and compares it with the President's statement, and asks is this the policy or, in the case of differences, is it not, and who is speaking for the United States? So it was decided that the matter had to be held in abeyance." [39]

The third reason for MacArthur's dismissal was that he "was not in sympathy with the decision to try to limit the conflict to Korea," and

Washington thought it was necessary "to have a commander more responsive to control of Washington." [40]

Administration officials had not forgotten MacArthur's previous liberal interpretations of his orders. He had interpreted his June 26 directive not to attack North Korean targets above the 38th Parallel as "permissive, not restrictive"; he had therefore given the appropriate orders in the belief that he possessed "the discretion normal to field command." He had given the same liberal interpretation to Washington's policy of establishing a buffer zone into which no non–South Korean forces were to be allowed. "Just as he violated a policy in this case," General Collins had said about that episode, "so perhaps the thing might be done in some other instance of a more serious nature." Given MacArthur's recent statements, this was precisely what the Administration feared. During the hearings, Secretary Acheson spoke this thought on behalf of all his colleagues, both civil and military.

Senator Morse . . . would it be fair for me to conclude that because it was felt in the State Department and by other Government officials here at home that General MacArthur was not in sympathy with the restrictions that were being imposed upon him as Commander to conduct a limited war in Korea, that you, as Secretary of State, became fearful that at this time there was a constant risk that General MacArthur, in exercising his field powers as commander, might initiate some action that would involve us in a war less limited than the policies of our country desired?

Secretary Acheson. Yes; I think that that would be fair for you to conclude . . . a theater commander must have very considerable latitude. He cannot be directed in meticulous detail: in exercising his discretion and authority I think there was worry on my part that he would exercise it in the direction of enlarging rather than confining the war.[41]

The reasons for Washington's apprehension were revealed at length during the General's testimony at the Senate hearings held upon his return to the United States. These were to be MacArthur's last official "Rendezvous with History."

PART THREE

THE MacARTHUR HEARINGS

XI

MacARTHUR RETURNS:
THE EAGLE RECLAIMED

The announcement of General MacArthur's dismissal stunned the American people. But the shock quickly turned to indignation. Americans in huge numbers immediately wired their representatives; telegrams began to pour into Congress. They ran ten to one against the President's decision. The latter's claim that MacArthur had threatened the supremacy of the civil government made little impression. As one prominent southern senator said shortly after MacArthur's relief, "The people in my part of the country at least, are almost hysterical." [1] So were the people in the rest of the country.

In San Gabriel, California, the President was burned in effigy. In Los Angeles, the City Council adjourned "in sorrowful contemplation of the political assassination" of General MacArthur. Automobiles appeared on downtown streets "plastered" with signs "Oust President Truman." [2] The Illinois Senate expressed its shock that the President had removed a foremost symbol of the free world's determination to resist totalitarian aggression, and resolved, "That we express our unqualified confidence in General MacArthur and vigorously condemn the irresponsible and capricious action of the President in summarily discharging him from command and that we further condemn such action without an opportunity to General MacArthur and others of his command to inform the people of our Nation of the true condition of affairs in Korea and the Far East; and be it further resolved, that we further criticize and condemn the policies of the present administration for withholding information, if any exists, to justify this action." [3] The Michigan, California, and Florida legislatures approved similar resolutions. The White House was bombarded with telegrams and letters, the overwhelming number of which informed the President in no uncertain terms that his decision had been mistaken. [4] When Mr. Truman, in his first public appearance after MacArthur's relief, attended the opening baseball game of the season to throw out the first ball, he was booed.[5]

The Republicans were not slow to exploit this groundswell of public sentiment. A few hours after the announcement of the General's dismissal, some of the party's major figures, including Robert Taft and Floor Leader Kenneth Wherry, met in the office of House Minority Leader Joseph Martin. Shortly after 10:00 A.M., Representative Martin emerged from his office and declared to the assembled newspaper reporters that the conference had agreed: first, that Congress should investigate the Administration's foreign and military policy "in the light of the latest tragic development"; and second, that General MacArthur should be invited to give his complete views to Congress. "In addition," Martin continued, "the question of possible impeachments was discussed." The reporters noted Martin's emphasis of the word "impeachments." While Martin refused to elaborate on this point, Republicans were saying in private that they had in mind not only President Truman but also Secretary Acheson and "possibly others."

On the floor of the Senate, Senator William Jenner charged "that this country today is in the hands of a secret inner coterie which is directed by agents of the Soviet Union. We must cut this whole cancerous conspiracy out of our Government at once. Our only choice is to impeach President Truman and find out who is the secret invisible government which has so cleverly led our country down the road to destruction." These words were greeted with applause from the public galleries. Senator Nixon proposed that the Senate censure the President and call upon him to restore General MacArthur to command; MacArthur's dismissal, Nixon stated, was tantamount to rank appeasement of World Communism. Senator McCarthy called the President a "sonofabitch" who must have made his decision while he was drunk on "bourbon and benedictine." McCarthy called upon the American people to fight the President's decision lest "Red waters may lap at all of our shores." Unless the public demanded a halt to "Operation Acheson," he warned, "Asia, the Pacific and Europe may be lost to communism." He called upon Democrats to help stop this trend; if they refused, they would be labeling their party as the "party of betrayal." Representative Orland K. Armstrong, Republican of Minnesota, called MacArthur's dismissal the "greatest victory for the Communists since the fall of China." [6] Representative Frederick R. Coudert,

Jr., Republican of New York, urged action on a proposed constitutional amendment by which a President could be removed from office or forced to stand for re-election by a two-thirds vote of no confidence by Congress. The Republican Policy Committee issued a unanimously approved manifesto asking whether "the Truman-Acheson-Marshall triumvirate" was preparing for a "super-Munich" in Asia. "As the authors of the 1945 decision to abandon China to the Communists," do they now presume themselves free to resume the course interrupted by the Korean conflict?" The committee failed, however, to elaborate on the reasons "the authors" had changed their mind to appease the Communists in the single case of Korea.[7] Brigadier General Julius Klein, consultant on national defense to the Republican National Committee, declared that not since Bataan had the nation been so humiliated. The Kremlin ought to fire a twenty-one gun salute in celebration.

It was just as well that the Kremlin did not heed General Klein's suggestion. The Russian salute would never have been heard above the din raised in the United States, while the country awaited Mac-Arthur's return from Tokyo. On Monday, April 16, an estimated crowd of 230,000 people, including school children who were given time off from school, witnessed MacArthur's last trip through that city. The Japanese paid their conqueror the highest possible honor: the Emperor personally visited MacArthur at the American Embassy. This was the first time in history that a Japanese monarch had called upon a foreigner who held no official capacity; the Emperor had visited MacArthur on several earlier occasions, but then MacArthur had been the Supreme Commander. At the Tokyo airport, MacArthur was greeted with a nineteen-gun salute, while eighteen jet fighters swooped and circled overhead and four Superfortress bombers flew across the airfield in formation.[8] In Hawaii, MacArthur's first stop on the flight back to the United States, a crowd of about 100,000 people lined the twenty-mile parade route and cheered its "heartfelt aloha." [9]

MacArthur landed at San Francisco at 8:29 P.M. on April 17.

"Mrs. MacArthur and myself have thought and thought of this moment for years," he told the approximately half a million people who greeted him. San Francisco had one of its worst traffic jams in history that evening. The trip from the airport to the downtown area, which normally takes no longer than thirty minutes, took the Mac-Arthur motorcade almost two hours. The deeper the cavalcade of official cars penetrated the city, the slower the progress. The cars had to halt at almost every street corner, so thick was the crowd. Another estimated three million people watched all this on television.[10]

The next day, April 18, a throng estimated to be at least as large as that of the previous evening, cheered the General during a two-hour tour of the city's financial and business district. Many of the viewers showered the bareheaded MacArthur with ticker tape, confetti, and torn television program guides. Some of the guests at the St. Francis, the hotel at which MacArthur was staying, even tore up their pillows and showered the General with feathers — a patriotic venture for which the management charged them fifteen dollars apiece.[11]

Characteristically, business tried to cash in on the public's massive acclaim. Plummer Ltd., of Fifth Avenue, New York, was already advertising the "General MacArthur Toby Jug, perfectly executed as to coloring and uniform. A great likeness of a great soldier. Height 7 ins., $10.50, 6¼ ins., $8.50, 5½ ins., $6.00, 4½ ins., $4.25, 3 ins., $2.75." And RCA Victor guaranteed prospective buyers that they would witness "the greatest single dramatic news event of the generation . . . [a] monumental climax [for which a] whole nation, indeed an entire world, stands poised in anticipation . . ." In tempting potential customers to buy a television set in order to watch the General's forthcoming speech to Congress, RCA asked: "His words — his gestures — the expression of his face — what will they mean to the destiny of the country? . . . You'll see it best and enjoy it most on RCA Victor." [12] Symbolically too, Senator Vandenberg died the same day.[13]

At Washington, where MacArthur landed just after midnight on April 19, the crowd at the airport received him with "an almost hysterical welcome." So tumultous was the reception that the official welcoming party, including Secretary of Defense Marshall, the Joint Chiefs of Staff and Major General Harry Vaughn, the President's personal representative, had barely time to extend its greeting before the crowd of 12,000 broke through the restraining ropes which had separated it from the official delegation. It swept the dignitaries aside as it surged around MacArthur's plane. Of the fifteen minutes he stayed on the airstrip, MacArthur spent thirteen fighting his way through the crowd to his car. The MacArthur family became separated; General Whitney, MacArthur's closest friend and adviser, lost his balance and fell. Some of the 300 reporters and photographers assigned to cover

MacArthur's arrival in the capital were better prepared: they wore football helmets! [14]

The nation's eyes were focused on Washington during this dramatic day upon which the General would address Congress. The House of Representatives assembled at its customary time, noon. Thirteen minutes later, Mrs. MacArthur entered the gallery. The whole House rose and cheered her. Five minutes later, young Arthur MacArthur came in with a line of officers who had served with his father; they sat in chairs ordinarily reserved for the President's Cabinet during a joint session. No Cabinet officers were present that day. At 12:20 P.M. anticipation rose as the floodlights were turned on and the senators marched into the chamber. Only MacArthur had still to arrive; the tension mounted as the minutes were agonizingly prolonged. Finally, at 12:31 P.M., General MacArthur entered, accompanied by a special escort of Senators and Representatives, and preceded by the House Doorkeeper. As the returning hero marched down the aisle toward the rostrum, the members of the House and Senate, and the great crowd in the public galleries, stood up and applauded loudly.

Then the Doorkeeper's voice rang out: "Mr. Speaker, General of the Army Douglas MacArthur." MacArthur took his place before the microphones in the spot usually reserved for Chiefs of State. Speaker Rayburn introduced the General. A demonstration lasting nearly two minutes followed.

As it died down, MacArthur began his speech:

Mr. President, Mr. Speaker, distinguished Members of the Congress, I stand on this rostrum with a sense of deep humility and great pride; humility in the wake of those great American architects of our history who have stood here before me; pride in the reflection that this forum of legislative debate represents human liberty in the purest form yet devised.

Here are centered the hopes, and aspirations, and faith of the entire human race.

I do not stand here as an advocate for any partisan cause, for the issues are fundamental and reach beyond the realm of partisan consideration. They must be resolved on the highest plane of national interest if our course is to prove sound and our future protected. I trust therefore that you will do me the justice of receiving that which I have to say as solely expressing the considered viewpoint of a fellow American. I address you with neither rancor nor bitterness in the fading twilight of life with but one purpose in mind, to serve my country.

Those who watched or heard the next half hour on television or radio are not likely to forget it. They may not remember what Mac-

Arthur said; they will always recall the image of the man which projected itself across the airwaves. It was a forceful image: Mac-Arthur's strength of character, deeply felt convictions, and unshakable self-confidence were apparent from his opening sentence. From his first words, it was clear that he was in complete command of the situation. His bearing was dignified and upright, his delivery stern and unhurried, yet the urgency of his message was evident throughout. His timing was calculated both to dramatize his views and impress his listeners; his sentences flowed easily and his words were eloquent. His use of emotional sentences and paragraphs combined with his-torical generalizations was highly effective.

. . . history teaches with unmistakable emphasis that appeasement but begets new and bloodier war. It points to no single instance where the end has justified that means — where appeasement has led to more than a sham peace. Like blackmail, it lays the basis for new and successively greater demands, until, as in blackmail, violence becomes the only other alternative. Why, my soldiers asked of me, surrender military advantage to an enemy in the field?

MacArthur paused, and then in a softer voice: "I could not answer."

Tactfully he paid his tribute to "your fighting sons," identified himself with their welfare, and the Administration with their plight. They had all met the test of battle, he said, and

I can report to you without reservation they are splendid in every way. It was my constant effort to preserve them and end this savage conflict honorably and with the least loss of time and minimum sacrifice of life. Its growing bloodshed has caused me the greatest anguish and anxiety. Those gallant men will remain often in my thoughts and in my prayers always.

Then MacArthur reached the climax of his speech; others, less rever-ent, might call it "pure corn."

I am closing my 52 years of military service. When I joined the Army even before the turn of the century, it was the fulfillment of all my boyish hopes and dreams. The world has turned over many times since I took the oath on the plains at West Point, and the hopes and dreams have long since vanished. But I still remember the refrain of one of the most popular bar-rack ballads of that day which proclaimed most proudly that —
    "Old soldiers never die; they just fade away." And like the old soldier of that ballad, I now close my military career and just fade away — an old soldier who tried to do his duty as God gave him the light to see that duty.
    Good-by.

It was an unforgettable performance.

But MacArthur was not to fade for a while yet. That afternoon, the General briefly visited Constitution Hall and the Daughters of the American Revolution. Afterwards, at a welcoming ceremony on the Mall, he received a silver tea service and the official key to the City of Washington. As the motorcade drove down Pennsylvania Avenue, jet fighters and bombers roared over the avenue in formation. Approximately a quarter of a million people watched all this. After the ceremony, MacArthur flew to New York City and a parade scheduled for the following day.[15]

New York outdid itself. "It roared and shrilled itself into near-exhaustion." For six hours and twenty-five minutes, "the metropolis formed a gigantic cheering section rocketing its shouts of approval for the 71-year-old soldier-statesman." An estimated seven and a half million people turned out; this was nearly twice the record crowd which had witnessed General Eisenhower's triumphal return from Europe in 1945. Everyone turned out to see MacArthur: New Yorkers, New Englanders, and New Jerseyites; babes in arms; school children and grandparents in wheelchairs. They lined up along the nineteen-mile parade route; many carried placards and banners reading "Welcome Home, MacArthur," "MacArthur Shall Never Fade Out," and "God Save Us from Acheson."

The ticker tape, confetti, and streamers showered upon MacArthur during this parade added up to 2,850 tons! Everywhere torn paper floated down from buildings to cover the returning hero. It looked as if New York had been hit by a snowstorm in April. In the background, harbor craft, trucks, and factory sirens added their own acclaim. As if this reception on ground and sea were not sufficient, the city had also hired fliers who spelled out "Welcome Home" and "Well Done" in heavenly letters two miles long.[16]

What accounted for this unrestrained and spontaneous welcome Americans gave MacArthur wherever he went? Why did Americans come out in the millions to see MacArthur? What made them stay away from baseball games or bring along portable radios to hear MacArthur's speech? Undoubtedly, one element was curiosity. MacArthur's opposition to the President, his dismissal, and his confrontation of Mr. Truman, added up to tense drama. People wanted to see for themselves what the challenger looked like. The cheers of greeting were also cheers of gratitude for a job well done during the years 1941–1945. In the Second World War, MacArthur had early established himself as a hero in the minds of a public hungrily seeking a hero. Amid the shock instilled by the disaster of Pearl Harbor and the defeat inflicted upon American forces in the Philippines, MacArthur's hopeless but defiant stand at Bataan symbolized American courage and staying-power. When the government ordered MacArthur to leave the Philippines for Australia, his famous vow, "I shall return," promised revenge and victory. MacArthur's soldierly skills contributed in great measure to that end and won him an everlasting place among America's greatest military leaders.

Of equal, if not of far greater importance however, was the reverse side of this hysterical enthusiasm for General MacArthur: the public's frustration with the country's continued participation in world affairs. First, there had been the intense efforts of World War II; these had been followed by the disappointment of the high wartime hopes for a lengthy period of peace. Then there had been the frustrations of the containment policy, which ran directly contrary to the American experience in world affairs. The cold war did not draw a clear-cut distinction between war and peace; it allowed the United States neither to abstain from foreign entanglement and preoccupy itself with domestic concerns, nor to harness its giant strength for one quick and convulsive all-out military effort to "punish" the enemy who had forced it to divert its attention from matters at home. Containment was not aimed at eliminating the Soviet danger once and for all by a clean-cut military blow, but only at improving the terms of coexistence and the possibility of survival by a long-run policy relying primarily on economic and political means. "Our name for problems is significant," Secretary Acheson had once said. "We call them headaches. You take a powder and they are gone. These pains [brought on by the world situation] are not like that. They . . . will stay with us until death. We have got to understand that all our lives danger, the uncertainty, the need for alertness, for efforts, for discipline will be upon us. This is new to us. It will be hard for us." [17]

It was also frustrating. Failure in foreign policy was a new experience. If the Truman Doctrine, the Marshall Plan, and NATO had stemmed the Red tide in Europe and given the American people a measure of security, the events of 1949 and early 1950 — the collapse of Chiang Kai-shek, the end of the American atomic monopoly, and the revelations of espionage in the government — deprived them of this security and left them disillusioned; the outbreak of the Korean

War and Chinese Communist intervention added greatly to this sense of insecurity and anxiety. By voicing these disappointments and frustrations of the American people as they uneasily adjusted themselves to their new role of world leadership, the conservative Republicans under Senator Taft's leadership had already gained wide-spread support; for a large number of Americans shared Senator Taft's yearning for the peace and tranquility of an earlier era and a desire to blame someone for having involved them in this "foreign mess." The dramatic figure of General MacArthur, upon his return, symbolized this frustration and gave voice to it in familiar words, one might even say "American" words: words of victory, holding forth a view of a quick and successful end to the bloodshed on the battlefield, words of confidence and praise for an America strong enough to accomplish anything she had the mind to do in this world, and words of condemnation for those who, driven by fear of Russia and troublesome allies, chained the proud and invincible American giant to the rock of "weakness" and "appeasement." Amid the frustrations of the cold war — frustrations brought out into the open and intensified by the Korean War — MacArthur thus became identified with traditional Americanism.

Samuel Lubell later told of an interview which he had held in 1950 with an elderly Ohioan couple named Hunter: "Although the Hunters saw no chance of agreement with Russia, they were reluctant to say that war is the only alternative. Nor were they content with the present nightmarish twilight of neither war nor peace. 'We ought to do something to show those Russians where they get off,' said Hunter. 'When Malik and Vishinsky say those things about us in the United Nations, someone ought to go up to them and slap their faces'! As I got ready to leave, Hunter tried to sum up his feelings, 'I guess what I've been trying to say is that it's time we got back to the American way of living.'" [18]

Letters written to newspapers after MacArthur's dismissal confirm the same mood of weariness with the cold war. One letter written by a real estate and insurance man in Pennsylvania was typical of the sentiments of many: "Let us cleanse ourselves. Let us rededicate ourselves. And cleansed, let us remember we are a great race, that we give orders, that we do not take orders. And if any power anywhere will challenge us, let us sweep them before us like chaff! Forward!" Another letter asked why the "Big Brass" did not support their colleague and "defy the bankrupt haberdasher" and the "traitorous" State Department who would "sell us down the river to Great Britain, Europe and the Communists." A lady from New Jersey enshrined MacArthur in her heart with George Washington, Abraham Lincoln, and Winston Churchill. The General, she wrote, had "the attributes of God; he is kind and merciful and firm and just. That is my idea of God." [19] Nor was this likeness of MacArthur to God limited to "average" Americans. After MacArthur's speech to Congress, Representative Dewey Short, educated at Harvard, Oxford, and Heidelberg, exclaimed, "We saw a great hunk of God in the flesh, and we heard the voice of God." [20] Herbert Hoover, more moderate in his appraisal, saw in MacArthur the "reincarnation of St. Paul into a great General of the Army who came out of the East." [21] MacArthur had struck the most responsive chord in the American temperament — "Americanism" with its religious, even mystical, overtones.

In these circumstances, all the Administration could do was to wait out the storm of public anger. This day too was to come. Eric Goldman tells of MacArthur's visit to the Polo Grounds to watch the Giants play the Phillies. The management, proud of its distinguished visitor, played a recording of a seventeen-gun salute; MacArthur's box was decorated with the Stars and Stripes, and the General told the crowd how happy he was "to witness the great American game of baseball that has done so much to build the American character." MacArthur and his party left before the other sports fans by walking across the diamond to the centerfield exit to the tune of "Old Soldiers Never Die." As the General neared the exit, a irreverent fan from the Bronx yelled: "Hey Mac, how's Harry Truman?" The crowd roared with laughter. [22]

This event could hardly have occurred before the Senate inquiry into MacArthur's dismissal. For it was this investigation which showed many Americans that perhaps MacArthur might not be right after all; for many others, it only proved that he had been right all along.

XII

THE GENERAL'S PROSECUTION:
REBEL WITH A CAUSE

It would have been foolhardy for the Democrats to oppose the Republican demand for a full-scale investigation into the Administration's Far Eastern policy. Such opposition would have been tantamount to political suicide. The Democrats did, however, oppose Republican insistence that the hearings be held by a special committee with equal representation from both parties and be open to the public. The result was a compromise: the inquiry would be conducted by the combined Senate Foreign Relations Committee and Armed Services Committee under the chairmanship of Senator Richard Russell; and the hearings would not be directly open to the public — that is, the proceedings were not to be televised or broadcast, but the witness' testimony would be released to the press after deletion of material that might endanger national security.

Senator Russell opened the "Greater Debate" in Room 318 of the Senate Office Building on May 3, 1951:

Gentlemen of the Committee on Armed Services and the Committee on Foreign Relations, today we are opening hearings on momentous questions. These questions affect not only the lives of every citizen, but they are vital to the security of our country and the maintenance of our institutions of free Government . . .
General of the Army Douglas MacArthur has consented to be the first witness at these hearings. I am sure it is unnecessary for me to attempt to recount in detail the deeds and services which have endeared General MacArthur to the American people.
On the permanent pages of our history are inscribed his achievements as one of the great captains of history through three armed conflicts; but he is not only a great military leader, his broad understanding and knowledge of the science of politics has enabled him to restore and stabilize a conquered country and win for himself and for his country the respect and affection of a people who were once our bitterest enemies.
The General is here today to counsel with our committees and to help us in the fulfillment of our legislative responsibilities . . .

The guiding light here today, and in the days to follow, must be the national interest, for the national interest transcends, in importance, the fortunes of any individual, or group of individuals.

Russell then swore MacArthur in, and invited him to open his testimony. But the General had no prepared statement. "My comments were made fully when I was so signally honored by the Congress in inviting me to appear before them. I appear today not as a voluntary witness at all, but in response to the request of the committee, and I am entirely in the hands of the committee." [1] Involuntary or not, MacArthur proved a most cooperative — and at times voluble — witness.

On the surface, MacArthur argued his case in strictly military terms. War, he said, indicated that "you have exhausted all other potentialities of bringing the disagreements to an end," and once engaged, "there is no alternative than to apply every available means to bring it to a swift end. War's very objective is victory — not prolonged indecision. In war there is no substitute for victory." Never before, MacArthur declared, had war been applied in a "piecemeal way"; you cannot fight a "half war." Present policy, which was based upon the assumption that "when you use force, you can limit that force," introduced "a new concept into military operations — the concept of appeasement . . ." But the very term "resisting aggression" indicated "that you can destroy the potentialities of the aggressor to continually hit you," and not "go on indefinitely, neither to win nor lose." [2]

The Administration's aim was obviously not victory. Its purpose was to "go on indecisively, fighting with no mission for the troops except to resist and fight in this accordion fashion — up and down — which means that your cumulative losses are going to be staggering." MacArthur condemned this course as bankrupt, whose net result could only be a "continued and indefinite extension of bloodshed." War, he admitted, was a gruesome thing, and he had never seen such devastation as in Korea. "I have seen, I guess, as much blood and disaster as any living man, and it just curdled my stomach the last time I was there. After I looked at that wreckage and those thousands of women and children and everything, I vomited. Now are you going to let that go on . . . ?" It would be better to surrender to the enemy and end the war on his terms, if his own military strategy were not adopted.[3]

MacArthur then turned to his alternative program which, he felt, would complete this war in the "normal way" and bring about a just and honorable peace with a minimum loss of life and in the shortest possible time. To begin with, the United States must defeat the Communist armies in the field. "When you say, merely, 'We are going to continue to fight aggression,' that is not what the enemy is fighting for. The enemy is fighting for a very definite purpose — to destroy our forces in Korea." To repel the enemy from this goal, the General repeated the recommendations he had outlined on several earlier occasions: imposing a naval blockade on China, tightening the economic embargo, lifting the "wraps" off Chiang Kai-shek, and bombing airfields, depots, and assembly points in Manchuria and China. He made it clear that if not permitted to destroy the enemy-built-up bases north of the Yalu, "if not permitted to utilize the friendly Chinese forces of some 600,000 men on Formosa, if not permitted to blockade the China coast to prevent the Chinese Reds from getting succor from without, and if there were to be no hope of major reinforcements, the position of the command from the military standpoint forbade victory." [4] He was positive that this program could be carried out without a great increase in ground troops; it needed only a "certain amount of Navy and Air." The primary need was the lifting of restrictions imposed on his air force." "You are a bridge player," he told one senator. "You know that the first rule in bridge is to lead from your strength."

Nor was he alone in believing that these measures would achieve military victory. His views were "fully shared" by all military commanders in the field as well as the Joint Chiefs of Staff. The latter had, in fact, embodied all of his suggestions, except for the bombing of Manchurian air bases and supply depots, in their recommendations of January 12, 1951, and "as far as I know, the Joint Chiefs of Staff have never changed these recommendations." Therefore, these recommendations must have been vetoed by either the Secretary of Defense or the Commander in Chief.

Senator Johnson. Has there been any other indication other than the documents of January the 12th to the effect that the Joint Chiefs support the program you advocate?

General MacArthur. Nothing in the writing that I know of.

Senator Johnson. Anything orally?

General MacArthur. Nothing that I know of.[5]

If adopted, his program would achieve victory in the least possible time and with a minimum of risk and casualties. Time and time again, MacArthur insisted that his way was the only way to achieve "a decisive end without the calamity of a third world war." Indeed, "I believe if you let it go on indefinitely in Korea, you invite a third world war. I believe the chances of the terrible conflict . . . would be much more probable if we practice appeasement in one area though we resist to our capacity along the line." [6]

To those fearing Communist China's huge resources of manpower, he pointed out that China lacked the "industrial base upon which modern war is based," and that the one railroad from the Soviet Union is "almost strained to the utmost . . . Communist China, its power to wage modern war, has been tremendously exaggerated." And he continued:

You must understand that in China itself, they have the greatest difficulty in merely supplying their present civilian population. I don't suppose there is a year in China that from 5 to 10 million people don't die of starvation or of the results of malnutrition. It is an economy of poverty, and the moment you disrupt it, you will turn great segments of its population into disorder and discontent [50 million people might well starve as the result, MacArthur estimated later], and the internal strains would help to blow up her potential for war . . .

They [the Chinese Communists] are peculiarly vulnerable to the process of blockade, and the process of internal disruption by bombing.

The minute you apply these factors, it becomes logistically more difficult, probably impossible, for them to maintain a foreign army on the march. [MacArthur had earlier testified that "after the breaking up of the distributive system," China would be unable to maintain more than a half to one million of her four to five million man army.]

A very modest effort, military effort, on our part, I believe, will have an excellent chance of bringing to an end the Korean slaughter. [7]

But, one senator wanted to know, if we embraced the new strategy and did manage to push the Chinese Communists out of North Korea, and then they refused to call a halt to the war, what course would he then advocate to end hostilities? "Such a contingency," MacArthur replied, "is a very hypothetical query. I can't quite see the possibility of the enemy being driven back across the Yalu and still being in a posture of offensive action." [8]

MacArthur was equally convinced that his strategy would not provoke Russian entry into the war. Asked whether the Soviet Union could afford to see Communist China defeated, he expressed the opinion that Russia had not "sufficiently associated" herself with the Korean War "to believe that the defeat of Red China to the extent of her being forced to evacuate Korea would necessarily produce a great prejudice to the Soviet cause in other parts of the world." Air attacks on Manchuria would not invite open Soviet intervention — unless the Soviet Union was determined to intervene anyway. A Soviet decision to commit its forces in the Korean War would more probably be the result of an estimate that the global balance of power was in its favor.[9] But there were certain factors in this power balance which would deter the Soviets from intervening in the struggle.

At a later date, MacArthur elaborated on these components. In a letter to Senator Harry F. Byrd, who was then inquiring into the charges that a lack of ammunition had impeded the conduct of the war, MacArthur wrote:

Underlying the whole problem of ammunition and supply has always been the indeterminate question as to whether or not the Soviets contemplate world conquest. If it does, the time and place will be at its initiative and could not fail to be influenced by the fact that in the atomic area the lead of the United States is being diminished with the passage of time. So, likewise, is the great industrial potential of the United States as compared with the Communist world. In short, it has always been my belief that any action we might take to resolve the Far Eastern problem now would not in itself be a controlling factor in the precipitation of a world conflict.[10]

Nor did MacArthur deem it "within the capacity of the Soviets to mass any great additional increment of force to launch any predatory attack from the Asian continent." The disposition of Soviet forces was "largely defensive." Soviet Far Eastern forces were not supported by a major industrial complex and the trans-Siberian railroad was already strained to the utmost maintaining Soviet forces at their present strength. While Russia could, of course, launch a destructive attack upon Japan, it was unlikely that she could invade it in the face of American naval and air superiority. The Soviet's air effort would probably not last very long either, since Russia suffered from a lack of maintenance facilities and petroleum in Siberia. And the majority of her submarines operating in the area of Vladivostok were of low radius and were being used largely for defensive purposes.[11] Seen from the Far Eastern Command's headquarters in Tokyo, therefore, the dimensions of Russian power did not seem too formidable —

certainly, less threatening than viewed from the other side of the world.

One senator drew MacArthur's attention to his equally adamant belief in October 1950 that the Chinese Communists would not intervene in the Korean War.

Senator McMahon . . . if you happen to be wrong this time and we go into an all-out war, I want to find out how you propose in your mind to defend the American Nation against that war.

General MacArthur. That doesn't happen to be my responsibility, Senator. My responsibilities were in the Pacific, and the Joint Chiefs of Staff and the various agencies of the Government are working day and night for an over-all solution to the global problem. Now I am not familiar with their studies. I haven't gone into it. I have been desperately occupied on the other side of the world, and to discuss in detail things that I haven't even superficially touched doesn't contribute in any way, shape, or manner to the information of this committee or anybody else.

Senator McMahon. General, I think you make the point very well that I want to make; that the Joint Chiefs and the President of the United States, the Commander in Chief, has to look at this thing on a global basis and a global defense.

You as a theater commander by your own statement have not made that kind of study, and yet you advise to push forward with a course of action that may involve us in that global conflict.

General MacArthur. Everything that is involved in international relationships, Senator, amounts to a gamble, risk. You have to take the risks.

The risk of Soviet intervention had been inherent in the original decision to defend the Republic of Korea, MacArthur continued, and in view of America's superior industrial power, larger atomic stockpile, and ability to deliver its new weapons, the risk seemed worth taking. Any policy which admitted that the United States could not defend every place in the world was tantamount to appeasement. "I say that we have the capacity to do it. If you say that we haven't, you admit defeat. If the enemy has the capacity and is divided on all these fronts, we should be able to meet it." [12] In a few years, this situation might change.

Consequently, MacArthur repudiated the idea that the United States was forced to buy time in Korea to strengthen its defenses and build up its forces in preparation for a major war in the years ahead. MacArthur denied this thesis not because the country was fully prepared for global warfare with the Soviet Union — indeed, he admitted that "from my general knowledge that we are rather inadequately prepared at the moment" — but because the basic premise of such a policy was the erroneous expectation "that relatively your strength is going up much more than the enemy's. That is a doubtful assumption . . ." [13] Time might not be on the side of the free world.

The United States could not, therefore, base its strategy in Korea on the assumption that time would correct the imbalance of force which, according to the Administration, existed then. Senator McMahon's advice to "stop, look, and listen, and see where we are before we plunge into a course that may take us over the precipice before we are ready" was false, and amounted only to a "sophistry of reasoning." To be sure, the Soviet Union might intervene; that was a possibility. But the perpetuation of the "slaughter" in Korea was a certainty — unless MacArthur's military program were adopted. "What I faced in the Pacific wasn't something that was speculative in the future. It's right now. What are you going to do to stop the slaughter in Korea? Are you going to let it go on? Does your global plan for defending this United States against war consist of permitting war indefinitely to go on in the Pacific?" [14]

To those who questioned his opinions, MacArthur reiterated his conviction that only a resolute effort to achieve victory would forestall a Russian attack.

. . . the best way to stop any predatory or surprise attack by the Soviet Union or any other potential enemy is to bring this war in Korea to a successful end, to impress upon the potential enemy that the power we possess is sufficient if he goes to war to overpower him. I believe that the evidences of weakness that we might show if we accept defeat, or this unconscionable continuation of slaughter with no definite mission at the end, will produce the very effect which you would of all others be most anxious to avoid.[15]

MacArthur was, of course, quite aware that America's European allies were reluctant to adopt his more vigorous military program. This attitude he found quite natural. "To the European the welfare and security of Europe is naturally paramount. He has no fear of attack from the West, solely from the East. It is not unusual therefore that he sees in every dedication of friendly resource toward the stabilization of Asia but a subtraction from that available for the betterment and security of Europe." Nevertheless, this reasoning was both short-sighted and fallacious. "Any breach of freedom in the East carries with it a sinister threat to freedom in the West. The issue is a global one and failure to comprehend this fact carries the germs of freedom's ultimate destruction." MacArthur emphasized that "If the fight is not waged with courage and invincible determination to meet the challenge here [in Asia] it will indeed be fought, and possibly lost, on the battlefield of Europe." [16] In short, Western Europe's first line of defense was in Korea, not in Germany; their adoption of Mac-Arthur's strategic proposals was in their own best self-interest — particularly since his recommendations would require few additional troops and little extra war matériel that would seriously detract from American power available for Europe.

But, MacArthur continued, if our principal allies were so paralyzed by their fear of Soviet Russia that they could not realize the futility of their course, the United States would have to "go it alone." This country could not disregard its own vital interests because the European powers "haven't got enough sense to see where appeasement leads." Our interest in Korea was the predominant one, and "if one nation carries 90 per cent of the effort, it's quite inappropriate that nations that only carry a small fraction of the efforts and the responsibility should exercise undue authority upon the decisions that are made." [17] Never, to paraphrase Sir Winston Churchill, had so many exercised so much authority for so little effort.

MacArthur, however, doubted that the United States would be deserted by her allies if his recommendations were adopted and implemented over their protests. In the final analysis, these nations were more dependent upon the United States than vice versa. But, he repeated, if this country had to sacrifice its vital interests for the sake of allied unity, such unity was valueless.[18] The substance of action could not — indeed, must not — be sacrificed to the form of unity.

MacArthur had presented his case, or so it would appear, in strictly military terms. He had declared that war's very objective was victory and not prolonged indecision, and that once hostilities had broken out, there was no alternative than to apply every available means to bring it to a close. Previously, he had talked of the "unprecedented military advantages of sanctuary protection for his [Chinese Communist] military potential against our counter attack," of "meeting force with maximum counterforce," and of the "abnormal military inhibitions" imposed upon his command. The logical conclusion of this line of argument was plain to see — the "politicians" should stop "interfering" with the military conduct of the war. MacArthur in this respect followed the advice of the Roman General Lucius Amelius Paulus.

. . . Commanders should be counselled, chiefly by persons of known talent; by those who have made the Art of War their particular study, and whose knowledge is gained from experience; by those who are present at the scene of action, who see the country, who see the enemy; who see the advantages that occasions offer, and who, like people embarked in the same ship, are sharers of the danger.

If, therefore, anyone thinks himself qualified to give advice respecting the war which I am to conduct . . . let him come with me. . . . But if he thinks this too much trouble, and prefers the repose of the city life . . . let him not . . . assume the office of pilot.[19]

How could men who were not professionally trained and who sat in offices thousands of miles from the scene of battle know what the situation demanded? Of course, Generals Collins and Vandenberg were professionally trained men and also sat in Washington, but at least these two members of the Joint Chiefs of Staff had visited Korea and learned about the military situation at first hand. Since MacArthur was also under the impression — or at least said he was under the impression — that he and the Joint Chiefs were agreed on certain military measures necessary to counteract Communist China's intervention, the failure to implement his recommendations could be due only to political "interference."

The implication was clear: since he, MacArthur, and the Joint Chiefs were fully agreed upon the means of defeating the enemy's forces, the President ought to have accepted their advice. The General presumably shared the American military doctrine that the military establishment was a politically neutral instrument whose operations should be guided exclusively by its own professional rules. The soldier was a nonpolitical figure who conducted his campaign in a nonpolitical and technically efficient manner. His only aim was victory, his sole objective the total defeat of the enemy's forces.

On closer reflection it seems doubtful that MacArthur really believed in such a sharp separation of military and political matters. It would certainly be difficult to classify some of his decisions and recommendations during the Korean War as completely nonpolitical. Prior to the Inchon landing, he had argued that the Korean War was a test for the free world. At stake was the West's reputation; only a quick and dramatic victory would redeem its prestige. "Oriental millions" were waiting to see who would be the winner. In late November, in refusing to halt his troops short of the North Korean–Communist Chinese frontier, MacArthur had informed the Joint Chiefs that the failure to unify all of Korea would be tantamount to a betrayal of the Korean people and a demonstration of weakness which would not only alienate the support of the people of Asia, but provoke Communist China's armies. And MacArthur's "military appraisal" of March 24 was apparently released to forestall the surrender of Formosa and Nationalist China's seat in the United Nations to Communist China. It would be a grave mistake, therefore, to interpret MacArthur's use of the term "victory" in a strictly military context.

MacArthur's political objectives after Communist China's intervention were, in fact, fourfold.[20] First, his mission had been "to clear out all North Korea, to unify it and to liberalize it." This objective had almost been achieved when the Chinese Communists had intervened. This turn of events "called for decisions in the diplomatic sphere to permit the realistic adjustments of military strategy. Such decisions were not forthcoming." Consequently, "I was operating in what I call a vacuum." In other words, MacArthur argued that he had been assigned a concrete policy objective — the military unification of Korea — and that he was unable to achieve this aim under the limitations imposed upon his forces, particularly his air power. He refused to accept this situation. As he had told the Joint Chiefs in November 1950, the failure to prosecute the military campaign to "its public and oft-repeated objective of destroying all enemy forces south of Korea's northern boundary . . . would be regarded by the Korean people as a betrayal of . . . the solemn undertaking the United Nations entered into on their behalf . . ."[21]

MacArthur's aim did not stop at driving the Chinese Communists out of Korea. His second objective was to counter the growing threat of Communist China. She was, as he had cabled Secretary of Defense Marshall on an earlier occasion,

a new and dominant power in Asia which for its own purposes has allied with Soviet Russia, but which in its own concepts and methods has become aggressively imperialistic with a lust for expansion and increased power normal to this type of imperialism . . . the aggressiveness now displayed not only in Korea, but in Indo-China, Tibet and pointing toward the south, reflects predominantly the same lust of power which has animated every would-be conqueror since the beginning of time.[22]

He wished, therefore, to "severely cripple and largely neutralize China's capability to wage aggressive war and thus save Asia from the engulfment otherwise facing it . . ." This purpose could be achieved without great risk, since the Soviet Union was unlikely to resort to war until its atomic and industrial power more nearly matched that of the United States. Communist Chinese expansion in the Far East must be stopped before this situation arose; the destruction of Red China's war-making potential would greatly weaken her government and threaten the Soviet Union's hold upon Asia.

On the other hand, failure to inflict heavy damage upon Communist China and the acceptance of a Korean stalemate and truce would simply transfer the strategic frontier in Asia from Korea to Indochina and allow the Peking regime to continue its expansion elsewhere. General Whitney claims that MacArthur foresaw the fate of the French possession and quotes him as saying, "This is the death warrant for Indochina," when informed of the Korean armistice.[23]

It is in this context that we must interpret one of the most misunderstood exchanges between General MacArthur and Senator McMahon.

> Senator McMahon. General, where is the source and brains of this [Communist] conspiracy?
> General MacArthur. How would I know?
> Senator McMahon. Would you think that the Kremlin was the place that might be the loci?
> General MacArthur. I might say that is one of the loci.[24]

Arthur Schlesinger, Jr., and Richard Rovere have suggested that MacArthur's reply indicated the General's belief that Soviet Russia was no greater a threat to world peace and American security than any other locus in the Communist orbit, since it was not any particular Communist state which was the enemy, but Communism *per se*. From this, they drew the conclusion that MacArthur was really advocating an ideological-military crusade to eradicate Communism from the earth's surface; and this conclusion, in their opinion, is warranted by MacArthur's definition of "Communism throughout the world" as our main enemy, and his refusal to accept any substitute for total military victory.[25]

Within the context of MacArthur's testimony and previous statements, his reply to Senator McMahon takes on a somewhat different meaning: Communist China was an imperialistic power in her own right; its threat must be met lest it expand to the rest of Asia; and the menace of Soviet Russia to Europe must divert attention neither from a recognition of Peking's grave threat to the future security of Asia, nor from the necessity to meet it while the global balance of power was still in our favor. Put in another way, the objective of MacArthur's military recommendations was not only to unify Korea, but to change the entire strategic picture in the Far East. This was undoubtedly the most important aim of the General's program.

MacArthur's third objective was the winning of Asian support for the democratic cause. The failure to prosecute vigorously the military against Communist China and attain a united Korea would be recognized as a token of weakness by the peoples of Asia and alienate their sympathies for the United States. This could not be allowed. MacArthur had long harbored somewhat of an apocalyptic vision of Asia's future. In 1951 MacArthur still held this view. He saw the "whole epicenter of world affairs" rotating back toward the area whence it had started. The future prosperity of the United States would largely depend upon trade with the new Asian states whose energies were almost totally devoted to raising themselves by their own sandal straps.[26]

His concern for Asia did not, MacArthur emphasized, spell a corresponding neglect of Europe — although he had on an earlier occasion cast a skeptical glance at Europe's value to the United States. Nevertheless, he now claimed that his program would offer Europe greater protection and security. The issues, he said, were global, "and so interlocked that to consider the problems of one sector oblivious to those of another is but to court disaster for the whole. While Asia is commonly referred to as the gateway of Europe, it is no less true that Europe is the gateway to Asia, and the broad influence of one cannot fail to have its impact upon the other."[27] Korea was *the* test of the Western alliance. The line against Communism must be held not only in Europe, but also in Asia. Red China's imperialism must be met with the same determination shown in the face of Russian expansion. Europe's line of defense was not at present in London or Paris or Washington, but in Korea. In Europe, the struggle between the free world and Communism continued by diplomatic means — or "words," as MacArthur so inappropriately appraised this effort — but in Asia, the war was already being fought with military weapons. If the war in Korea were lost, the democracies would have suffered a first-class political and psychological setback, and they would have demonstrated a lack of determination and courage which could not but fail to embolden Communist efforts to undermine the Western nations, possibly by a third world war. On the other hand, if the war were won, Europe would probably be saved from war and stay free, because the line would have been held and all breakthroughs blocked.

These, then, were the four principal objectives — perhaps three and a half, since the defense of Europe seemed almost incidental — which constituted the political substance of the term "victory." MacArthur's use of this all-inclusive designation was a shrewd tactic to maximize support for his point of view; for the term appeared to promise a quick decision and favorable end to the war. It allowed MacArthur to pose as a simple military officer wishing only to conduct the war in the normal professional manner, unencumbered by bumbling amateurs in Washington who were too afraid of the Russians and Chinese and too sensitive to the opinions of their allies. It allowed him to taint his civilian superiors as "politicians," which as a term of reproach is used with greater effectiveness in only one Western democracy, France. Indeed, they were not merely "politicians," they were "politicians" who did not seem to grasp the importance of Asia to the security of the United States. Their horizons were so limited to the Atlantic Ocean that they might well be called "North Atlantic isolationists"; [28] and he was the innocent victim of their ignorance.

MacArthur's separation of political and military matters does not, therefore, indicate that he really believed in the sharp dividing line which he had himself suggested. It would appear, rather, that he hoped to strengthen his appeal to the public and the Congress by stating the issue in this clear-cut and decisive fashion. The myth that political policy and military force are distinct elements of policy is probably nowhere stronger than on Capitol Hill; and the appeal of a swift, clear-cut victory was general, since American experience drew a clear-cut distinction between peace and war as two mutually exclusive states of affair. When the nation was at peace, foreign policy took little account of military force; the peace was to be kept by the diplomats and a diplomacy divorced from military considerations. When the nation was at war, suddenly diverted from its normal preoccupation with domestic concerns, military factors became dominant to the virtually total exclusion of all political policy; the only aim was a speedy military victory, to punish the aggressor who had been rash enough to attack it and disturb its enjoyment of the American way of life.

But by presenting his case in "military" terms, MacArthur was also justifying his revolt against the Administration. For just as rebels in ancient times invoked natural law to justify their revolts against constituted authority which they claimed had forfeited the right to govern by violating the traditional restraints on power, so MacArthur was placing the responsibility for his revolt upon the Administration; it was not he who was not acting in accordance with the traditional rules of warfare, but the government. It was not he who, therefore, deserved stricture — even though he was committing a democratic heresy by challenging the supremacy of civilian authority — but Washington, which by its "untraditional" and even "un-American" conduct of the war had turned him into a rebel, at least in thought and spoken word, if not in action. Only the professional experience of many years and keen awareness of the strategic factors involved led him to adopt his new cause.

There can be no doubt on this score; MacArthur was verbally in open revolt against his government. His failure to change Washington's policy through regular channels had led him to face the most painful question which the soldier can ever confront: how could he be true to his oath to the Constitution and serve the best interests of the United States as he understood them, and yet remain faithful to the Administration in power? To MacArthur, these two courses were mutually exclusive; he could not serve the Constitution and the government without betraying his duty to one or the other. He was intensely convinced that the United States government was pursuing a Far Eastern policy which was detrimental to American interests — even if that would become obvious only in future years — and that he understood the national interest of the United States, at least in the Pacific, better than Washington itself. Perhaps MacArthur felt like General De Gaulle in 1940 when the latter "rebelled" against his government by refusing to lay down his arms. For MacArthur and De Gaulle resembled one another closely: both identified themselves with their country's national destiny, both possessed a strong sense of personal mission and an immense superiority complex, and both believed in strong executive leadership and aloofness. "The man of character," De Gaulle has written in a passage which might well have been written by MacArthur, "is distant because authority does not go without prestige, and prestige does not go without distances being kept. In relation to his superiors, he finds himself in a difficult position. Sure of his own judgment and conscious of his strength, he makes no concessions to the desire to please. He . . . is not capable of passive obedience . . . More than that: those who do great things must often ignore the conventions of a false discipline. Thus in 1914 Lyautey kept Morocco despite orders from above; and after the battle of Jutland, Lord Fisher bitterly commented on Jellicoe's dispatches: 'He has all Nelson's qualities, except one: he has not learned to disobey.' " [29] (It is interesting to note in this connection that De Gaulle was just about the only European leader who openly condemned French and European leaders who attacked MacArthur — "a foreign military leader whose daring was feared by those who profited by it." Europe's statesmen should rather "pay deserved tribute to the legendary service of a great soldier.") [30]

In any case, whether MacArthur was inspired by sentiments akin to those of De Gaulle or not, MacArthur drew a sharp distinction between his loyalty to the state and those who temporarily held its power:

> I find in existence a new and heretofore unknown and dangerous concept that the members of our armed forces owe primary allegiance or loyalty to those who temporarily exercise the authority of the Executive Branch of the Government rather than to the country and its Constitution which they are sworn to defend. No proposition could be more dangerous.[31]

While this statement is meant to represent MacArthur's justification for his course, it still fails to answer why, unable to "rectify" Washington's policy through the legally established channels, he did not resign his command,[32] return to the United States, and then arouse public opinion during the inevitable tour of leading cities which would undoubtedly wish to honor him. That he was not incapable of such a task was shown after his dismissal. One possible answer to this question might be that MacArthur felt that his appeals over the head of the Administration to the American public, and particularly to Congress, could be more effectively directed if he remained in Tokyo. Certainly, as a private citizen roaming the width and breadth of the United States, he would be unable to exert the same degree of political leverage on Washington than as Commander in Chief, Far East — if only because in the former capacity he would then have deprived Mr. Truman of the most difficult political decision and act of his whole career, namely, dismissing him. While he remained in office, he left the Administration with two alternatives: one, to fire him, which was politically almost impossible, and two, to be caught between himself, and possibly the Joint Chiefs, on one side, and strong congressional opposition and public criticism on the other. Neither alternative was an attractive one, since both courses might in the end force the Administration to adopt, reluctantly to be sure, the policy of its critics. MacArthur might well have believed that since the first was unlikely, the second would effect the desirable changes he had long advocated. After all, the General was never less than self-confident; unfortunately for him, he, like so many others in their time, underestimated the President's courage.

MacArthur's case was persuasively argued and well presented. Nevertheless, it suffers from three weaknesses and inconsistencies. These were inherent in his argument, since as a theater commander he was challenging what Secretary Acheson called the bedrock of American foreign policy. First, the General declined to accept Washington's estimate of Soviet intentions, or what elsewhere he referred to as Washington's "political intelligence." Yet, previously he had absolved himself from any blame for his forecast that Communist China would not intervene in the Korean struggle, since Peking's decision to fight was a political decision beyond the confines of a military estimate in Korea. The "intelligence that a nation is going to launch a war," MacArthur said, "is not an intelligence that is available to a commander, limited to a small area of combat. That intelligence should have been given to me. The agencies that the controlling powers had, which received reports from all over the world . . . gave a much wider and a much broader basis upon which to make those concepts." Washington should have given him this information! [33]

MacArthur was now, however, arguing that the "Soviet will not necessarily mesh its actions with our moves. Like a cobra, any new enemy will more likely strike whenever it feels that the relativity in military or other potential is in its favor on a world-wide basis." [34] Does this mean that all of a sudden, when it suited MacArthur's convenience, it was possible for the theater commander to predict the political course of another nation? If so, he was, by his own admission, in no position to make this type of judgment. Only Washington was; only Washington had available to it the "political intelligence" which could forecast the future course of another nation. The government's failure to predict Communist China's course does not resolve the self-contradiction of MacArthur's argument.

Second, the General at no time abandoned his pose as a theater commander, and he never accepted the global consequences of his recommendations:

Senator McMahon. General, as I take it, you have no opinion to give us to when we will be best prepared for a war that would include the Soviet Union, if one had to come?

General MacArthur. Such studies, as that, Senator, are made [by] higher authority than my own . . .

Senator McMahon. And, as former Chief of Staff of the Army, you realize that those higher in authority have to take into account many factors which a theater commander cannot take into account?

General MacArthur. Unquestionably . . . It is inherent in their command position.

Senator McMahon. If they show up here and say that they have weighed all those factors, and they believe that the policy which we are pursuing in the east is the correct one, I assume that you would agree with them inasmuch as you have not studied those factors which will influence the opinion of these competent men?

General MacArthur. Any decision they'd make, Senator, are like all other human decisions. They have to pass before the high court of public opinion.

No decisions, ended MacArthur, are infallible. They are not correct simply because they have been decided by a group in authority.[35]

This explanation, however, begs the real question: the issue involved is not whether the Joint Chiefs of Staff are fallible or not, but whether the Joint Chiefs on the basis of the global intelligence available to them are in a better position to determine the course of policy than the theater commander. MacArthur said they were, but at the same time implied that he also, despite his more limited responsibilities, could predict the Soviet Union's intentions and American capabilities. If the Joint Chiefs disagreed with him, it was they who were in the wrong, not he.

MacArthur, of course, never admitted that such differences of opinion had existed between himself and his military superiors. Instead, he argued — although all the evidence belies it — that he and the Joint Chiefs had been in "full agreement" on the recommendations of January 12, 1951. These had not been implemented because they had apparently been vetoed by the politicians.[36]

MacArthur's third inconsistency lay in the suggestion that since he and his military superiors were in agreement on the means of defeating the Chinese Communists in Korea, the President and his political appointees ought to stop "interfering" with the professionals' conduct of the war. Here MacArthur was caught on the fork of his own philosophy — "Surprised and amazed how wise I was," the General had to listen to Senator McMahon reading a statement which he, MacArthur, had once delivered as Army Chief of Staff. "The national strategy of any war," he had then declared, involves "decisions that must be made by the head of the state, acting in conformity with the expressed will of the Government. No single departmental head, no matter what his particular function or title, could or should be responsible for the formulation of such decisions." Should the President delegate this right to "any subordinate authority," this attempt "would not constitute delegation but rather abdication." [37] In short, MacArthur agreed with Clemenceau — and Truman — that wars were too serious a matter to be left in the hands of generals alone.

XIII

THE ADMINISTRATION'S DEFENSE: THE MEEK SHALL INHERIT

MacArthur had condemned the Administration's Korean and Chinese policy in forthright and unequivocal terms. "I was operating in what I call a vacuum. I could hardly have been said to be in opposition to policies which I was not aware of even. I don't know what the policy is now." No doubt MacArthur overstated his case somewhat for dramatic effect, but his words illustrate the intensity of his frustration after Communist China's intervention. Washington was fighting an accordion war — up and down — at a "staggering" cost. "It isn't just dust that is settling in Korea . . . it is American blood." [1] His own plan, he maintained, would be decisive, and it would quickly achieve the desired results — victory in the field, a united Korea, and an end to hostilities. His only requirement was that the restrictions imposed upon him by the politicians in Washington should be lifted. It is to these two themes — the Administration's indetermination and his own resolution — to which MacArthur constantly returned. His course was positive; Truman's negative. He stood for victory; the President for stalemate. The choice was clear, the alternatives simple.

The Truman Administration, not unnaturally, saw MacArthur's strategy in a different light. It would, as Secretary of State Acheson emphasized, accept the "large risk of war with China, risk of war with the Soviet Union, and a demonstrable weakening of our collective-security system — all this in return for what? In return for measures whose effectiveness in bringing the conflict to an early conclusion are judged doubtful by our responsible military authorities." [2] The United States could not, therefore, allow its field commander's desire to achieve military victory in a local area to govern its entire global foreign policy, particularly since his strategic recommendations were militarily unfeasible and politically undesirable.

To clarify these points, to emphasize them, and then once more to re-emphasize them, the Administration brought an impressive array of witnesses before the committee; Secretary of Defense Marshall, the Joint Chiefs of Staff, the Secretary of State, and ex-Secretary of Defense Louis Johnson. Altogether, they testified for almost a month, from May 7 to June 7. MacArthur had testified for three days.

During his days on the witness stand, MacArthur had argued that his military program to defeat Communist China had received the endorsement of the Joint Chiefs of Staff, and that the limitations imposed upon him were political. The Joint Chiefs quickly denied both of these notions. They made it quite clear that they had opposed an extension of the war on strictly military grounds; in other words, their professional opinion was that MacArthur's program was militarily impracticable. Perhaps the most important military testimony in this respect came from the Air Force Chief of Staff. His testimony has suffered from gross neglect, partly no doubt, because it came near the end of the hearings when public interest was rapidly waning. Nevertheless, what General Hoyt Vandenberg had to say remains significant because he dismissed once and for all the notion that the Joint Chiefs had allowed their views to be colored by considerations not strictly professional.

In declaring his opposition to the bombing of Manchuria, General Vandenberg prefaced his remarks with the comment that the role of air power was not well understood in the United States. Strategic air power, he said, should be employed only for the destruction of the enemy's industrial centers. He did not doubt that the air force could lay waste the cities of Communist China and Manchuria, but the result might not be conclusive. In war, there could first of all be no guarantee, no certainty. More important, Communist China's arsenals lay in the Soviet Union; despite large-scale bombing of Manchuria and continental China, therefore, the Russians would still be in a position to supply the weapons of war from across the Manchurian border.[3]

Destruction of Red Chinese and Manchurian cities would, in addition, require "full" application of the Strategic Air Command's power. Anything less would be unable to achieve the task, since the rate of attrition would be too high. The air force would lose planes and crews more quickly than they could be replaced. The resulting loss would deprive the air arm of its capacity for "massive retaliation" against the Soviet Union. ". . . The United States Air Force, if used as a whole, can lay waste Manchuria and [the] principal cities of China, but . . . the attrition that would inevitably be brought about upon us would leave us, in my opinion, as a Nation, naked for several years to come . . ." The bombing of Manchuria would require twice the number of bombers then available to the Strategic Air Command. Under present circumstances, therefore, the air force could not afford to "peck at the periphery." SAC must be kept ready for its principal role — to deter the Soviet Union from attack and to preserve the global balance of power; or, if it did not succeed in this task, to destroy the heart of international Communism's power, the Soviet Union's industrial complex. "While we can lay the industrial potential of Russia today [to] waste, in my opinion, or we can lay the Manchurian countryside [to] waste, as well as the principal cities of China, we cannot do both, again because we have a shoestring Air Force [87 wings]. We are trying to operate a $20 million business with about $20,000." [4]

It was, therefore, better to concentrate on the 200 miles of supply line in North Korea — "we can exercise very concentrated attacks on that supply line. If you extend the length another hundred miles back into Manchuria, you can get certain other bases, but with the same air power you would thin out your present attacks against the 200 miles of supply line that is Korea." [5]

Not only could the country not afford to attack Manchuria because the rate of attrition which the air force would suffer would undermine its deterrent capacity, but "going it alone" would seriously effect its over-all strength in another way. If we "went it alone" in Asia, we probably would have to "go it alone" in Europe. This would deprive the United States of its bases in both Europe and North Africa. The advantages of keeping these bases were obvious: bombers stationed near to the Soviet Union would have to load less gasoline and would be able to carry more bombs than planes flying in from farther away. Bombers striking from the continental United States would have to be refueled two or three times per mission. At that rate, a plane could render only two to three missions per month; from Europe and North Africa, the same plane could carry out fifteen to twenty missions every thirty days. Vandenberg estimated that minus its overseas bases, the United States would require an air force five to six times the size it at present possessed. European bases, while not therefore "absolutely essential," were "highly desirable." [6]

An economic blockade too would be limited in its effectiveness in bringing enough pressure to bear upon Communist China to quickly end the war. The limitation was, according to Admiral Sherman, dictated by two factors. The first consideration was the nature and stage of Communist China's economic development. This was still sufficiently lacking in industrialization and specialization that a blockade would not have the same immediate impact as it would on a more highly industrialized country. A blockade could only be an effective long-run weapon, since the urban and military segments of the Chinese economy were dependent on imports and exports. Cutting off such items as rubber, petroleum, petroleum products, industrial chemicals, pharmaceuticals, machine tools, machinery, industrial and automotive spare parts, metals, electrical and electronic equipment would create unemployment and unrest, hinder industrial production, and cause serious financial difficulties. This in turn would gravely hamper China's ability to continue the war, particularly since the Communist regime was almost entirely dependent upon imports for its heavy military equipment, transportation equipment, automotive spare parts, all manufactured material for replacing or augmenting her heavy industry, and many of her medical supplies. Halting of the vast drug shipments, for instance, would be a particularly effective measure, since it would make it difficult for the Chinese Communists to cope with contagious diseases; the result would be to curtail the mobility of their armies.[7]

The second consideration limiting the effectiveness of a blockade of Communist China was the thoroughness with which China could be cut off from the essential supplies she had to import. The long Sino-Russian border would make any blockade incomplete. Admiral Sherman stressed that the loss of imports enforced by a naval blockade would force Communist China to rely more upon the Soviet Union, and thereby place an increasing drain on both the Soviet economy and the Trans-Siberian railroad. This long railway, which was subject to easy disruption by bombing, sabotage, or naval raiding parties, was already overtaxed and could not therefore adequately replace the supplies stopped on the sea; moreover, it could attempt to do so only at the expense of supplying the Soviet Union's own forces in the Far East.[8] The other members of the Joint Chiefs were less optimistic than Admiral Sherman. General Bradley, the chairman of the Joint Chiefs, qualified Sherman's analysis: the Trans-Siberian railroad could handle

17,000 tons a day in addition to its own tonnage-maintenance requirements. Russia had also built up supply depots and certain war industries to relieve the railway of some of its load during wartime. The implication was clear: Russian forces in the Far East had a "considerable military capacity": they could for a time get along with fewer supplies. This available tonnage could be switched to supply Communist China.

A blockade by itself could not, therefore, speedily terminate hostilities. A blockade could necessarily yield only slow results since it relied for effects principally on starvation and attrition. Only if combined with other military measures, such as air bombardment, could a naval blockade yield immediate results; short of such supplementary means, a blockade could not seriously hamper China's capacity to continue its conduct of the war. The Admiral also emphasized that the key to an effective United Nations naval blockade would be the wholehearted cooperation of our allies. Any effective blockade must include Port Arthur and Dairen, over which the Soviet Union exercised certain military rights and privileges under the Sino-Soviet treaty. The Russians would "very probably" demand unimpeded access to both ports; stopping her ships might provoke her entry into the war.[9] "If the United Nations should declare a naval blockade, the Russians would probably respect it, as they did the United Nations blockade of Korea. If the United States should declare a blockade unilaterally, the Russians might not respect it, and it is conceivable that they might oppose it by force."[10]

The implication of Admiral Sherman's words is clear: a unilateral blockade by the United States would signify the isolation of this country from its allies. Since this would for all practical purposes neutralize the United States Air Force, Moscow might be tempted to break the blockade of Dairen and Port Arthur. With NATO's massive retaliation nonexistent, the Strategic Air Command could, in the event of war, operate at only 15 to 20 per cent of its effectiveness. If, on the other hand, the United States imposed the blockade in cooperation with its Atlantic allies, any Soviet counteraction would risk the possibility of an immediate reaction by NATO, or more specifically, American strategic air power based on Western European and North African soil. "The fact is that our allies have been unwilling to join in a naval blockade of China, and have been slow to establish a tight economic blockade."[11]

Another reason for the need of a United Nations blockade was equally obvious; most of the strategic imports and ships carrying goods to Communist China bore the flags of non-Communist United Nations members. Sherman recommended that greater effort be concentrated on increasing the effectiveness of the economic blockade. In recent weeks, he said, United States efforts along these lines had been successful. The British government had prohibited any further sales of rubber for the rest of the year,[12] and the General Assembly had on May 18 by a vote of forty-five to four approved a resolution calling for an embargo on arms, ammunition, petroleum, and other materials of war, although as Secretary Acheson stressed, "Many countries were already doing this . . . ; others were not."

In expanding this point, Acheson emphasized that as early as 1948 the United States had agreed with its allies to draw up a number of lists of such items as arms, ammunition, implements of war and atomic energy whose export to the Soviet bloc would be restricted. These lists were expanded in 1949, so that by the end of that year the participating European nations had embargoed shipments to the Soviet bloc of about two-thirds of the industrial items which American experts then regarded as being of primary strategic significance. In both of the following years, the number of categories of goods not to be exported to the Communist sphere was augmented by approximately 50 per cent and the total number of items restricted, or closely supervised to prevent excessive shipment, was increased threefold. The result was that by early 1951 about 90 per cent of the items the United States considered to be of strategic importance were already on the embargo lists. Since late 1949, moreover, certain specialized petroleum products, such as aviation gasoline and special lubricants, had also been embargoed to the Sino-Soviet bloc by the United States, England, and other governments. Acheson stressed that ever since the Chinese Communists consolidated their grip on the Chinese mainland, for many months before the outbreak of the Korean War, the British government had cooperated with the United States and the principal American and British oil companies in restricting shipment of petroleum products to those types and quantities clearly intended for civilian use. Immediately after the Communist attack in Korea, the British Admiralty had taken over all British oil stocks in the Far East and secured agreements by British companies to follow a sales policy parallel to that of American companies. The Hong Kong government had reinforced this policy by closely supervising the bunkering of vessels in Hong Kong and rationing shipments to Macao to prevent leakage to Communist China, by numerous seizures of illicit cargoes, confiscation of the ships involved, and the levying of severe fines on smugglers. It was possible that despite these measures small amounts of petroleum products may have been smuggled into the mainland, but, Acheson said, it "can̄ be stated flatly, however, that . . . no significant shipments of petroleum products of military usefulness have been exported to Communist China from or through any place in the free world." Thus the "facts show there already exists on the part of the major industrial countries of the free world an economic embargo with respect to materials of primary strategic significance." The economic blockade made the naval blockade much less important. "I think it is clear that we cannot get nations to go further in regard to a naval blockade than they are willing to go on an economic blockade, since it is a more drastic sanction." [13]

Thus the Administration, particularly its military advisers, doubted the efficacy of winning the Korean War through the application of air power and the imposition of a naval blockade. MacArthur had always denied that his prescription would need few extra ground troops. General Collins, Army Chief of Staff, did not agree. The successful implementation of MacArthur's strategy would require the United States to send "considerably" more troops to Korea.[14] General Bradley, indeed, thought that a decision could be effected only if American troops were actually sent into China proper.

Chairman Connally . . . if we have an all-out war, and the war should expand to include China, would it not almost inevitably follow that at some time in the future development of that, we would have to put ground troops on Chinese soil?

General Bradley. To get decisive results, in my opinion you would . . . if you go to an all-out war with China, I think you would have to do something like the Japanese did. Go in and try to get a decision. I do not believe you could get any decision by naval and air action alone.

Chairman Connally. Well, naval and air action as against China without ground troops would mean just sort of a holding proposition, would it not?

General Bradley. Well, I think it would be a rather long-drawn-out affair in which you would try to knock out their centers of communication and knock out as much of their industry as possible, possibly try to limit on supplies and food without taking any positive action inside China itself.[15]

The Communist army in Korea could be decimated; but it could not be defeated without hitting its center of power. The air force and navy could hamper China's capacity to fight; but they could not destroy it. If there were no alternative to military victory, there could also be no substitute to military invasion and occupation. MacArthur had himself recognized at the time of the North Korean aggression that air and naval forces alone would not suffice to halt the Communist attack; ground troops would be needed. If this was true for a Soviet satellite, it was certainly true for Communist China.

In any case, even if it were not necessary to employ American troops inside continental China, large reinforcements would be needed. An all-out war with Communist China would require "substantially" more naval, air, and ground power, as well as an increase in supply and service troops to support the forces at the front. These could not, however, be furnished without a more intensive program of mobilization and greater effort to produce the ammunition and other implements of war.[16]

Could these troops not be supplied by Nationalist China? The Joint Chiefs thought not. Chiang would need his troops to safeguard Formosa; and his soldiers were anything but first-class. General MacArthur's mission to Formosa had "indicated a state of readiness which didn't seem to be conducive of successful action by those troops . . ." The Nationalist troops "had very limited capabilities, particularly for offensive action. As General MacArthur himself had pointed out, they would have to have almost complete logistical support from ourselves, transportation furnished . . . their leadership, equipment, and training were all of such a state that they would be of limited use in offensive operations." [17] Any diversionary action against continental China would, in addition, require excessive United States naval and air support — excessive, that is, to the returns that could be expected from such an investment.[18] Nor was the reason purely the military's unfavorable estimate of Chiang's troops. Of greater importance, although not explicitly stated during the hearings, was the Administration's evaluation of Chiang Kai-shek's political prospects on the continent. The only circumstances under which Nationalist troops might reconquer vast portions of China, if not the whole mainland, would be if upon their landing, the Chinese Communist army rallied to Chiang Kai-shek as the French people and the Bourbon army had rallied to Napoleon upon his return to French soil from Corsica. In the Administration's opinion, it was precisely this confidence of the masses which Chiang lacked; its loss had accounted for his defeat in the first place, for his fall in four short years from "the undisputed leader" of the Chinese people to a "refugee" on a small island off the coast of China. It was extremely doubtful that a year's absence had restored the Chinese people's affection for their old leader.

There was, in short, no substitute for American troops. But concentrating American armed power in Korea meant stripping other areas of their forces, lowering the deterrent to Soviet intervention in these parts of the world and increasing their vulnerability to attack. In fact, the attrition of American military strength, particularly air and ground strength, might well deprive the United States of its ability to counter emergencies elsewhere, and perhaps even weaken the United States sufficiently to attract a Soviet attack. This country could not therefore afford to engage "too much of our power in an area that is not the critical strategic prize." Yet, this is precisely what MacArthur's strategy would entail; nothing would probably delight the Kremlin more. It would, in General Bradley's famous phrase, "involve us in the wrong war, at the wrong place, at the wrong time, and with the wrong enemy." [19]

Indeed, it might also involve us with the right enemy, since bombing Communist China and inflicting a severe defeat upon the Soviet Union's closest and strongest ally would probably leave the Kremlin no alternative but to intervene. As Secretary Acheson said:

> We know of Soviet influence in North Korea, of Soviet assistance to the North Koreans and to Communist China, and we know that understandings must have accompanied this assistance. We also know that there is a treaty between the Soviets and the Chinese Communists. But even if this treaty did not exist, China is the Soviet Union's largest and most important satellite. Russian self-interest in the Far East and the necessity of maintaining prestige in the Communist sphere make it difficult to see how the Soviet Union could ignore a direct attack upon the Chinese mainland.

To be sure, General MacArthur had argued that the Soviet Union would not intervene if the United States and its allies acted with determination and without hesitation; the Administration, however, remembered that he had said the same thing just before Communist China had entered the battle. (It might have added that MacArthur's foresight had proven itself equally fallible on other occasions. In 1939, he had declared Japan would not attack the Philippines; proponents of such a view, he had said, failed to understand "the logic of the Japanese mind." If Japan did covet the islands, however, his Filipino forces would prove themselves more than a match for the invading army. In early 1941, he had doubted that the Japanese would commit suicide by attacking as mighty a naval power as the United States, but if Japan should launch such an attack, American, British, and Dutch forces could handle her with half the forces they then had in the Far East!) Admittedly, the Administration had shared MacArthur's mistaken estimate of Peking's intentions before November 24; but it was unwilling to take a second chance. "I cannot accept the assumption," said Secretary Acheson, "that the Soviet Union will go its way regardless of what we do. I do not think that Russian policy is formed that way any more than our own policy is formed that way. This view is certainly not well enough grounded to justify a gamble with the essential security of our Nation."

There were a number of courses the Russians could follow. Acheson believed that "They could turn over to the Chinese large numbers of planes with 'volunteer' crews for retaliatory action in Korea and outside. They might participate with the Soviet Air Force and the submarine fleet." Or, the "Kremlin could elect to parallel the action, taken by Peiping and intervene with a half million or more ground-force 'volunteers'; or it could go the whole way and launch an all-out war. Singly, or in combination, these reactions contain explosive possibilities, not only for the Far East, but for the rest of the world as well." [20]

Hostilities with the Soviet Union at the present time had, however, to be avoided. Not only was a war unnecessary because Soviet imperialism had been contained and denied the fruits of its aggression; it was also undesirable because the United States might have to fight such a war alone. Our allies, as Secretary Acheson said,

are understandably reluctant to be drawn into a general war in the Far East — one which holds the possibilities of becoming a world war — particularly if it developed out of an American impatience with the progress of the effort to repel aggression, an effort which in their belief offers an honorable and far less catastrophic solution.

If we followed the course proposed, we would be increasing our risks and commitments at the same time that we diminished our strength by reducing the strength and determination of our coalition.

We cannot expect that our collective-security system will long survive if we take steps which unnecessarily and dangerously expose the people who are in the system with us. They would understandably hesitate to be tied to a partner who leads them to a highly dangerous short cut across a difficult crevasse.

In relation to the total world threat, our safety requires that we strengthen, not weaken, the bonds of our collective-security system.

The power of our coalition to deter an attack depends in part upon the will and the mutual confidence of our partners. If we, by the measures proposed, were to weaken that effort, particularly in the North Atlantic area, we would be jeopardizing the security of an area which is vital to our own national security.[21]

Allied fears of a large-scale war in the Far East and a corresponding shift of American power from Europe to the opposite side of the world — or World War III, which would probably see the Russians occupying their countries — were not the only reason for Washington's reluctance to test MacArthur's opinions about Soviet intentions. Even if the United States were willing to "go it alone" and alienate its allies, it had to resist this temptation for one simple reason — the United States was unready to fight a global war.

Senator Johnson. General, from an over-all standpoint of the disposition of our forces throughout the world, are we sufficiently strong to fight a successful holding action in the event the Soviet Union attacks at an early date?

General Collins. Not as of the moment; no, sir. That applies particularly to Europe. I think that we have sufficient forces out in the Far East to hold there. I think that we have sufficient forces in Alaska to hold there. I do not think we have sufficient forces in Europe.

General Bradley was even more emphatic: "I would not be a proponent of a policy which would ignore the military facts and rush us headlong into a show-down before we are ready." [22]

Even in Asia, the Russians possessed the capacity to intervene and put up a good fight; contrary to General MacArthur's opinion, Administration witnesses considered Soviet power in the Far East "a very serious matter." They had "many thousands of planes in the other areas of Vladivostok, Dairen–Port Arthur, in Harbin, Manchuria, and troop concentrations at Sakhalin near to Japan." The Russians had over the past few years also been building up their Far Eastern industries, and they had "undoubtedly" been accumulating sufficient supplies to sustain their divisions "for a considerable length of time." [23]

Refusal to accept MacArthur's military program did not, therefore, in the opinion of the chairman of the Joint Chiefs, constitute "appeasement."

There are those who deplore the present military situation in Korea and urge us to engage Red China in a larger war to solve this problem. Taking on Red China is not a decisive move, does not guarantee the end of the war in Korea, and may not bring China to her knees. We have only to look back to the five long years when the Japanese, one of the greatest military powers of that time, moved into China and had almost full control of a large part of China, and yet were never able to conclude that war successfully. I would say from past history one would only jump from a smaller conflict to a larger deadlock at greater expense. My own feeling is to avoid such an engagement if possible because victory in Korea would not be assured and victory over Red China would be many years away . . .

Some critics of our strategy say if we do not immediately bomb troop concentration points and airfields in Manchuria, it is "appeasement." If we do not immediately set up a blockade of Chinese ports — which to be successful would have to include British and Russian ports — it is appeasement. These same critics would say that if we do not provide the logistical support and air and naval assistance to launch Chinese Nationalist troops into China it is "appeasement."

These critics ignore the vital questions:

Will these actions, if taken, actually assure victory in Korea?

Do these actions mean prolongation of the war by bringing Russia into the fight?

Will these actions strip us of our allies in Korea and in other parts of the world?

From a military viewpoint, appeasement occurs when you give up something, which is rightfully free, to an aggressor without putting up a struggle, or making him pay a price. Forsaking Korea — withdrawing from the fight unless we are forced out — would be an appeasement to aggression. Refusing to enlarge the quarrel to the point where our global capabilities are diminished, is certainly not appeasement but is a militarily sound course of action under the present circumstances.[24]

Did the rejection of MacArthur's program mean that the Administration would continue to "go on as before"? Would it continue to sacrifice American lives, as MacArthur had charged, "without justified purpose"? The answer to the first question was "yes," to the second "no." American lives in Korea had not been sacrificed in vain.

The operation in Korea has been a success. Both the North Koreans and the Chinese Communists declared it to be their purpose to drive the United Nations forces out of Korea and impose Communist rule throughout the entire peninsula. They have been prevented from accomplishing their objective.

It has been charged that the American and allied forces in Korea are engaged in a pointless and inconclusive struggle.

Nothing could be further from the fact. They have been magnificent. Their gallant, determined, and successful fight has checked the Communist advance and turned it into a retreat. They have administered terrible defeats to the Communist forces. In so doing, they have scored a powerful victory.

Their victory has dealt Communist imperialist aims in Asia a severe setback.

The alluring prospect for the Communist conspiracy in June 1950 —

the prospect of a quick and easy success which would not only win Korea for the Kremlin but shake the free nations of Asia and paralyze the defense of Europe — all this has evaporated.

But the achievements gained by the United States and her friends were not simply negative:

> Instead of weakening the rest of the world, they have solidified it. They have given a more powerful impetus to the military preparations of this country and its associates in and out of the North Atlantic Treaty Organization.
>
> We have doubled the number of our men under arms, and the production of material has been boosted to a point where it can begin to have a profound effect on the maintenance of the peace.
>
> The idea of collective security has been put to the test, and has been sustained. The nations who believe in collective security have shown that they can stick together and fight together.
>
> New urgency has been given the negotiation of a peace with Japan, and of initial security arrangements to build strength in the Pacific area.
>
> These are some of the results of the attack on Korea, unexpected by — and I am sure most unwelcome to — the Kremlin.[25]

Korea had thus been a success. But how could fighting now be ended? Could this really be achieved without carrying the war into China as General MacArthur had recommended? Could the hostilities actually be concluded without risking the dire consequences pointed out by the government's witnesses? Their testimony seemed to suggest that the United States would continue to fight indefinitely, that is until Communist China finally tired of the war; this impression, needless to say, was not welcome to the American public, and must be attributed largely to the Administration's inability to clarify the nature of previous cold-war clashes and their relationship to the present war in Korea.

A comprehensive presentation of Administration policy would have clarified that in each of the East-West conflicts which had preceded Korea, both sides had aimed only at limited objectives and pursued these aims by limited means. The Soviet rulers had in no case aimed at a knock-out blow of the Western powers, since this purpose could have been achieved only by means of total war. Each Communist challenge had been met by the Western powers, particularly the United States, with an equally limited response; the West, too, had been reluctant to resort to global hostilities.

Each side had been unwilling to precipitate atomic warfare. The almost equal distribution of power between them and the very destructiveness of modern weapons had limited the objectives which they could safely seek. Both blocs had therefore surrendered the notion that they could impose their respective wills upon one another; neither pursued total military victory nor unconditional surrender.

The means, in short, had limited the end, and necessity had become the mother of moderation. Consequently, the Administration believed: first, that the United States must restrain its efforts to counter expansionist Soviet moves to the restoration of the *status quo;* and second, that the Soviet government acted upon the assumption that if the Western nations resisted its thrusts successfully, it was safest to break off the engagement and accept the pre-crisis situation. In this context, the American government viewed the intermittent American-Soviet trials of strength as a series of conflicts whose aim it was to determine the precise location of the boundary which divided the Communist states from the free world; American containment would allow no further Russian encroachment beyond this line, and Soviet imperialism could satisfy its ambitions only at the risk of all-out war.

Berlin was an obvious case in point. The Russians had hoped to drive the Western allies out of the former German capital, and they had expected to achieve their objective by a land blockade of the city. The Western allies had refused to be intimidated, since they could have not withstood the political and psychological consequences of Berlin's fall. At the same time, the Atlantic allies had shared the Soviet Union's reluctance to pay the price of a full-scale war for a limited aim. Consequently, they had not tried to reopen the corridor into Berlin by sending tanks and troops to challenge the Red army; instead, they had limited themselves to the air lift. The Soviets had not challenged this effort, for they had realized that to have done so would have precipitated the total war which both sides hoped to avoid. The United States and the Soviet Union had been unwilling to take a risk of this magnitude in order to achieve a decisive result in Berlin. Consequently, the issue had been settled on the basis of the *status quo.* Neither side had won a victory in the traditional sense of the word; instead, both sides had accepted the stalemate.

Nor had the blockade been settled quickly; it had taken fifteen months for the crisis to pass. Patience, firmness, and determination had been needed to execute this policy, since it had required the application of just enough pressure to achieve its objective, but not so much pressure that it would have precipitated a world war. As Secretary Marshall explained, "We have brought to bear whatever has been necessary, in money and also manpower, to curb the aggressor; and we have sought in every possible way to avoid a third World War." Berlin had been an expensive operation; nevertheless, it had been a better alternative than a total war and the vast destruction which such a holocaust would have inflicted upon all sides.[26]

Korea fell into the same category as Berlin. It was "only the latest challenge in this long, hard, continuing world wide struggle. We are applying there the same policy that has been successfully applied in the attempted aggressions that preceded it elsewhere in the world." [27] This war, too, was being fought under certain ground rules. The Chinese Communists possessed a "privileged sanctuary" in Manchuria, but the United States possessed a similar sanctuary in Japan, Okinawa, and South Korea, particularly around the main port of Pusan. "They are not bombing our ports and supply installations," said General Bradley, "and they are not bombing our troops." [28]

The objective too was limited. The purpose of the fighting was to restore the situation that had existed before the North Korean attack on June 25, 1950. When Senator Alexander Smith said that he was "a little bit confused" by the idea of "stopping where we began," Acheson replied:

Senator, if you accomplish what you started out to do, I don't think that is synonymous with saying you stopped where you began.

We started out to do two things. One is repel the armed attack and the other is to restore peace and security in the area.

Now, if we do these two things, we have done what we started out to do, and I should think that is success.

Thus, without admitting outrightly that the Administration had abandoned the goal of a militarily unified Korea, the Secretary of State informed the Communists that it was willing to call a cease-fire on the 38th Parallel. The price for a united Korea was too high; the *status quo* was therefore acceptable.[29]

To be sure, Acheson had always insisted that the United States had never harbored any other aim, but this explanation will not withstand critical examination. That the attempt to unify Korea by force had been made, but that circumstances had necessitated acceptance of the present solution, is evident from General Bradley's testimony:

General Bradley . . . as we went farther north and the United Nations again came out with a resolution to establish a unified Korea, united and free Korea; that was the mission they gave to General MacArthur in late September. [Actually the United Nations resolution was approved on October 7, though Bradley is correct when he says that the mission was originally assigned to MacArthur by Washington in late September.]

Senator Cain. And yet to carry out that mission from a military point of view or that objective from a political point of view, it will, before we are through, if we do not change that mission, be required to defeat the enemy and to repel him, not from South Korea but we must repel the enemy from Korea, or otherwise, sir, how can we make Korea a free, independent, and democratic nation?

General Bradley. Well, I think we could have an intermediate military objective . . .[30]

In late September and early October, the Administration had argued that the parallel had to be crossed to safeguard South Korea's security; for if North Korea were not defeated, South Korea might be subjected to a further attack at some future date when the enemy had recovered his strength and reorganized his army. Administration witnesses did not repeat this argument after Communist China's intervention, even though the threat to South Korea's future existence remained — only, of course, on a more potent scale. This time they explained that although a cease-fire on the 38th Parallel would only reaffirm the position that had existed at the time of the initial challenge, it could be made to contain safeguards to deter another invasion. Why such an arrangement had not been considered in October of 1950 was not said; but the implication was that it had not then been a question of accepting such a cease-fire or nothing. The opportunity for a militarily united Korea had been rendered possible by the destruction of the North Korean army. Circumstances had now changed. The *status quo* had been restored at the 38th Parallel and the Administration was willing to call an end to the fighting on this line.[31]

There remained only one question: would the Chinese Communists, as the Russians before them, settle on the basis of the 38th Parallel, the line from which the North Korean advance had originally started? Secretary Acheson believed they would, although he could not predict the time when this would happen. But Berlin had taken fifteen months to settle; Greece eighteen months; Korea was then in its tenth month. Hope for an early finish of the fighting, however, was good for several reasons. First, "the offensives of the enemy have been broken and thrown back with enormous enemy casualties. These defeats . . . present grave problems for the Communist authorities in China. While the manpower resources of China are vast, its supply of trained men is limited. They cannot cover up their casualties. They cannot gloss over the draft of more and more men for military service." Second, the "Chinese Red leaders have betrayed their long-standing pledge of demobilization and the military demand for man power has, instead, been increased." And third, "Peiping has also broken its promises of social and economic improvement. In the great cities, dependent on imported materials, unemployment increases. The regime has not lightened the burdens of the people. It has made them. heavier." The dissatisfaction caused by this increasing toll of dead and injured, as well as by the broken pledges, were already "reflected in a sharp increase in repressive measures, and in propaganda to whip up the flagging zeal of their own people. In the light of all these factors," Acheson concluded, "I believe that the aggression can best be brought to an end with a minimum risk and a minimum loss, by continuing the punishing defeat of the Chinese in Korea." The infliction of heavy casualties on the Chinese army, the destruction of its morale and "trained fabric" would, in other words, bring the Chinese Communists to negotiate an end to hostilities without the risk of World War III.[32]

Shortly after Acheson made this statement, the Communists made their first move to end the war. On June 23, 1951, the Russian delegate to the United Nations, Jacob Malik, intimated that the Soviet Union was ready for a cease-fire in Korea. The Communists, therefore, having also tried unsuccessfully to conquer the entire Korean peninsula, had finally decided to incorporate the stalemate on the 38th Parallel into the almost global stalemate along the line determined in previous engagements.

The meek had inherited; they had restored the Republic of Korea to its prewar boundaries; they had managed to avoid an enlarged war and its attendant dangers in the Far East; they had preserved the unity of the Atlantic community and through the rearmament program increased their power several times; and they had husbanded their strength to balance Russian power and to create "unassailable barriers" in the path of Soviet expansion. They had refused to dissipate their military power on the periphery of the Communist empire, but had conserved it for its primary function, the continued denial of Communist ambitions and the encouragement of trends within the Soviet political and social system which would so increase its strains and stresses that they would moderate the ambitions of its leaders.

It was this article of faith upon which the Administration's case, in the final analysis, rested: Soviet imperialism could be contained without the horror of another global conflict, that the indefinite frustration of the Kremlin's appetite would cause the regime to become more accommodating and negotiate outstanding issues, and to accept a live-and-let-live attitude based upon the realities of military strength and the necessity of compromising with power. "For no mystical, Messianic movement — and particularly not that of the Kremlin," George Kennan had predicted, "can face frustration indefinitely without eventually adjusting itself in one way or another to the logic of that state of affairs." United States containment policy, therefore, "has it in its power to increase enormously the strains under which Soviet policy must operate, to force upon the Kremlin a far greater degree of circumspection than it has had to observe in recent years, and in this way to promote tendencies which must eventually find their outlet in either the break-up or the gradual mellowing of Soviet power." [33] Or, as Secretary Acheson expressed it during the hearings: ". . . what we must do is to create situations of strength, then I think that the whole situation in the world begins to change so far as the potentialities of the Soviet Union being able to achieve its present purposes is concerned; and with that change there comes a difference in the negotiating positions of the various parties, and out of that I should hope that there would be a willingness on the side of the Kremlin to recognize the facts which have been created by this effort of ours and to begin to solve at least some of the difficulties between east and west." [34] Time, in short, *was* on the side of the United States and her allies — if the Western powers could remain united, contain further Communist expansion, and preserve the balance of power on the basis of the *status quo.*

XIV

TRUMAN VERSUS MacARTHUR:
ACHILLES REBOUND

Prior to the North Korean attack in June 1950, the Administration's foreign policy was based upon the fundamental assumption that the Soviet Union presented the chief threat to American security; Moscow's leaders were committed to the elimination of all non-Communist nations. George Kennan compared Soviet expansion to

> a fluid stream which moves constantly, wherever it is permitted to move, toward a given goal. Its main concern is to make sure that it has filled every nook and cranny available to it in the basin of world power. But if it finds unassailable barriers in its path, it accepts these philosophically and accommodates itself to them. The main thing is that there should always be pressure, unceasing constant pressure, toward the desired goal. There is no trace of any feeling in Soviet psychology that the goal must be reached at any given time.[1]

The American task was, therefore, to erect "unassailable barriers" in the path of Soviet power to contain its further spread. The Truman Doctrine, the Marshall Plan, the Berlin Airlift, NATO, were all part of this policy.

The principal aim of this "long-term, patient but firm and vigilant containment of Russia's expansive tendencies" was not the destruction of the Soviet Union and its satellites, but the creation of a balance of power to effect this "containment." The objective of this policy was to deter the Kremlin from attempting to achieve world domination by resort to total war, lead it instead to the negotiating table, and to settle the principal cold war issues. A second characteristic of containment was its assumption that such a "situation of strength" could be attained by the United States only in association with its principal NATO allies. American independence and security had traditionally required a balance of power in the interior of Europe to check any nation which possessed ambitions to conquer the sea-bordering states as a prereq-

uisite to first eliminating England and then proceeding to world conquest. Consequently, the collapse of NATO could not be tolerated.

The military heart of this containment policy was the almost complete reliance upon strategic air power to deter or win World War III.
The Western armies stationed in Europe were not sufficiently large
to prevent the Russian army from reaching the English Channel. The
NATO army was primarily a "plate-glass" which would set off the
burglar alarm and send the United States Strategic Air Command flying toward its Soviet targets. The assumption was that the only kind
of war possible was a total war which would begin the moment the
Soviet Union struck a surprise blow at either the United States or
America's "first line of defense" in Western Europe.

It was this reliance upon a strategy of total war which had been
responsible for the Joint Chiefs' recommendation to withdraw American troops from South Korea and for Secretary Acheson's and General
MacArthur's exclusion of the Republic from the Pacific defense perimeter. For in an all-out war South Korea would indeed be neither
strategically vital to the United States nor defensible; its fate would
be determined by the results of the conflict fought in other theaters.
The limited war with which the North Koreans faced the President
and his advisers on June 25, 1950, therefore presented the Administration with an agonizing dilemma.

On the one hand, the Communist invasion of South Korea struck
at the basic presuppositions of American policy. If the primary purpose of containment was to prevent further Soviet expansion, American inaction in the face of Soviet aggression could only encourage
further such acts in the future. The appetites of dictators were in-
satiable; one meal only whetted their palates and increased their
hunger. If the aim of containment was also to hold together the
Western powers, American refusal to rescue a friend in distress would
disintegrate NATO. Our European allies would have believed that
in a similar crisis they would be abandoned in a similar manner;
consequently, they would have dismissed American treaty pledges as
valueless, turned to neutralism for safety, isolated the United States,
and deprive the Strategic Air Command of a large measure of its
deterrent power.

On the other hand, the limited Soviet challenge in Korea did not
fit our strategic doctrine. South Korea was certainly not "worth" the
price of total war; massive retaliation upon Moscow was not the answer

to the shrewd Russian exploitation of the government's one-sided concentration upon air-atomic striking power. A more limited response was needed. Fortunately, the United States had several undermanned and "undertrained" divisions in near-by Japan. Ironically, therefore, the Administration was compelled to fight a limited war to preserve its total-war policy; it was forced to respond by less than total means to a Soviet satellite in order to prevent the disintegration of a policy predicated upon massive retaliation as the principal means of deterring or winning a total war with the Soviet Union.

The price for American unpreparedness to fight a less than total war was strategic improvisation. Administration officials, still deeply imbued with the belief that the main contest would be with the Soviet Union and fought over the possession of Western Europe, thought of the Korean War only as a strategic diversion cleverly planned by the Kremlin as a means to weaken American power and divert it from Europe. Thus, while the government's political and military leaders knew that the limited Soviet attack in Korea left the United States with no alternative but to respond to it, they were determined that the fighting in the "far-off" Asian peninsula be kept as limited as possible. The Korean War was a necessary war: to teach the Soviet leaders that aggression would not pay; to hold together the Western alliance; and to preserve the military basis of containment. Nevertheless, it remained a "peripheral" war.

During the first stage of the conflict the objective was the restoration of the Republic of Korea to its prewar status. General MacArthur's magnificent amphibious operation at Inchon transformed the character of the war; his military victory changed it from a defensive war seeking only to re-establish the *status quo* to an offensive war attempting to affect a permanent change in the *status quo.* The North Koreans had been defeated; the military situation favored the fulfillment of an American goal of several years' standing: the unification of the whole of Korea. The Administration thereupon shifted its emphasis from containing the expansion of Soviet power to the forceful liberation of a Soviet satellite.

At the same time, the Administration abandoned the two assumptions upon which it had based its strategy in previous clashes with the Soviet Union: first, that the United States had to limit its efforts to contain Soviet expansionist moves to the restoration of the *status quo;* and second, that if the United States managed to re-establish the old equilibrium, the Russian leaders broke off the engagement and accepted the pre-crisis situation. After Inchon, however, the United States government made no attempt, as it had, for instance, after its successful resistance in Berlin, to negotiate an end to the hostilities through diplomatic channels. The Administration offered the Soviets only the total elimination of their satellite; in accordance with its own conclusion that it was dangerous to extend its reaction to Russian moves beyond the re-establishment of the *status quo,* the government must have expected the rejection of its demand for North Korea's unconditional surrender. Secretary Acheson had himself stated that governments do not negotiate their own survival. American insistence upon the military unification of Korea thus assured the continuation of hostilities.

This objective was officially proclaimed on October 7, 1950. Prior to that day the aim of the campaign had been only the restoration of the *status quo:* since a non-Communist South Korea had existed before the outbreak of the Korean War, the threat to Communist China of a liberated Republic of Korea was no greater than that before June 25, 1950. But on October 7, as American-led forces surged northwards toward the Manchurian border, the threat to Communist China's industrial center became one of far greater magnitude. But the Administration believed that it was politically safe to drive into North Korea and free the Soviet satellite from Communist domination. The Chinese Communists were believed to be Chinese first and Communist second; moreover, they were allegedly already involved in such an intense struggle with the Soviet Union to prevent the latter from detaching Northern China, Manchuria, and Sinkiang, that Peking's anxious eyes were turned to the Northern provinces, not to Korea; China's traditional enemy was Russia, not the United States.

The resulting attempt of the Democrats to practice in October and November 1950 what the Republicans were only to preach two years later, led Communist China to intervene in order to redress the balance. The rapid change in the resulting military situation quickly led the Administration to deny its revisionist objective and revert once more to its *status quo* guise. The continued division of Korea was inherent in the Administration's rejection of MacArthur's military proposals to counter China's intervention.

One of the reasons for this rejection was the Administration's concern lest the Soviet Union might precipitate World War III. The government insisted that the United States must not offer the Russians any pretext for intervention. "Every decision I made in connection with the Korean conflict," the President wrote later, "had this one aim in mind: to prevent a third world war and the terrible destruction it would bring to the civilized world. This means that we should not do anything that would provide the excuse to the Soviets and plunge the free nations into full-scale all-out war . . . The points that appeared most critical [in the middle of December 1950] were Berlin, Western Germany, Indo-China, Yugoslavia, and Iran. In each of these areas a minor incident could easily be created which would give the Russians an excuse for open intervention . . . and the Kremlin might not be bluffing and might have decided that the time was in fact ripe for a general war with the United States." [2] In the Administration's opinion, MacArthur's strategy to bomb Communist China, blockade her ports, and sanction Chinese Nationalist attacks upon the mainland would provide the Kremlin with just such an excuse.

But even if the Soviet Union should remain a spectator, the United States could not extend the war; it had to avoid becoming engaged in a "war of attrition" with Chinese manpower. Korea would "bleed us dry" and make it impossible to build a strong military defense in Europe. A large-scale commitment of American power in Asia would not only expose Europe to Soviet armies; it might incite such an attack at a moment of maximum American weakness on the continent. Nothing, General Bradley asserted, would delight the Kremlin more than the "enlargement of the war in Korea to include Red China . . . It would necessarily tie down additional forces, especially our sea power and air power, while the Soviet Union would not be obliged to put a single man into the conflict . . . A 'limited war' with Red China would increase the risk we are taking by engaging too much of our power in an area that is not the critical strategic prize. Red China is not the powerful nation seeking to dominate the world . . ." It was for this reason that MacArthur's strategy would involve us in the wrong war, at the wrong place, at the wrong time, and with the wrong enemy. The President stressed the same point: ". . . I never allowed myself to forget that America's principal enemies were sitting in the Kremlin, or that we could not afford to squander our reawakening strength as long as that [of] the enemy was not committed in the field but only pulling the strings behind the scenes." [3] The United States had, therefore, to conserve its strength to check the main danger — Soviet Russia which *was* "the powerful nation seeking to dominate the world" — and not waste its power in a peripheral area.

This view was shared by Britain and France. America's chief allies were reluctant to see American power directed to the Far East before Europe was secure against Russian assault; they had no desire to risk the outbreak of World War III so soon after the second had ended for an area that was to them of minor strategic significance; and they hoped that their friendly attitude would hasten the split between the Chinese Communists and the Kremlin, as well as identify at least Britain and France with the new trends in Asia, social progress and national independence. Thus, if the United States decided to carry the war to Communist China, it would have to "go it alone." But the premise of creating "situations of strengths" and balancing Soviet might or winning a total war was NATO's unity and combined strength. It "is of transcendent importance," Secretary Acheson stressed, "that in our policies in all parts of the world, where danger may be created, we work absolutely in hand with our allies." [4]

For these reasons, American policy-makers were willing to settle the war on the 38th Parallel. The Communists had attempted to erase the parallel and expand their power by incorporating South Korea into the Communist bloc; neither the North Koreans nor the Chinese Communists had achieved this objective. The Communists had also hoped to destroy the Western alliance and isolate the United States; in this too they had failed. NATO had been preserved and greatly strengthened by the new rearmament program and the addition of four American divisions. And Korea's primary purpose, to put the Communists on notice that the Western powers would not tolerate Communist expansion by military force, had been achieved. The wisest course was thus to end this strategic diversion, to conclude this peripheral war, and once again concentrate on the main task: the strengthening of air-atomic striking power to deter the Soviet Union from precipitating total war and the building of a "situation of strength" in Western Europe.

MacArthur's fundamental charge against the Administration was that its restrictions kept him from achieving "victory" in the field. Inherent in this accusation was MacArthur's repudiation of the Administration's basic assumptions, above all the supposition that the

Soviet Union might be ready and willing to fight a total war, and that the United States, therefore, must not provide an eager Kremlin with any excuse for attack.

MacArthur contended that the Administration divorced theory from practice. In theory, American foreign policy was based upon the assumption that the United States held sufficient power, above all air-atomic striking power, to deter the Soviet Union from launching an all-out war; in practice, American policy-makers acted upon the assumption that a limited extension of the war would hand the Soviets an excuse for precipitating World War III. On the one hand, the Kremlin was allegedly reluctant to engage in global hostilities with the United States because of America's greater retaliatory strength, inherent primarily in the destructive power of the Strategic Air Command; on the other hand, the Kremlin regarded our purported deterrent power with so little respect that it would deliberately risk total war rather than suffer a limited defeat of Communist China (a limited defeat would preclude the unconditional surrender and overthrow of Peking, and leave it weakened but nevertheless in control of the Chinese mainland).

MacArthur failed to see any consistency between the Administration's rationale of its foreign policy, based upon the atomic impact of massive retaliation, and its failure to act upon its own premise. If it were true that the United States held the atomic balance — as he believed and the Administration professed — then his recommendations for air attacks and a naval blockade of Communist China could be safely executed. SAC would continue to deter the Soviet Union and ensure that the limited hostilities, although somewhat extended, would remain confined to the Chinese-Korean theater; our superior strategic air power would provide the umbrella under which this expanded limited war could be fought. It was sheer fantasy, MacArthur charged, to suppose that American air attacks upon Manchuria would provide an eager Kremlin the opportunity to enter the battle. The Soviet Union possessed far inferior retaliatory power (the Russians did not begin to develop their long-range air force until 1954); why should it, therefore, be allowed to handcuff American strength? The United States possessed the superior atomic sanction; why should it not take advantage of this greater power? MacArthur pointed to the paradox that the side with the smaller strategic strength had paralyzed the will to act of the side which possessed the more effective striking force. The Administration's fear to act upon his recommendations to attack across the Yalu and the resultant impasse on the Korean battle-field was not a military stalemate, but a stalemate between the Soviet leaders *militarily incapable* of destroying the center of free world power and American policy-makers *psychologically reluctant* to exploit the advantage of the very atomic balance which they claimed was the primary safeguard of peace.

If the Russian leaders were really militarily capable of winning a total war and were merely seeking a convenient pretext to launch World War III, they would hardly need the United States to furnish the excuse; they were perfectly capable of manufacturing their own. If they were, however, restrained by American air power, they would rather tolerate a limited defeat of their chief ally than risk suicide. North Korea was no more "worth" the cost of an all-out conflict to the Soviet Union than South Korea had been to the United States; nor was Communist China's position in North Korea "worth" that price as long as American objectives remained confined to the Korean peninsula.

MacArthur also dissented from the Administration's assumption that even if an attack upon Communist China would not precipitate World War III, this country must not become engaged in a "war of attrition" lest this course would weaken NATO and provoke a Soviet attack. The General denied that the Korean War was a Russian maneuver to draw American strength away from Europe and dissipate it against Chinese manpower, a strategic diversion which must be ended as soon as possible at minimum cost to the central effort to strengthen our total-war deterrent.

Not only was the "real" challenge against the enemy's number-one team in Europe hypothetical, for it was "Russia's policy . . . not to sacrifice its own troops but to use those of friends," but:

Mr. Truman failed abysmally to comprehend the Soviet Strategy in the latter's continuing and relentless effort to control the world . . . He failed to understand that the global panorama has long encompassed three great areas of potential struggle: In the center, Europe; on the flanks, Asia to the north and Africa to the south. Mr. Truman apparently thought of the center as the area of supreme interest and potential struggle, believing that if it could be held safely all else would fall into place . . .

What the Soviets sought were the economic frontiers of the world — Asia to the north, Africa to the south — frontiers which possessed such a mighty reservoir of the world's potential wealth in raw resources. The center represented little in economic advance, the flanks everything. The Soviet strategy was merely to defend in Europe but to advance by way of the flanks; to cause the free world to concentrate its resources at the center to the neglect of the vital ends.[5]

Korea was, therefore, the right war at the right place at the right time, and above all else, with the right enemy. For Communist China was Soviet Russia's chief ally and most powerful friend in Asia. Therefore, a defeat inflicted upon Communist China, however limited that defeat might be, would affect both Soviet strength in Asia and the global balance of power between the Western and Communist blocs. The defeat of the Chinese Communists in Korea would strengthen the friendship and support of the Asian peoples, particularly the Japanese and Filipinos, for the United States; the loss of American prestige in an acceptance of the stalemate would alienate their sympathies. Conversely, Communist China's status would be recognized as "the military colossus of the East"; America's fear to demonstrate its superior strength would make our friends feel less secure and drive the neutral nations deeper into neutralism; for they would feel more threatened as a result of Peking's unchallenged recognition as a strong and menacing neighbor and therefore look upon the Communists states with a more friendly, if also a more apprehensive, eye. The destruction of Communist China's industrial complex, military depots, and communication network would gravely weaken Sino-Soviet offensive strength in the Far East and deter Moscow and Peking from initiating any further aggressive adventures; confining hostilities to the Korean peninsula and concluding the war on the basis of the *status quo* would leave Sino-Soviet power intact and encourage it to exploit the West's weakness and lack of determination in other areas. Indeed, if the war in Korea were "lost" — by MacArthur's definition — the Western democracies would have suffered such a first-class political and psychological defeat that the Soviets could not but be emboldened to new efforts to undermine Western Europe. But to drive the Chinese Communists out of Korea in accordance with his strategy, MacArthur asserted, would demonstrate to the Western nations that even the Sino-Soviet alliance shrank from certain risky steps; victory would raise Europe's self-confidence by showing the limits of Communist power and the superior strength of the United States. It is for this reason that MacArthur insisted that Korea was *the* test of NATO and that Europe's first line of defense was not in Germany but in Korea.

His war in Korea was not, therefore, a sideshow; it was at the center of the world-wide struggle. The war, to be sure, contained its risks, but this was inherent in the nature of international politics and the original decision to fight in Korea; the conflict also presented a great opportunity to inflict a limited yet severe defeat upon the Sino-Soviet bloc, demonstrate American determination and power, raise Western resolution and self-assurance, and forestall the disaffection of friendly Asian nations. This opportunity outweighed all the risks, particularly since these risks were minimized by the deterrent power of America's superior atomic air-striking power.

MacArthur also emphasized that an alliance could act decisively only if its members were agreed on the nature of the danger facing them. If they were not animated by such a common realization, they not only did not add to the security of the United States; they detracted from it by restraining the United States from taking the steps necessary to safeguard its interests. The argument that the Administration could not accept his recommendations because it could not afford to isolate itself in the face of the Soviet threat toward Europe, was invalid; it was not the existence of the alliance which would deter the enemy's aggression, but the resolution which bound it together in concrete instances which called for vigorous action. When such determination and will-power were lacking, the United States must protect its own interests. The Administration's unwillingness to risk the loss of its allies allowed American policy to be dictated by the weaker members of the alliance. Under these circumstances, the achievement of allied unity became self-defeating; for the price of continued cooperation was the substance of action.[6] In MacArthur's opinion, this price was too high and was paid upon the false assumption that unilateral action by the United States in Asia would undermine NATO, isolate this country, and encourage a Soviet attack in Europe. MacArthur believed that this prejudged the issue because it presumed that the United States was more dependent for its security upon its European allies than they upon the United States.

Since he was unwilling to accept formal unity for inaction or half-hearted effort, MacArthur advised that in order to forestall the disastrous effects he foresaw from an acceptance of a Korean stalemate, the United States "go it alone." European reluctance to become involved in major hostilities in the Far East ought not to prevent the Administration from taking actions which were in America's interest;

the Administration could not give global scope to an alliance whose conflict of interests in areas outside of Europe paralyzed it.[7]

The United States was sufficiently strong to fight the Korean War by herself; she had to act unilaterally if necessary, and pursue alone those policies which aimed at the preservation of a favorable balance of power. The United States must not allow this balance to be overturned by subordinating her strategy to allied fears; for in the final analysis, the security of Europe depended upon this country's ability to maintain this equilibrium. After the North Korean invasion, the United States had not first asked its allies whether they would approve of American intervention; the American government had acted in accordance with the dictates of national security. Allied consent had subsequently been extended, but it had not been a precondition for action. The Administration ought now to act upon its own precedent.

Communist China's appearance on the battlefield thus brought into the open the almost total disagreement between the Administration and its Commander in Chief, Far East, a disagreement which had, of course, never lain far below the surface and had irritated the relationship between Washington and Tokyo from the beginning of the war. Since shortly after the outbreak of hostilities, MacArthur had openly advocated that the United States maximize its commitment to Chiang Kai-shek and take a strong stand against Communist China; and his repeated "military" criticisms of the Administration's preoccupation with Europe and alleged neglect of American interests in the Far East were hardly new.

But these frequent and vigorous challenges of Administration policy after China's intervention were, however, incompatible with the President's continuing civilian supremacy and authority as chief diplomat and Commander in Chief to formulate and implement the policies the Chief Executive considered necessary to ensure the nation's self preservation. MacArthur embarrassed the Administration by giving the world the impression that the United States spoke with two voices — one civilian, one military — on foreign policy; he confused our allies and increased their reluctance to follow American policy because they feared that the government could not control him; and his March 24 statement actually forestalled the execution of Presidential policy. This situation was intolerable and left Mr. Truman no choice but to dismiss his field commander. But the price the President paid included, among other things, the adoption of a stronger anti-

Mao and pro-Chiang policy along the lines advocated by the "old soldier" who refused to fade away.

The Administration's political weakness and vulnerability in Congress was a further cause for the Truman-MacArthur controversy; the President's lack of strength was particularly noticeable in the Senate. The reason for this was that in early 1950 the leadership of the Republican party in Congress on matters of foreign policy returned from the liberal eastern wing of the party to the traditional and predominantly middle-western conservatives, who constitute the majority of Republicans in Congress. These conservative Republicans rejected "bipartisan" cooperation. They believed that partisanship in foreign policy was politically expedient; "me-tooism" in international affairs, as in domestic affairs, resulted in defeat at the polls. Policies stamped with the Administration trade-mark were credited by the electorate to the party in power, and not to the "loyal" opposition which had supported them. In addition, Taft Republicans were convinced that the Democratic party, aided by the "heretical" eastern wing of their own party, were destroying the foundations of the American political and economic system, and that this process could be halted only by the restoration to power of the heirs and custodians of the "true" Republican tradition with its belief in a strong legislature, a balanced budget, and a minimum of government intervention in business. Thus partisanship in foreign policy was also an ideological necessity.

The conservative Republicans focused their criticisms upon the New Dealers. The latter's crimes were many: they had fathered "Socialism" and the Welfare State in America; they had involved the United States in World War II; they had "sold out" China and Eastern Europe at the wartime conferences with Stalin; and they had allowed Communist agents and "sympathizers" to infiltrate the American government. In short, the New Dealers were responsible for altering the traditional libertarian American system, entangling the United States in the complications of the international world, and aiding, either unwittingly or deliberately, the forces of World Communism. This conspiratorial interpretation of American domestic and foreign politics could not have been advanced at a more appropriate moment in American postwar history. Popular frustration with the cold war was widespread.

Republican mid-term election successes appeared to prove to orthodox party strategists that opposition *per se* was good politics, and that their pre-election estimate that attacks upon foreign policy were politically profitable was correct. As a result, after November 7, 1950, they no longer confined their broadsides to Yalta, Teheran, and Potsdam; Alger Hiss and other cases of espionage; the Administration's "loss" of China and responsibility for the war in Korea; they now attacked the whole scope of American foreign policy, particularly the European policy. General MacArthur's close link to this group, among whom such leaders as Taft, Wherry, Bridges, and Knowland were largely oriented toward Asia, lent it great prestige and strengthened its criticisms.

These attacks had even before June 25, 1950, imposed an increasing inflexibility upon American Far Eastern policy; they had prevented the Administration from initiating its Mao Tse-tito policy and forestalled the complete abandonment of Chiang Kai-shek. The Administration's protection of Formosa after the outbreak of North Korean aggression satisfied the opposition only temporarily. As the war progressed, their assaults became increasingly vociferous in their demands for a stronger anti-Mao and pro-Chiang policy; and their electoral gains, together with Communist China's intervention, added to the pressure exerted upon the Administration to adopt General MacArthur's proposal to extend the war and hit across the Yalu River.

These attacks were not, however, powerful enough to achieve this aim; but they were sufficiently strong to place American diplomacy in a domestic political straightjacket which foreclosed negotiations as a means to end hostilities, brought the Administration to endorse a large-scale military-aid program for Chiang, to announce a rather doubtful enthusiasm for his regime, and even to issue a call for a revolution within Communist China. Thus, in May and June 1951, during the Senate inquiry into MacArthur's dismissal, the extraordinary and ridiculous situation arose in which, on the one hand, the Administration was defending its limitation of the war and its dismissal of General MacArthur for advocating the opposite course, and at the same time renouncing its acceptance of the *status quo* and the implicit recognition of Peking's existence which this implied, and presenting the key issue as the survival of the Chinese Communist regime itself. Since regimes do not, however, negotiate about their own survival, this issue could only have been settled by the total war with Communist China — and perhaps with the Soviet Union — which the Administration had already rejected as too dangerous a course. Thus, if the government's call for an internal revolt within Communist China had been taken seriously by Peking, it would have committed the United States to an interminable war with no possibility of ending it through negotiations or a cease-fire.

Walter Lippmann subsequently wrote that the situation had been so serious that President Truman

was not able to make peace, because politically he was too weak at home. He was not able to make war because the risks were too great. This dilemma of Truman's was resolved by the election of Eisenhower . . . President Eisenhower signed an armistice which accepted the partition of Korea and a peace without victory because, being himself the victorious commander in World War II and a Republican, he could not be attacked as an appeaser. President Truman and Secretary Acheson, on the other hand, never seemed able to afford to make peace on the only terms which the Chinese would agree to, on the terms, that is to say, which Eisenhower did agree to. The Democrats were too vulnerable to attack from the political followers of General MacArthur and of the then powerful Senator McCarthy, and indeed to attack from the whole right wing of the Republican party.[8]

Thus the separation of powers exaggerated the peculiar American tendency to define foreign policy objectives in abstract and ideological terms; for to gain congressional and popular support for their policies, presidents must oversell their policies. This they do, not by presenting the key issues as enlightened — yet nevertheless, "selfish" — national interests, but as the highest moral principles and aims.

Whereas interests can, however, be compromised, principles cannot. Their integrity, indeed their survival, can be guaranteed only by the total destruction of the enemy and the complete elimination of the evil which threatens to contaminate, if not to abolish, them. Anything less than the full application of "righteous power," and the achievement of complete victory, creates an embarrassing discrepancy between expectation and reality, and leaves in its wake widespread disillusionment.

The Administration's political weakness was evident, however, not only in its acceptance of much of its critics' policy and its apparent inability to sign an armistice on or near the 38th Parallel, but also in its failure to take effective measures to restrict MacArthur's discretionary powers. Nowhere was this more vividly demonstrated than in North Korea after the first signs of Chinese Communist intervention.

MacArthur believed that boldness and a show of force would convince Peking that Korea's fate had already been settled; any hesitation would be interpreted as weakness and an invitation to full-scale intervention. The Administration proposed that only South Korean troops be sent into the area along the Manchurian frontier and northeastern provinces bordering the Soviet Union; by this means it expected to reassure Peking that American troops would not invade Manchuria. But MacArthur advanced the proper "purely military" considerations which he claimed necessitated his advance to the Yalu, and the government surrendered meekly. The reason it later advanced for its laxness was the American tradition granting generals great latitude in determining the tactical means to gain their objectives. This was primarily a rationalization; American policy-makers could hardly have been blind to the interrelationship of tactical means on the one hand and strategic concepts and political consequences on the other. A more reasonable explanation would attribute their paralysis to the Administration's fear of being accused of "softness" toward Communism, its uncertainty that MacArthur could not again carry off a "tremendous gamble" as at Inchon, its field commander's heightened prestige since that brilliant victory and Republican mid-term victories.

This is not to say that MacArthur's determination to launch his "end of the war" offensive, or the Administration's failure to stop him, were responsible for Communist China's full-scale intervention. The key decision determining the intervention was probably the crossing of the parallel; this is not, however, to excuse Washington's relaxation of political control as MacArthur advanced into North Korea. In seeking allied support for the crossing of the parallel, the Administration had given assurances that it would direct its military operations in North Korea with circumspection, that it would conduct itself with caution and avoid all acts with which might provoke either Russia or China. MacArthur's operations, in the view of the allies, hardly supported this understanding; in their opinion, MacArthur's "belligerent" statements, together with his advance to the Yalu, gave Peking reasonable grounds for suspicion of American intentions and at least a partial justification for its intervention. Consequently, London and Paris refused to sanction an extension of the war beyond the Yalu, and slowed down and later eviscerated the Administration's condemnation of Communist China. This one incident, they believed, had shown both

MacArthur's liberal — perhaps more appropriately, unwarranted — interpretation of his orders, and the Administration's inability to exert effective control over him. Thus Truman's domestic weakness was one of the principal causes for the lack of allied confidence and insistence upon restraint.

The intensity of the executive-legislative battle not only allowed MacArthur to inject himself into this conflict and exploit his strong legislative support, but made it incumbent upon the Administration to invoke the Joint Chiefs' public support for its policies. Thus, ironically, the President's main reason for dismissing MacArthur, the necessity to preserve the principle of civilian control of the military, had to rely for its defense almost completely upon General Bradley and his three colleagues. The Joint Chiefs, widely regarded as a strictly professional and disinterested body, could command senatorial attention, for they combined the roles of World War II heroes and technical experts; consequently, they bore the chief burden of explaining to the inquiring senators the relationship of military strategy to political objectives, the respective contribution of Europe and Asia to our national security, and the value and role of allies in American policy. Secretary Acheson, despite the articulate, organized, and persuasive presentation of his testimony, could command no such reception; his Congressional audience received him in a more hostile and skeptical mood.

If the Administration's political vulnerability left the Joint Chiefs little choice but to lend their glamor to the government's policies, it also squandered much of their wartime prestige and reputation for political neutrality. Senator Taft's announcement, shortly after General MacArthur's dismissal, that he no longer possessed any confidence in General Bradley's professional judgment — as if "purely military" evaluations were ever without political implications! — is symptomatic of this change of attitude. Apparently the Senator believed that Bradley's opinions were warped by a purported pro-Democratic bias. Taft's criticism, however, even if it were true — and all the evidence belies it — would hardly be germane; for he is not disputing the fact that military men speak for or against national issues of a highly controversial nature in public, but the fact that General Bradley agreed with the President's policy, and disagreed with his, Senator Taft's, views. His point was not that a criticism of his and former President Hoover's almost exclusive reliance on air and sea power for the defense of the American Gibraltar should have been the task of the military's civilian superiors; his point was that General Bradley had found his strategy wanting. His concern was not, therefore, with the problem that partisan alignment of generals implied for the future of civilian supremacy; he was merely incensed that there were also "Democratic Generals," like the chairman of the Joint Chiefs, not just "Republican Generals," like MacArthur.

Nonetheless, the Senator's hostility to General Bradley does draw attention to the manner in which the separation of powers between the President and Congress draws military leaders into political conflict. The danger in this is not that military officers belong, as Senator Taft seemed to believe, to one or the other of the two principal parties. The real threat lies elsewhere: that the generals' independent judgment lends itself to exploitation by both parties; and that this will signal, as Walter Lippmann has written, "the beginning of an altogether intolerable thing in a republic: namely a schism within the armed forces between the generals of the Democratic Party and the generals of the Republican Party"; [9] and that the result will considerably weaken civilian control and presidential direction of foreign policy.

Our study of the Truman-MacArthur controversy has shown that the preservation of civilian control is not merely a simple matter of maintaining a number of appropriate constitutional and institutional safeguards. Indeed, the word "control" is in itself somewhat vague, for it implies that to avert a threat from the professionals of the sword restraints need be applied only to them; this is not necessarily true. At a time of high international tension, such as 1950–1951, during which the population and their elected officials are intensely preoccupied with security, the dominance of the military and "military" attitudes among civilians both in and out of government may become overriding. This is particularly true if such a period of crisis should last a relatively long time, or be followed rapidly by successive crises. Under such circumstances, American democracy may be transformed into a "garrison state" in which all power is concentrated in the Executive, authority flows downward, and democratic liberties are merely memories. This state of affairs, as Louis Smith has emphasized, may come "not by willful usurpation by the military but by successive adaptations for defense having the support of public opinion. It may be ushered in, not by conspiracy, but by plebiscite. It may come into

power, not over the wreckage of the civil organs traditionally expected to repress it, but with their respective support." [10]

This points to what is thus the principal as well as the most easily
perceptible factor determining the effectiveness of civilian control:
the quality of the nation's civilian leadership, that is, the ability of
the politically responsible officials to recognize threats to their supremacy and their courage to act in order to preserve their control, no
matter how unpopular their steps.

> Only to the extent that civilian leaders are committed to democratic
> values and procedures and the necessity for a civilian point of view can the
> requisite supremacy be maintained. Their intelligence and understanding,
> their clarity of purpose and direction, and their courage and confidence in
> the face of various anxieties and exigencies of a "cold war" and even full-
> scale war itself seem to be crucial . . . civilian apathy and ignorance may as
> effectively subvert civilian supremacy as a deliberate attempt by the military
> to augment their supremacy.[11]

Another factor of key importance during a period of war is a field
commander who is not violently opposed to the policies he is expected
to execute, at least not so violently that he will refuse to restrict his
objections to constitutionally authorized channels. No government
can allow a military officer to challenge its whole foreign policy
publicly; such toleration would undermine its authority to determine
the nation's policy, divide the domestic support it needs, and alienate
the allies it desires.

This need for a field commander more in sympathy with official
strategy becomes even more urgent in view of the latitude the United
States has traditionally granted its military officers. Since it is not
customary for an Administration to issue specific orders to a military
executive thousands of miles away, the latter can, owing to poor
judgment or deliberate design, make decisions whose political and
strategic consequences may well prevent the achievement of the
government's objectives, if not undermine them. Necessity may, therefore, compel a re-examination of the tradition of military freedom lest
it excuse us into disaster. In limited warfare not only military strategy,
but on occasions even military tactics, have important political reper-
cussions.

Imposing such restrictions on the man in the field will require a
change in the traditional American attitude that war is a purely
military instrument. The military, as well as their civilian superiors,

will have to recognize that Clausewitz' definition of war as a political tool means that military operations are not only subordinate to political aims, but that there is no such thing as an autonomous sphere in which military operations are conducted in a strictly military manner unencumbered by "outside interference." None of the other generals who directed the Korean War, with the sole exception of General Ridgeway, understood war in any broader sense than their own narrow professional definition. James Van Fleet, Mark Clark, Turner Joy, all took MacArthur literally and echoed his calls for a military victory; after all, was MacArthur not voicing merely the obvious? [12]

Not until military men as a whole accept the need for close political direction will they be less likely to issue public statements voicing their displeasure at the "political interference" with their conduct of a limited war; indeed, until they abandon their notion that war is a military tool they will find it difficult wholly to accept the concept of limited warfare. Military men seem sometimes to forget that they are servants of the state and that they will not be judged by the nature of the policies they implement, only by how well they implement these policies. Their civilian superiors are responsible for the actual formulation of political strategy, not they. It is not their function to take their disagreements into the public forum for national debate.

Indeed, unless the soldier observes more carefully the limitations imposed upon him by his professional obligations and responsibilities, he will in fact be helping to undermine the control his civilian superiors exercise over him. For the separation of powers provides, as one writer has aptly phrased it, "a perpetual invitation, if not an irresistible force, drawing military leaders into political conflicts." [13] In these circumstances, it will be a rare political opposition that will resist taking the field commander's criticisms (or the criticisms of one or more members of the Joint Chiefs) to the nation in order to capture political power by exploiting the American public's temperamental inability or unwillingness to fight anything less than total war. As it is, the institutional and psychological jealousies between the President and Congress, the irresponsible opposition which profits politically from Administration weaknesses and failures, the weak party discipline, and the possibility of a mid-term upset, seriously limit even a strong chief executive's degree of "peacetime" diplomatic freedom and ability to carry on his own foreign policy without succumbing, at least to some degree, to his opponent's program. The link between the opposition party and the general in the field, particularly a popular general, will intensify this tendency.

But basically the problem of preserving effective civilian control and minimizing the possibilities of the soldier–opposition party liaison is a question of how rapidly the American people adjust their traditional approach to foreign policy under the pressures and tensions of the cold war: how quickly they learn that they cannot at one moment preoccupy themselves with domestic affairs to the almost complete neglect of foreign policy, and at the next moment, when the enemy menace has become clear, focus all their attention and energies upon his utter destruction; how soon they accept the constantly recurring limited challenges, even limited wars, without the kind of intense and desperate frustration which might spill over either into total war or isolation. The process of learning is necessarily a slow one. "Taken as a whole," Robert Osgood has said, "the American record in foreign policy since 1945 is a remarkable adaptation to novel and challenging circumstances." Nevertheless, this record "does not show a real adjustment, either in its underlying conceptions of force and politics or in its concrete policies, to the imperatives of a strategy capable of resisting limited aggression by limited means. Such adaptation is bound to be encumbered by the weight of traditional habits of mind resisting the pressure of unprecedented events." [14]

The time of such adaptation can, however, be shortened in the armed forces through education. Officers should receive a broader training than they have in the past so that they become aware of the wider context in which military policies have to be decided. Some civilians may fear that military men with a fuller understanding of the political and economic conditions that affect military strategy will be able to present their military points of view more effectively and thereby undermine civilian authority. In fact, such officers, precisely because they are aware of the broader framework of policy, are least likely to threaten civilian supremacy. The MacArthur case, to be sure, might prove otherwise; but the MacArthurs, who are willing to challenge their governments openly in an effort to change official policy to one more in accordance with their own political predilections, are a rarity. The Mark Clarks, Van Fleets, and Turner Joys, with their strong belief that war is a nonpolitical instrument and that wars can only be won if the politicians and diplomats do not "interfere" in them are not a rarity. The traditional American view that military and non-military factors can be considered independently of each other may not have been harmful during a period of isolation; but it cannot fail to be harmful, even disastrous, at a time of global involvement. For the issue at stake is no less than the preservation of limitations on limited war.

Limitations are arrived at by a complex and subtle process of informal negotiations with the enemy in which the two sides never sit down at a diplomatic table and formally negotiate these limitations with one another. Instead, they tacitly agree about these limitations by mutual example. Thus, the United States will permit China to possess a "privileged sanctuary" beyond the Yalu River; American fighters and bombers — let alone troops — do not cross the Korean–Chinese frontier. Similarly, the Chinese do not attack the allied armies in the field with fighters or bomb the supply ports. Had the U. N. forces, however, bombed the Manchurian supply depots, troop-concentration points, and roads and railroad tracks leading to Korea, thereby perhaps jeopardizing the ability of the Chinese army to withstand a sustained U. N. offensive, the Chinese might have been compelled to attack the U. N. forces and South Korean ports from the air. Mutual self-restraint helps to prevent hostilities from escalating. This is not to say that a particular limitation can never be changed or, that once lifted, the war will automatically escalate immediately into total war. Limitation should be discarded only after careful consideration, only if absolutely necessary, and only if accompanied by a full knowledge of the risks involved. The greater the number of limitations that are lifted, the greater the possibilities of escalation, and the very event which impels both sides to try and keep the hostilities limited — a total strategic nuclear war — may be precipitated.

The United Nations' decision to cross the 38th Parallel is an obvious example of the risks undertaken when one side violates a tacit limitation. In a limited war the political objectives are limited. At the beginning of the Korean hostilities, the objective was to restore the *status quo*. While the objective seemed negative (to prevent South Korea from falling under Communist domination), it also served certain positive political purposes. It demonstrated America's reliability to her friends and allies. It also showed the Soviets and Chinese the futility — and risks — of using force to transform the balance of power. The political objective then was to demonstrate American determination to stop the Communists from extending their power by force. Once the United Nations force marched across the 38th Parallel, however, the objective became the total elimination of the North Korean government and the unconditional surrender of its armed forces. But Korean unification under United Nations control would have threatened Chinese security. Thus the invasion precipitated her intervention — just as the attempt to overthrow the South Korean government and the Communist threat to Japanese security precipitated American intervention. The invasion to the north, therefore, escalated the war by removing one of the most important limitations.

The problem of preserving these limitations is a question of "communication." It is precisely because they are not formally negotiated that they must somehow be clearly drawn and "obvious." These limitations may make no sense militarily. In fact, from a military point of view, when the aim is the destruction of the enemy's forces, sanctuaries such as Manchuria or Pusan are roadblocks in the way of a military victory. From the point of view of achieving political objectives, however, these limitations make eminently good sense.

Nothing better illustrates the conflict between the political objective of limited war and the military objective of victory than the problem of who should control the use of tactical nuclear weapons. Militarily, their use is likely to be advocated because of their greater and more "efficient" killing potential. Politically, however, their use may be disastrous. How many invaded states will wish to be "saved from Communism" by being devastated by such destructive weapons? There will be little left to be saved. The threatened use of tactical nuclear weapons *may* encourage the victims of aggression *not* to call for American help.

More significantly, the distinction between nuclear and nonnuclear weapons is obvious, as apparent as a frontier line and not subject to varying interpretations. But if this distinction were discarded and a new one made, say between tactical and strategic nuclear weapons, just where *would* the line be drawn: at 2 kilotons, 20 kilotons (the yield of the Nagasaki bomb), or 2 megatons? Not using tactical nuclear weapons is a simple recognizable limitation and therefore easy to observe; any other distinction raises more problems than it solves.

A field commander like a MacArthur, whether his motives are political or strictly military, will only endanger these limitations. In pursuing "victory," he will press for the lifting of limitations imposed upon him — limitations that are, in a military sense, admittedly illogical and impediments to victory. But in his cry that "there is no substitute for victory," is the danger of escalation. It is particularly for the MacArthurs, therefore, that Clausewitz wrote

The art of war in its highest point of view becomes a policy, but, of course, a policy which fights battles instead of writing notes. According to this view, it is an unpermissible and even harmful distinction, according to which a great military event or the plan for such an event should admit a *purely military judgment;* indeed, it is an unreasonable procedure to consult professional soldiers on the plan of war, that they may give a *purely military opinion.* . . . For war is an instrument of policy; it must necessarily bear the character of policy; it must measure with policy's measure. The conduct of war, in its great outlines, is, therefore, policy itself, which takes up the sword in place of the pen, but does not on the account cease to think according to its own laws.[15]

These are wise words to remember in an age in which nuclear bombs have outmoded total war as suicidal and made the world safe only for limited wars.

NOTES

I. MacARTHUR RETURNS

1. John Spanier, *American Foreign Policy Since World War II*, rev. ed. (New York: Frederick A. Praeger, 1962), pp. 1–13.

2. *Military Situation in the Far East,* Hearings before the Committee on Armed Services and the Committee on Foreign Relations, United States Senate, 82nd Cong., 1st Sess. (Washington, Government Printing Office, 1951), p. 45, 289. This document will hereafter be referred to as *Senate Hearings.*

3. Louis Smith, *American Democracy and Military Power* (Chicago: Chicago University Press), 1951, p. 15.

4. Robert E. Osgood, *Limited War* (Chicago: Chicago University Press, 1957, pp. 176–177; see also pp. 28–45 for Osgood's analysis of the American approach to war.

5. Karl von Clausewitz, *On War,* Modern Library ed. (New York: Random House), pp. 596–601, 16–17; also Samuel P. Huntington, *The Soldier and the State* (Cambridge: Harvard University Press, 1957), pp. 55–97.

II. THE NORTH KOREAN ATTACK

1. Courtney Whitney, *MacArthur: His Rendezvous with Destiny* (New York: Knopf, 1956), p. 331.

2. "The United Nations Commission on Korea to the Secretary-General," State Department, *United States Policy in the Korean Crisis* (Washington: Government Printing Office, 1950), p. 21.

3. "The Acting Chairman of the United Nations Commission on Korea to the President of the Security Council," *ibid.,* pp. 21–22.

4. *Senate Hearings,* p. 2371.

5. Harry S. Truman, *Memoirs, Vol. II: Years of Trial and Hope* (New York: Doubleday, 1956), pp. 325–326; *New York Times,* November 3, 1952.

6. *Senate Hearings,* pp. 242–243. This factor is not mentioned in the General's explanation of why he had once himself defined the United States defense perimeter in exactly the same terms as Acheson later outlined it. See MacArthur's letter to the *New York Times,* February 4, 1956, in reply to John Carter Vincent's letter, *ibid.,* January 30, 1956.

7. *Ibid.,* March 2, 1949.

8. Joseph M. Jones, *The Fifteen Weeks* (New York: Viking, 1955), pp. 90–91.

9. *Ibid.;* also *Senate Hearings,* p. 382.

10. Truman, II, 325–326.

11. *Senate Hearings,* pp. 242–243.

12. The Russian-occupied Kurile Islands are an unmentioned break in the chain.

13. "Crisis in Asia — An Examination of U.S. Policy," *State Department Bulletin,* XXII (January 23, 1950), 115–116.

14. *Senate Hearings,* pp. 1991–92. General Willoughby, MacArthur's

Chief of Intelligence, claims that Tokyo warned Washington of the imminence of an attack for over six months. Willoughby does not, however, include any of the qualifying comments that Acheson quoted. Charles Willoughby and John Chamberlain, *MacArthur, 1941–1951* (New York: McGraw-Hill, 1955), pp. 351–352.

15. *Senate Hearings,* p. 2589.

16. *New York Herald Tribune,* July 5, 1950.

17. *New York Times,* June 27, 1950.

18. I. F. Stone, *The Hidden Story of the Korean War* (New York: Monthly Review Press, 1952), p. 65.

19. *New York Times,* June 27, 1950.

20. Osgood, p. 165.

21. "A Militaristic Experiment," *State Department Bulletin,* XXIII (July 10, 1950), 50.

22. *New York Herald Tribune,* June 27, 1950.

23. "Korean Attack Opens New Chapter in History," *State Department Bulletin,* XXIII (August 7, 1950), p. 208.

24. Whitney, p. 322; Truman, II, 336.

25. State Department, *Korea, 1945 to 1948* (Washington: Government Printing Office, 1948); Truman, II, 316–330.

26. "The Korean Experiment in Representative Government," *State Department Bulletin,* XXIII (July 3, 1950), 13; also Dean Acheson, "Review of U.N. and U.S. Action to Restore Peace," *ibid.* (July 10, 1950), 46.

27. Arthur M. Schlesinger, Jr., and Richard Rovere, *The General and the President* (New York: Farrar, Straus and Young, 1951), p. 242n.

28. Waltz, *New York Times,* June 26, 1950.

29. Truman, II, 332–333; Bradley, *Senate Hearings,* p. 958; Krock, *New York Times,* July 2, 1950; Alsops, *New York Herald Tribune,* June 27, 1950.

30. The reasons for resisting the North Korean attack are explicitly set forth in the President's message to MacArthur on January 13, 1951. See below, Chapter VIII.

31. Truman, II, 339–340.

32. *Ibid.,* p. 334.

33. *Ibid.,* pp. 337–339.

34. Whitney, p. 332.

35. For the decisive role played by MacArthur in the commitment of ground troops, see Bradley, *Senate Hearings,* p. 1122, and MacArthur, pp. 235–236.

36. "Press Release by the White House, June 30, 1950," *United States Policy in the Korean Crisis,* pp. 24–25.

37. "Statement by the President, June 26, 1950," *ibid.,* p. 17; Beverley Smith, "The White House Story: Why We Went to War in Korea," *Saturday Evening Post,* November 10, 1950, p. 80.

38. *Ibid.;* Reston, *New York Times,* June 28 and July 3, 1950.

39. *New York Herald Tribune,* June 30, 1950.

40. "The American Ambassador in the Soviet Union to the Soviet Minister of Foreign Affairs," *United States Policy in the Korean Crisis,* pp. 63–64.

41. Albert Warner, "How the Korean Decision Was Made," *Harpers' Magazine,* June 1951, p. 104.

42. "Statement Read to the American Ambassador in the Soviet Union

by the Soviet Minister of Foreign Affairs, June 29, 1950," *United States Policy in the Korean Crisis*, p. 64.

43. Smith, "White House Story," p. 88; Truman, II, 342.

44. Truman, II, 341, 343; Baldwin, *New York Times*, June 28, 1950; Smith, "White House Story," p. 78.

45. Truman, II, 343.

46. *Senate Hearings*, pp. 231–232.

47. United Nations, *Official Records of the Security Council*, Fifth Session, 473rd Meeting, June 25, 1950, pp. 7–8. Hereafter cited as *Security Council Records*.

48. *Ibid.*, 474th Meeting, June 27, 1950, p. 4.

49. "The United Nations Commission on Korea to the Secretary-General," *United States Policy in the Korean Crisis*, p. 21.

50. Truman, II, 337–339.

51. "Statement of Deputy Foreign Minister A. A. Gromyko on American Armed Intervention in Korea," *U.S.S.R. Information Bulletin*, July 28, 1950, pp. 420–423.

52. "Soviet Allegation of Illegality of United Nations Security Council," *United States Policy in the Korean Crisis*, pp. 61–63.

53. *House of Commons Debates*, Fifth Series, vol. 477, col. 485–495.

54. Truman, II, p. 339.

55. United Nations, *Yearbook of the United Nations* (New York, 1951), pp. 226–229. Luxemburg, also a member of the U.N., sent an infantry unit to Korea early in 1951.

56. Leland M. Goodrich, "Korea: Collective Measures against Aggression," *International Conciliation*, October 1953, p. 146.

57. *Security Council Records*, Fifth Session, 473rd Meeting, June 25, 1950, p. 4.

58. Arnold Wolfers, "Collective Security and the War in Korea," *Yale Review*, XLIII (Summer 1954), 487.

III. DOMESTIC POLITICS AND FORMOSA

1. *State Department Bulletin*, XXIII (June 28, 1950), 805.

2. Arthur H. Vandenberg, Jr., and Joe A. Morris, *The Private Papers of Senator Vandenberg* (Boston: Houghton Mifflin, 1952), p. 551.

3. *Ibid.*, pp. 552–553.

4. The best works analyzing the conservative Republicans are: John P. Armstrong, "The Enigma of Senator Taft and American Foreign Policy," *Review of Politics*, XVII (April 1955); William S. White, *The Taft Story* (New York: Harpers, 1954), and "What Bill Knowland Stands For," *New Republic*, February 27, 1956; Arthur M. Schlesinger, Jr., "The New Isolationism," *Atlantic*, May 1952; Selig Adler, *The Isolationist Impulse* (New York: Abelard-Schuman, 1958); Robert Taft, *A Foreign Policy for Americans* (New York: Doubleday, 1951); Eric Goldman, *The Crucial Decade* (New York: Harper, 1956).

5. Bradford H. Westerfield, *Foreign Policy and Party Politics* (New Haven: Yale University Press, 1955), pp. 259–268, 343–376.

6. State Department, *United States Relations with China, 1944–1949* (Washington: Government Printing Office, 1949), p. xv.

7. Wedemeyer's speech may also be found in *Senate Hearings*, pp. 3238–42.

8. *United States Relations with China,* pp. xiv, xvi.

9. Vandenberg, pp. 525–527.

10. "Transcripts of Round Table Discussions on American Policy toward China in the Department of State, October 6, 7, and 8, 1949," *Institute of Pacific Relations,* Hearings before the Subcommittee to Investigate the Administration of the Internal Security Act and Other Internal Security Laws of the Committee on the Judiciary, United States Senate, 82nd Cong., 1st Sess. (Washington: Government Printing Office, 1951–52), pp. 1551–1682.

11. "Crisis in Asia — An Examination of U.S. Policy," *State Department Bulletin,* XXII (January 23, 1950), 113–114 (italics mine).

12. *United States Relations with China,* pp. xvi–xvii.

13. Bert Andrews, *New York Herald Tribune,* June 28, 1950; speech by Senator Taft to the Senate on June 28, 1950, *Congressional Record,* 81st Cong., 2nd Sess. (Washington: Government Printing Office), pp. 9319–23.

14. *Senate Hearings,* pp. 1671–72.

15. *Ibid.,* pp. 1770–71.

16. *Institute of Pacific Relations,* pp. 1580–81.

17. *Senate Hearings,* pp. 1674–75.

18. *Ibid.,* p. 2578.

19. *State Department Bulletin,* XXII (January 16, 1950), 79.

20. *Ibid.,* p. 80.

21. Entire document, *Senate Hearings,* pp. 1667–69.

22. *Ibid.,* pp. 1673–74.

23. United Press story from Tokyo on that day, *ibid.,* pp. 1675–76.

24. *New York Times,* January 4, 1950; *Congressional Record,* 81st Cong., 2nd Sess., p. 83.

25. *Congressional Record,* 81st Cong., 2nd Sess., p. 89.

26. *New York Times,* January 4, 1950.

27. *Congressional Record,* 81st Cong., 2nd Sess., pp. 298–299.

28. Smith's letters to Acheson, November 4, December 27, 1949, and report of his visit to the Far East, *Senate Hearings,* pp. 3314–26.

29. *Senate Hearings,* pp. 3255–57.

30. Westerfield, pp. 367–368, 388.

31. "Statement by the President," *Senate Hearings,* p. 3369; "The President's Message to the Congress, July 19, 1950," *ibid.,* p. 3467.

32. These interchanges may be found in *Congressional Record,* 81st Cong., 2nd Sess., pp. 9228–29, 9537–40.

33. *Ibid.,* pp. 9319–23.

IV. MacARTHUR, FORMOSA, AND INCHON

1. *State Department Bulletin,* XXIII (July 17, 1950), 83; "Statement by the President," *United States Policy in the Korean Crisis,* p. 67.

2. Vandenberg, pp. 75–89.

3. *Congressional Record,* 81st Cong., 2nd Sess., p. 10554.

4. Walter Millis, ed., *The Forrestal Diaries* (New York: Viking, 1951), pp. 17–18.

5. "Excerpts from Documentary Report on Soviet Entry into War against Japan," *New York Times,* October 20, 1955, pp. 10–14.

6. For instance, Dean Acheson, "Crisis in Asia — An Examination of U.S. Policy," *State Department Bulletin*, XXII (January 23, 1950), 112.

7. See Harriman's telegram informing the President of his discussions with MacArthur, in Truman, II, 350–353.

8. See below, Chapter IX.

9. Truman, II, 342–343.

10. *State Department Bulletin*, XXIII (October 16, 1950), 607.

11. Whitney, pp. 369–370.

12. *Ibid.*, p. 371; Truman, II, 349.

13. "Response of the United States to the Chinese Nationalist Government's Aide-mémoire of June 29, 1950," *Senate Hearings*, p. 3383.

14. *Ibid.*, pp. 123, 23.

15. Whitney, pp. 372–373.

16. *New York Times*, August 12, 1950 (italics mine).

17. Whitney, pp. 373–374.

18. Truman, II, 349–53.

19. Whitney, p. 375.

20. Truman, II, 352.

21. *Ibid.*, p. 354; Whitney, pp. 369–370, 376. Whitney dates this directive as August 5 (Truman, August 14), and he adds that the Joint Chiefs also favored the Nationalist bombardment of the mainland.

22. *Senate Hearings*, pp. 3477–80, 182–184; Whitney, pp. 377–380.

23. Whitney, p. 380, claims that the message was sent to the Department of the Army ten days before the expected delivery. Willoughby, p. 420, makes no such claim, nor did the Administration witnesses during the Senate Hearings.

24. *Senate Hearings*, p. 111.

25. Truman, II, 354–355.

26. Whitney, p. 374.

27. Truman, II, 352.

28. *Senate Hearings*, pp. 2002–03.

29. See below, Chapter IX.

30. Truman, II, 355–356.

31. *Ibid.*, pp. 356–358.

32. Whitney, pp. 377, 380–382.

33. *New York Times*, July 9, 1950.

34. Whitney, p. 319.

35. The planning for Inchon is covered by Whitney, pp. 319, 342–345.

36. George C. Kenney, *The MacArthur I Know* (New York: Duell, Sloan and Pierce, 1951), pp. 211–212.

37. *Ibid.*, p. 212; *New York Times*, September 15, 1950; Reston and Baldwin in *New York Times*, September 24 and October 30, 1950, respectively.

38. For the MacArthur–Joint Chiefs conference, Whitney, pp. 345–350.

39. According to the *New York Herald Tribune*, September 16, 1950, the Inchon invasion was actually "one of the worst-kept secrets" of the war. "It has been whispered and blabbed all over Korea and Japan. If the North Koreans did not know where we were going and when we would arrive, they were the only people in Asia who didn't. Army field commanders used news of the invasion to bolster troop morale all along the front. They promised

that if we can hold on until mid-September there will be landings behind enemy lines which will destroy him completely. It was impossible to hide the loading at the port of embarkation, where thousands of troops and their equipment were put aboard ship in full view of the local population, known to be infested with Communist agents."

40. Whitney, pp. 350, 351–353.

41. *Ibid.,* pp. 342–343.

42. "MacArthur's Statement Replying to Mr. Truman's Charges in His War Memoirs," *New York Times,* February 9, 1956.

43. Whitney, pp. 337–338.

V. CROSSING THE 38TH PARALLEL

1. *New York Times,* July 30, 1950.

2. Whitney, p. 345.

3. Royal Institute of International Affairs, *Documents of International Affairs, 1949–50* (London: Oxford, 1953), p. 658.

4. *Ibid.,* p. 659; *State Department Bulletin,* XXIII (October 16, 1950), 607.

5. *New York Times,* August 28, 1950.

6. *Ibid.,* August 29, 1950.

7. *State Department Bulletin,* XXIII (October 16, 1950), 610.

8. See for instance Werner Levi's account of the National Campaign Week against U.S. Aggression, July 17–24, 1950, in *Modern China's Foreign Policy* (St. Paul: University of Minnesota Press, 1953), pp. 296–297. Levi comments, "An accumulation of hate was produced that must have been a record even for a Communist country."

9. *New York Times,* September 24, 1950.

10. *Ibid.,* September 25, 1950.

11. K. M. Panikkar, *In Two Chinas* (London: Allen and Unwin, 1955), p. 108.

12. *New York Times,* October 1, 1950.

13. *Ibid.,* October 2, 1950.

14. *Ibid.,* October 10, 1950.

15. *Security Council Records,* Fifth Session, 527th Meeting, November 28, 1950, pp. 23–24.

16. John Dille, *Substitute for Victory* (New York: Doubleday, 1954), p. 20.

17. *State Department Bulletin,* XXIII (October 9, 1950), 579–580.

18. United Nations, *Official Records of the General Assembly,* Supplement no. 20, Resolution 376(V), pp. 9–10. Hereafter cited as *General Assembly Records.*

19. "Review of U.N. and U.S. Action to Restore Peace," *State Department Bulletin,* XXIII (July 10, 1950), 46.

20. Frederick H. Hartmann, *The Relations of Nations* (New York: Macmillan, 1957), p. 383.

21. *Senate Hearings,* pp. 1782, 1735, 1929.

22. *Ibid.,* p. 36.

23. *Ibid.,* p. 2258.

24. Truman, II, 383–384.

25. *Ibid.,* pp. 365–366; *Substance of Statement Made at the Wake*

Island Conference (Washington: Government Printing Office, 1951), p. 5.

26. Whitney, pp. 392–395.

27. *Ibid.* These qualifications are not to be found in the statements compiled from the notes taken by General Bradley and checked for accuracy by the rest of the presidential party. MacArthur did not challenge the correctness of these notes until after his dismissal, when he claimed that they had been taken by a stenographer "lurking behind the door," who "could record only what she could hear through the small door" of the door. Thus her account was "at best sadly inadequate" (Whitney, pp. 391–392).

General Bradley testified that various people took notes because this was a historic conference. He had taken them because he had to report back to the Joint Chiefs. While he had not been aware that Mr. Jessup's secretary had been taking notes as well — apparently on her own responsibility — Bradley stated that "we would have had practically as full notes without hers. It was very helpful to have checked them against hers . . ." Bradley could not understand why anyone should object to the taking of notes at such an important meeting (*Senate Hearings*, pp. 925–929, 950, 952, 959, 979). The answer: it allowed MacArthur to claim that this woman had taken the *only* notes, that these notes were inadequate if not false, and that they had deliberately left out his qualifications on possible Chinese intervention.

28. Whitney, pp. 393–394, 455–457.

29. Truman, II, 359; paraphrased text, *Senate Hearings*, p. 718.

30. Whitney, p. 397.

31. See above, Chapter III.

32. C.B.S. Interview, *State Department Bulletin*, XXIII (September 18, 1950), 463.

33. "Strategy of Freedom," *ibid.*, XXIII (December 18, 1950), 963; Truman, *ibid.*, XXIII (November 27, 1950), pp. 852–853.

34. Panikkar, pp. 108–110.

35. *New York Herald Tribune*, October 2, 1950.

36. Truman, II, 362.

37. *General Assembly Records*, 294th Meeting, October 7, 1950, p. 230.

38. *State Department Bulletin*, XXIII (September 18, 1950), 463 (italics mine).

39. *Senate Hearings*, p. 1835.

40. Whitney, p. 397.

41. Stone, pp. 109–115; Truman, II, 361.

42. Whitney, p. 399.

43. *New York Times*, September 29, 1950.

44. *New York Herald Tribune*, September 30, 1950.

45. *General Assembly Records*, First Committee, 347th Meeting, September 30, 1950, pp. 11–12.

46. *Ibid.*, Plenary Meeting, 294th Meeting, October 7, 1950, p. 232.

47. *Ibid.*, 350th Meeting, October 3, p. 32.

48. *Senate Hearings*, p. 340.

VI. WAKE ISLAND

1. *Senate Hearings*, pp. 3483–84.
2. *New York Times*, October 15, 1950.
3. Whitney, p. 387.
4. *New York Times*, October 21, 1950; Truman, II, 365.
5. Truman, II, 365–367; *Substance of statement made* . . .
6. *Senate Hearings*, p. 1115.
7. Truman, II, 367.
8. Whitney, p. 395.
9. See below, p. 111.
10. Whitney, p. 326.
11. *Senate Hearings*, p. 3490; Truman, II, 354.
12. *New York Times*, October 12, 1950 (italics mine).
13. *Senate Hearings*, pp. 3486–91.
14. *Ibid.*, p. 3486.
15. Truman, II, 362–363.
16. *New York Times*, October 11, 1950.
17. Truman, II, 363.
18. Whitney, pp. 340–341.
19. *New York Times*, October 10, 1950.
20. *Ibid.*, October 11, 1950.
21. *Ibid.*, October 20, 1950; Stone, *Hidden Story*, has also drawn attention to the relationship between the attack and the Wake Island meeting.
22. Whitney, p. 388.
23. *New York Times*, October 16, 1950.
24. "President's Speech at San Francisco upon His Return from Wake Island," *Senate Hearings*, p. 3490.

VII. THE "HOME BY CHRISTMAS" OFFENSIVE

1. *New York Times*, October 22, 1950. Baldwin's warning indicates that he was aware of the Central Intelligence Agency memorandum, dated October 20, which reported that the Chinese Communists would enter North Korea for the limited purpose of protecting the power plants along the Yalu. The State Department reaction to this memorandum was a suggestion that General MacArthur issue a statement declaring that he would not interfere with the operation of these installations. But both the Joint Chiefs and MacArthur rejected such an announcement as undesirable (Truman, II, 372; Whitney, pp. 401–402).
2. *New York Times*, October 26, 1950.
3. *Ibid.*, October 28, 1950.
4. *Ibid.*
5. *Ibid.*, October 31, 1950.
6. *Ibid.*, November 3, 1950.
7. *Ibid.*, November 4, 1950.
8. *Ibid.*
9. *Ibid.*, October 29, 1950.
10. *Ibid.*, November 1, 1950.
11. *Ibid.*, November 2, 1950.

12. Samuel L. A. Marshall, *The River and the Gauntlet* (New York: Morrow, 1953), pp. 14–16.

13. Truman, II, 373.

14. *Senate Hearings*, pp. 3492–93.

15. *New York Times*, November 6, 1950.

16. Truman, II, 377.

17. *New York Times*, November 8, 1950.

18. *Ibid.*, November 9, 1950.

19. *Ibid.*, November 8, 1950.

20. Text, *State Department Bulletin*, XXIII (November 27, 1950), 853.

21. *New York Times*, November 16, 1950.

22. *Ibid.*, November 17, 1950.

23. *Ibid.*, November 12, 1950.

24. *Ibid.*, November 21, 1950.

25. "Special Communiqué of General MacArthur, November 24, 1950," *Senate Hearings*, pp. 3491–92; Marguerite Higgins, *The War in Korea* (New York: Doubleday, 1951), pp. 174–175.

26. *Senate Hearings*, p. 19.

27. *Ibid.*, pp. 1216–17, 1230, 3193; Truman, II, 360.

28. Truman, II, 372; *Senate Hearings*, p. 1241.

29. *New York Times*, October 26, 1950.

30. *Ibid.*, October 27, 1950.

31. *Senate Hearings*, p. 1240.

32. *Ibid.*, p. 1241.

33. Whitney, pp. 413–414, 420–421; Willoughby, pp. 397–398.

34. *New York Times*, November 20, 1950.

35. *Senate Hearings*, p. 3492.

36. Whitney, p. 416.

37. *Ibid.*, pp. 417–418, and paraphrase, *Senate Hearings*, p. 1229.

38. Whitney, pp. 418–419; paraphrase, *Senate Hearings*, pp. 1229–30.

39. *New York Times*, November 25, 1950.

40. *Ibid.*, November 27, 1950.

41. *Ibid.*, November 30, 1950.

42. *Senate Hearings*, p. 3495 (italics mine).

43. *Ibid.*, p. 1369; General Marshall (p. 17) also pointed out that the Eighth Army "had no expectation that it would be strongly resisted."

44. *Ibid.*, pp. 1311, 1312.

45. *Ibid.*, pp. 1240–41, 1251, 1302.

46. *Ibid.*, pp. 1299–1302, 1231, 1312–13.

47. *Ibid.*, pp. 1337, 1312.

48. Whitney, pp. 411–412.

49. *Senate Hearings*, pp. 21, 29–30.

50. Whitney, pp. 418–419.

51. *Ibid.*, pp. 413–414; Willoughby, pp. 396–397.

52. *New York Times*, November 10, 1950.

53. Willoughby, p. 393.

54. *New York Herald Tribune*, December 6, 1950.

55. Willoughby, p. 388; Whitney, p. 413.

56. *New York Times*, November 26, 1950.

57. *Ibid.*, November 20, 1950.

58. *Ibid.*, November 28, 1950.

59. *New York Herald Tribune*, December 11, 1950; *Senate Hearings*, p. 972.

60. *New York Times*, November 30, 1950.

61. See below, Chapter VIII.

VIII. THE MacARTHUR-TAFT ALLIANCE

1. Sherman, *Senate Hearings*, p. 1628.

2. Truman, II, 391–393; Whitney, pp. 424–426.

3. *Senate Hearings*, pp. 47–48.

4. *Ibid.*, p. 1617.

5. *Ibid.*, pp. 429–430; paraphrase, pp. 2179–80.

6. Whitney, pp. 432–434; paraphrase, *Senate Hearings*, pp. 2180–81. The passages in italics will be discussed below, Chapters XII and XIII.

7. Whitney, pp. 434–435.

8. *Ibid.*, pp. 435–436.

9. *Senate Hearings*, pp. 1583, 882, 1119, 324–325.

10. Truman, II, 435–436; *Senate Hearings*, pp. 503–505.

11. *Senate Hearings*, pp. 324, 331–332, 735–738.

12. *Ibid.*, pp. 13, 247; Whitney, p. 462 (italics mine).

13. Whitney, p. 462; *Senate Hearings*, pp. 247–248.

14. *Senate Hearings*, p. 14; Marshall's denial, p. 332.

15. *Ibid.*, pp. 1189, 1210–11, 1220–21, 111, 1392.

16. Whitney, p. 439.

17. *Ibid.*, pp. 440–457.

18. *New York Herald Tribune*, December 6, 1950.

19. Kenney, pp. 240–241.

20. *Senate Hearings*, pp. 3491–95, 3532–35; Whitney, pp. 449–450.

21. Willoughby, p. 403.

22. Truman, II, 384.

23. *Senate Hearings*, p. 3536.

24. For a particularly illuminating analysis of the political atmosphere of 1950, see Goldman, *The Crucial Decade*, pp. 112–144.

25. *New York Times*, November 8, 9, 1950.

26. Council on Foreign Relations, *The United States in World Affairs, 1950*, ed. Richard C. Stebbins (New York: Harpers, 1951), pp. 411–413.

27. Samuel Lubell, "Is America Going Isolationist Again?" *Saturday Evening Post*, June 7, 1952.

28. *New York Times*, November 9, 1950.

29. *U.S. News and World Report*, XXIX (November 17, 1950), 26–27. In the same issue (pp. 28–33), Senators Nixon, Dirksen, and Milliken support Taft's views. Reston, *New York Times*, November 9, 1950.

30. White, pp. 173–174.

31. *Ibid.*, pp. 102–103.

32. Westerfield, pp. 372–373.

33. This certainly seems to have been the principal motivation of Senators Bridges and Knowland in exerting pressure upon the Eisenhower Administration for the release of the Yalta Papers prior to the 1954 election.

34. Elmer Davis, "Harry S. Truman and the Verdict of History," *Reporter*, February 3, 1953, p. 20. Walter Lippmann (*New York Herald*

Tribune, December 14, 1950) contends that the attacks upon Acheson were partly the fault of the President and the Secretary of State himself for not debating candidly and openly with Senator Knowland and his colleagues the issue of American interests in Asia. Messrs. Truman and Acheson "tried instead to smother the dispute by conceding bits and pieces here and there when the heat became too great, hoping somehow they could fob off the opposition without adopting its policy . . . the result was to infuriate and not to placate the opposition. Holding their conviction passionately, the attempt to deal with them cleverly rather than openly led enormous support to the false and malicious charges against Mr. Acheson and the State Department. The insincerity was not due to sinister and hidden influences. It was due to the fact that Mr. Truman . . . and Mr. Acheson . . . tried to play politics with a question of the highest national significance. They sought to deal with General MacArthur and Senator Knowland and the Republicans in Congress as if a great issue in foreign policy were like an appropriation or a tariff bill that could be compromised and logrolled . . . when the stakes are life and death the attempt to make a policy by the method of the pork barrel will lead to disaster abroad and disunity at home."

35. Douglas Southall Freeman's introduction to McGeorge Bundy, *The Pattern of Responsibility* (Boston: Houghton Mifflin, 1952), p. xx: "Any distortion of statement was permissible if it was directed against him; but if he did not spell out the last letter of the obvious in answer, there were mumblings about half-truths. He had to fight, so to say, with one hand tied behind him. The handicap of being a gentleman cost him at least one lap before he got underway."

36. Westerfield, pp. 327–329.

37. Reston, *New York Times*, November 9, 1950.

38. *Ibid.*, November 14, 1950.

39. *State Department Bulletin*, XXIII (November 27, 1950), 839.

40. *Congressional Record*, 82nd Cong., 1st Sess., pp. 58–59.

41. *Ibid.*, p. 94.

42. *Ibid.*, pp. 54–61; Taft, *A Foreign Policy*, pp. 99–100. Most of Taft's book is a compilation of speeches he delivered on the floor of the Senate.

43. *Ibid.*, pp. 91–92, 100–101.

44. *Ibid.*, pp. 101, 99. Herbert Hoover's views are collected in his *Addresses upon the American Road, 1950–1955* (Stanford: Stanford University Press, 1955), pp. 3–31.

The Administration's views are summed up in the excerpts from the testimony of Secretaries Acheson and Marshall and General Bradley, and these may be found in the *State Department Bulletin*, vol. XXIII, February 26, 1951. The ablest presentation was delivered by General Eisenhower in his reports to the Congress and the nation, *ibid.*, February 12 and 19, 1951; see also Bundy, pp. 82–100.

45. *Congressional Record*, 82nd Cong., 1st Sess., pp. 3254–82.

46. Jean Jacques Servan-Schreiber, *Reporter*, May 1, 1951, p. 14.

47. Taft, p. 112.

48. Speech of June 28, 1950, *Congressional Record*, 82nd Cong., 1st Sess., pp. 9319–23.

49. "Speech delivered to the Yale Club of New York City on April 12, 1951," *ibid.*, Appendix, p. 2031.

50. Taft, p. 107.

51. *Ibid.,* pp. 108–109.

52. John Ballantine, *Formosa* (Washington: Brookings Institute, 1952), pp. 128–129.

53. *Senate Hearings,* p. 903.

54. *Ibid.,* pp. 1934–35, 1728–29, 3204–10, 1755, 351, 470–471, 531.

55. Rusk's speech is reprinted, *ibid.,* pp. 3191–92.

IX. THE ALLIES SEEK PEACE

1. *New York Times,* December 1, 1950; Truman, II, 395–396.

2. *H. C. Deb.,* Fifth Series, vol. 481, col. 1439.

3. *The Times* (London), December 4, 1950.

4. Attlee actually also represented the Commonwealth, particularly India, *H. C. Deb.,* vol. 481, cols. 1353, 1361; vol. 482, cols. 1456–57. Leon D. Epstein, *Britain — Uneasy Ally* (Chicago: Chicago University Press, 1954, pp. 206–207.

5. *Ibid.* p. 235; Bevin, *H. C. Deb,* vol. 482, col. 1458; editorial, *The Times,* December 1, 1950.

6. *H. C. Deb.,* vol. 481, cols. 1335–36. The editorial in *The Times,* December 1, 1950, expressed its belief that not since the most critical days of World War II had Churchill so ably and fully reflected British opinion.

7. *H. C. Deb.,* vol. 481, foreign policy debate of November 29 and 30, 1950, cols. 1162–1277, 1330–1440; vol. 482, debate of December 14, 1950, cols. 1350–1463.

8. Under Secretary of State for Foreign Affairs, *ibid.,* vol. 481, col. 1357; Attlee, vol. 482, col. 1353.

9. Bevin, *ibid.,* vol. 481, col. 1167.

10. *Ibid.*

11. For the British point of view during the Truman-Attlee conference, Truman, II, 394–413.

12. *Economist,* CLIX (July 22, 1950), p. 153; Attlee, *H. C. Deb.,* vol. 476, col. 2160.

13. Paton of Norwich, *ibid.,* vol. 482, cols. 1419–20.

14. *Ibid.,* cols. 1364–65; vol. 481, cols. 1335–36.

15. Mikardo, *ibid.,* col. 1257; *New Statesman and Nation,* XL (December 2, 9, 16, 1950); Epstein, p. 218.

16. Epstein, pp. 219–220.

17. *Senate Hearings,* pp. 51, 122.

18. Royal Institute of International Affairs, *Documents of International Affairs, 1951* (London: Oxford University Press, 1954), pp. 564–570; Schlesinger and Rovere, pp. 222–223n.

19. *New York Times,* June 30, 1950.

20. *Ibid.,* August 14, 1950. In General, Nehru thought that the West's approach was too militaristic, and too preoccupied with the problem of Communism, which he said was a "trivial question" against the background of Asia in general (October 4, 1950).

21. *State Department Bulletin,* XXIII (July 31, 1950), 170–171.

22. *Ibid.*

23. *Ibid.*

24. *General Assembly Records,* Plenary Meetings, vol. I, 324th Meet-

ing, December 14, 1950, p. 660. Nationalist China abstained, *State Department Bulletin*, XXIII (December 25, 1950), 1005.

25. Annex I to the "Report to the General Assembly from Group on Cease-Fire in Korea, January 2, 1951," *Senate Hearings*, pp. 3509–13.

26. *New York Times*, January 13, 1951.

27. *General Assembly Records*, First Committee, Summary Records of Meeting, vol. II, 424th Meeting, January 13, 1951, p. 475.

28. *New York Times*, January 13, 1951.

29. *Senate Hearings*, pp. 1967–68.

30. *State Department Bulletin*, XXIV (January 29, 1951), 165–166.

31. *Ibid.*, p. 164.

32. *General Assembly Records*, 426th Meeting, January 18, 1951, pp. 523–524.

33. *Ibid.*, 429th Meeting, January 22, 1951, p. 525.

34. *Ibid.*, 431st Meeting, January 25, 1951, pp. 544–545.

X. CHINA'S CONDEMNATION AND MacARTHUR'S DISMISSAL

1. Truman, II, 398–417.

2. *State Department Bulletin*, XXIII (December 15, 1950), 963.

3. Truman, II, 403.

4. *Ibid.*, pp. 382–383; see below, Chapter XII.

5. *Ibid.*, p. 403.

6. *Ibid.*, pp. 420–421.

7. *Ibid.*, p. 421.

8. "The President's Communiqué of December 8, 1950, Regarding his Conference with Prime Minister Attlee," *Senate Hearings*, p. 3503.

9. Acheson, *ibid.*, p. 1719; see below, Chapter XII.

10. *State Department Bulletin*, XXIV (May 14, 1951), 765 (italics mine).

11. *Senate Hearings*, pp. 2006, 1783–84.

12. Truman, II, 398, 403, 404, 407–408.

13. *Senate Hearings*, pp. 3510–11.

14. *General Assembly Records*, First Committee, 432nd Meeting, January 26, 1951, p. 559.

15. "Resolution of General Assembly of United Nations Declaring Communist Government of China as Aggressor," *Senate Hearings*, pp. 3513–14.

16. *H. C. Debs.*, vol. 483, col. 41.

17. *General Assembly Records*, First Committee, 453rd Meeting, January 27, 1951, pp. 569–570.

18. *Ibid.*, Plenary Meeting, February 1, 1951, p. 692.

19. Whitney, p. 462.

20. "Statement of General MacArthur, February 13, 1951," *Senate Hearings*, pp. 3539–40.

21. Whitney, p. 461.

22. *Senate Hearings*, p. 77.

23. *Ibid.*, pp. 1790–92; Truman, II, 438, 440.

24. Truman, II, 438–439; *Senate Hearings*, p. 1193, 343.

25. Truman, II, 439–440.

26. *Ibid.*, pp. 440–441; "Statement of General MacArthur, March 24, 1951," *Senate Hearings*, pp. 3541–42.

27. *Senate Hearings,* pp. 69–71, 285, 72.

28. MacArthur's address to the American Legion, *New York Times,* October 18, 1951. Frazier Hunt, *The Untold Story of Douglas MacArthur* (New York: Devin-Adair, 1954), pp. 507–509: "It was obvious [from the Joint Chiefs' message] that a big sell out was about to take place . . . this was his last chance to help check a political move that might well be disastrous to both Korea and America . . . he was cutting squarely across what was probably a devious and far-fetched plan by the U.N. for an appeasement settlement . . . Certainly [he] forestalled any half-way measure for appeasement . . ." Whitney, pp. 467–468, agrees that such a plot was "definitely a fact."

29. Reston, *New York Times,* May 9, 1950.

30. Hunt, pp. 507–508: "The Eighth Army, with its air arm still tied behind its back, was advancing and ready to cross the 38th parallel. He might still press for a conclusion of the war, despite the intrigues of Washington and in the General Assembly of the U.N."

31. *Senate Hearings,* pp. 3193–94.

32. *Ibid.,* pp. 3543–44; Whitney, pp. 463–464; Truman, II, 445–446.

33. *Senate Hearings,* p. 113.

34. *Ibid.,* pp. 380, 1336.

35. Truman, II, 444, 442.

36. "After MacArthur," *Economist,* April 14, 1951, p. 843.

37. Both these points are covered by Bradley, *Senate Hearings,* pp. 878–879; Truman, II, 442–445.

38. Quoted in *The Observer* (London), April 8, 1951.

39. *Senate Hearings,* pp. 1774–75, 989–990, 325, 344, 349, 376–377.

40. *Ibid.,* p. 325, 878.

41. *Ibid.,* pp. 1789.

XI. *MacARTHUR RETURNS*

1. *New York Times,* April 12, 1951.

2. *Ibid.*

3. *Senate Hearings,* p. 3298.

4. Schlesinger and Rovere, pp. 8–9.

5. *New York Times,* April 21, 1951.

6. *Ibid.,* April 12, 1951.

7. *Ibid.,* April 13, 1951.

8. *Ibid.,* April 16, 1951.

9. *Ibid.,* April 17, 1951.

10. *Ibid.,* April 18, 1951.

11. *Ibid.,* April 19, 1951.

12. *Ibid.,* April 18, 1951.

13. *Ibid.,* April 19, 1951.

14. *Ibid.*

15. *Ibid.,* April 20, 1951; the speech may also be found in *Senate Hearings,* pp. 2553–58.

16. *New York Times,* April 20, 1951.

17. Address to the Harvard Club of Boston, State Department Press Release 377, June 3, 1946.

18. Samuel Lubell, *The Future of American Politics* (New York: Doubleday Anchor, 1956), p. 166.

19. *New York Times*, May 6, 1951.

20. *Congressional Record*, 82nd Cong., 1st Sess., p. 4129.

21. *New York Herald Tribune*, April 27, 1951.

22. Goldman, pp. 209–210.

XII. THE GENERAL'S PROSECUTION

1. *Senate Hearings*, pp. 1–3.

2. *Ibid.*, pp. 39–40, 67–68, 3557.

3. *Ibid.*, pp. 30, 39, 67, 82.

4. *Ibid.*, pp. 30, 68, 13, 49, 10, 207, 3557.

5. *Ibid.*, pp. 13, 48.

6. *Ibid.*, p. 81.

7. *Ibid.*, pp. 42–43, 58, 136–137.

8. *Ibid.*, p. 211, 258.

9. *Ibid.*, pp. 9, 69, 130, 131, 250.

10. Whitney, pp. 536–537, 512, quotes the Alsop column of June 13, 1954, with relish: " . . . MacArthur was right in feeling as he obviously did that the time of Chinese intervention in Korea was the right time for a showdown in the world struggle between the Soviet and the free halves of the world. In the simplest terms, the United States already possessed decisive air-atomic striking power, while the Soviet air-atomic power was still virtually nil in 1950–51. The Communist enemy had then proved his aggressive intentions. Our one major weapon then had its fullest value. That value was already being impaired by the Soviet air-atomic build-up. Logic demanded a showdown without further delay." Hunt writes on p. 497: "To MacArthur . . . it was abundantly clear that Russia needed several more years to build her long-range bomber planes and stockpile her atomic bombs."

11. *Senate Hearings*, pp. 6–8.

12. *Ibid.*, pp. 75–76, 80, 83, 120.

13. *Ibid.*, pp. 217, 80, 291.

14. *Ibid.*, pp. 80, 12, 75–76.

15. *Ibid.*, p. 221.

16. "MacArthur's Message to Hugh Baillie, December 1, 1950," *ibid.*, p. 3535.

17. *Ibid.*, pp. 42, 111.

18. *Ibid.*, p. 297; Whitney, pp. 545–546.

19. *Ibid.*, pp. 428–429; John Gunther, *The Riddle of MacArthur* (New York: Harper, 1950), pp. 55–56.

20. See below, Chapter XIV.

21. *Senate Hearings*, pp. 19, 167; Whitney, p. 418.

22. Whitney, pp. 410, 431, 433, 537; *Senate Hearings*, p. 3555.

23. Whitney, p. 509.

24. *Senate Hearings*, p. 100.

25. Schlesinger and Rovere, pp. 224–226.

26. Speech in Seattle, *New York Times*, November 14, 1951; Whitney, p. 496.

27. *Senate Hearings*, p. 3553.

28. Whitney, p. 307; speech in Seattle, *New York Times*, November 14, 1951.

29. Charles de Gaulle, *Le Fil de l'épée* (Paris, 1946), pp. 46–47, quoted by Alexander Werth, *France, 1940–1955* (New York: Holt, 1956), p. 206.

30. Speech in Seattle, *New York Times*, November 14, 1951.

31. Address to the Massachusetts legislature, *New York Times*, July 26, 1951.

32. *Senate Hearings*, pp. 389, 1194, 1283.

33. *Ibid.*, pp. 18–19.

34. *Ibid.*, p. 3558.

35. *Ibid.*, p. 102.

36. *Ibid.*, p. 13.

37. *Ibid.*, p. 105.

XIII. THE ADMINISTRATION'S DEFENSE

1. *Senate Hearings*, p. 30.

2. *Ibid.*, pp. 325, 351, 354.

3. *Ibid.*, pp. 1378, 1402, 744, 887, 943.

4. *Ibid.*, pp. 1398, 1399, 1379, 1385, 1393.

5. *Ibid.*, pp. 887, 744, 507.

6. *Ibid.*, pp. 1386, 884.

7. *Ibid.*, pp. 1512–13.

8. *Ibid.*

9. *Ibid.*, pp. 1525, 1518, 1521, 1189.

10. *Ibid.*, pp. 1514, 1517, 742.

11. *Ibid.*, pp. 1523, 1570, 1514, 882.

12. *Ibid.*, pp. 1515–16.

13. *Ibid.*, pp. 1726–27.

14. *Ibid.*, p. 1219.

15. *Ibid.*, p. 745.

16. *Ibid.*, pp. 882–883.

17. *Ibid.*, pp. 619, 337, 673–674, 742, 886, 903.

18. *Ibid.*, pp. 1584, 1620.

19. *Ibid.*, pp. 731–732, 1219.

20. *Ibid.*, pp. 1719, 741, 751.

21. *Ibid.*, p. 1719.

22. *Ibid.*, pp. 1212, 1188, 1218, 732, 742, 745, 883–884, 896.

23. *Ibid.*, pp. 360, 743, 1002–03, 1588.

24. *Ibid.*, p. 733.

25. *Ibid.*, pp. 1716–17.

26. *Ibid.*, pp. 365–366, 731.

27. *Ibid.*, p. 366.

28. *Ibid.*, pp. 751, 892.

29. *Ibid.*, p. 1786.

30. *Ibid.*, p. 955.

31. *Ibid.*, pp. 1053–54.

32. *Ibid.*, pp. 1717–18.

33. Kennan, pp. 127–128.

34. *Senate Hearings*, p. 2083.

XIV. *TRUMAN VERSUS MacARTHUR*

1. Kennan, p. 118.
2. Truman, II, 345, 420–421.
3. *Ibid.*, p. 456; *Senate Hearings,* pp. 731–732.
4. *Ibid.*, pp. 1763–64.
5. "Text of MacArthur's Statement in Reply to Charges Made by Truman in His Memoirs," *New York Times,* February 9, 1956. Although this passage was written almost five years after MacArthur's dismissal, his point of view here is no different from that voiced during the Korean War.
6. Whitney, pp. 545–546. Kennan arrived at the same conclusions, pp. 99–100.
7. During the last fifty years, British and American interests in the Far East have rarely been identical, often in conflict. Britain's principal efforts in the twentieth century have been exerted against European powers — first Germany, then Russia — who have attempted to upset the European balance of power; after that, her main efforts have been directed to the defense of India. While the United States has approached the Orient through China, Britain has approached it through India. This has led to fifty years of Anglo-American conflict in the Far East, for to protect India against Japan, Britain has always been willing to make concessions at China's expense. For instance, in the Anglo-Japanese alliance of 1904 against Russia, Britain managed to divert Japanese pressure away from India to China; by thus concentrating Japan's expansionist drive to China, more specifically Manchuria, Britain also forced Russia to lessen its pressure on India in order to counter Japan's growing strength in Manchuria and Northern China. This British policy, dictated by British interests and not by any so-called "immorality," was in complete opposition to the American Open-Door policy which was aimed at preserving China's territorial integrity and political independence (on this policy, see also above, Chapter III).
8. *New York Herald Tribune,* August 24, 1956.
9. *Ibid.*, April 30, 1951.
10. Smith, *American Democracy and Military Power,* pp. 8–9.
11. Burton M. Sapin, and Richard C. Snyder, *The Role of the Military in American Foreign Policy* (New York: Doubleday, 1954), p. 57.
12. *Interlocking Subversion in Government Departments.* Hearings before Subcommittee to Investigate the Administration of the Internal Security Act and Other Internal Security Laws of the Committee on the Judiciary, United States Senate, 83rd Cong., 1st Sess. (Washington: Government Printing Office, 1954); among other articles written by Van Fleet and Mark Clark, see the characteristically entitled "You Can't Win if Diplomats Interfere," *U.S. News,* August 20, 1954.
13. Huntington, p. 177.
14. Osgood, p. 45.
15. Clausewitz, pp. 599, 601; for the progress being made in the education of the military, see John W. Masland, and Laurence Radway, *Soldiers and Scholars* (Princeton: Princeton University Press, 1957).

CRITICAL BIBLIOGRAPHY

This bibliography is not meant to be exhaustive, and includes only those books, pamphlets, and articles which the author found useful.

PRINTED SOURCES
Official Documents

UNITED STATES

Congress. *Congressional Record.*

———— *Institute of Pacific Relations.* Hearings before the Subcommittee to investigate the Administration of the Internal Security Act and Other Internal Security Laws of the Committee of the Judiciary, United States Senate, 82nd Congress, 1st Session. Washington: Government Printing Office, 1951–52.

———— *Interlocking Subversion in Government Departments.* Hearings before the same subcommittee, 83rd Congress, 1st Session. Washington: Government Printing Office, 1954–55. Generals Van Fleet, Clark, Almond, Joy, and Stratemeyer all confess their belief that the Korean War was "lost" because the politicians in Washington — often referred to as "appeasers" — handcuffed the military.

———— *Military Situation in the Far East.* Hearings before the Armed Services Committee and Foreign Relations Committee, United States Senate, 82nd Congress, 1st Session. Washington: Government Printing Office, 1951. These five volumes are indispensable. Though both Truman and Whitney in their respective volumes elaborate on certain facts of the war and quote in greater detail the paraphrased communications between Toyko and Washington included here, little has been added on the basic issues of the war and outline of the campaign since these hearings were held.

———— *Substance of Statements made at Wake Island Conference on October 15, 1950, compiled from notes kept by the conferees from Washington.* (Compilation by General Bradley.) Washington: Government Printing Office, 1951.

———— *The United States and the Korean Problem, Documents, 1943–1953.* Washington: Government Printing Office, 1953.

Department of State. *State Department Bulletin.*

———— *United States Policy in the Korean Crisis.* Washington: Government Printing Office, 1950. Review of the crisis in June 1950.

———— *United States Policy in the Korean Conflict.* Washington: Government Printing Office, 1951. Review of the first six months of fighting.

———— *United States Relations with China, 1944–1949.* Washington: Government Printing Office, 1949. The State Department's justification of its claim that the fall of Chiang was his own doing and could not have been prevented by this country.

GREAT BRITAIN

Parliament. *Debates. House of Commons.*

UNITED NATIONS
Official Records of the General Assembly.
Official Records of the Security Council.
United Nations Bulletin.
Yearbook of the United Nations, 1950.
Yearbook of the United Nations, 1951.

Unofficial Collections of Documents

Royal Institute of International Affairs. *Documents of International Affairs, 1949–50.* London: Oxford University Press, 1953.
———— *Documents of International Affairs, 1951.* London: Oxford University Press, 1954.

NEWSPAPERS AND PERIODICALS

American: *Newsweek, New Yorker* (Richard Rovere's letters from Washington), *New York Herald Tribune, New York Times, Reporter, Time, U.S. News.* British: *Economist, Manchester Guardian Weekly, New Statesman and Nation, The Times* (London).

BOOKS AND ARTICLES

Adler, Selig. *The Isolationist Impulse.* New York: Abelard-Schuman, 1958. A history of a long impulse.
Allen, H. C. *Great Britain and the United States: A History of Anglo-American Relations, 1783–1952.* New York: St. Martin, 1955. A short analysis of the Korean War crediting the Administration for its courage in meeting the threats posed by the North Koreans and MacArthur. Critical of American policy toward Communist China.
Almond, Gabriel. *The American People and Foreign Policy.* New York: Harcourt Brace, 1950. A superb study of the relationship of public opinion to foreign policy. Almond concludes that the American people are not deeply concerned with the world's problems, and that their reaction to discussions of foreign policy has neither depth nor structure.
Armstrong, John P. "The Enigma of Senator Taft and American Foreign Policy." *Review of Politics,* vol. XVII, April 1955. A definitive analysis of the domestic basis of Taft's approach to foreign policy.
Ballantine, John. *Formosa.* Washington: Brookings Institute, 1952. A valuable analysis of American policy since 1949 toward the Nationalist regime on the island.
Bell, Coral. "Korea and the Balance of Power." *Political Quarterly,* vol. XXV, no. 1, January-March 1954. A fine analysis of United States–USSR tug of war over Korea, including some realistic words about the role of the United Nations.
Berger, Carl. *The Korean Knot.* Philadelphia: University of Pennsylvania Press, 1957. Useful introduction to post-World War II Korea.
Brogan, Denis W. "The Illusion of American Omnipotence." *Harper's Magazine,* December 1952. Brogan relates how, when American policy is not successful, this illusion gives rise to the hunt for those who allegedly betrayed American interests through incompetence or disloyalty.
Bundy, McGeorge. *The Pattern of Responsibility.* Boston: Houghton Mifflin, 1952. A convenient collection of Secretary Acheson's major pro-

nouncements on various aspects of American foreign policy including China, Formosa, and Korea.

Cheever, Daniel S., and H. Field Haviland. *American Foreign Policy and the Separation of Powers*. Cambridge: Harvard University Press, 1952. In their balanced treatment the authors conclude that the separation of powers is not an insuperable barrier hindering the conduct of foreign relations.

Clark, Mark. *From the Danube to the Yalu*. New York: Harper, 1954. Includes the former Far Eastern Commander's criticisms of American policy in the Far East.

———— "You Can't Win a War if Diplomats Interfere." *U.S. News*, August 20, 1954. Title suggests content.

Claude, Inis. *Swords into Ploughshares*. New York: Random House, 1956. This is the best book yet available on the United Nations. It analyzes critically, yet temperately, the theoretical assumptions underlying both the various organs of the world organization and the purposes to which they are dedicated, such as collective security.

Clausewitz, Karl von. *On War*. Modern Library ed. New York: Random House, 1943. O. J. Matthijis Jolles' translation of the soldier's bible.

Cottrell, Alvin J. and James E. Daugherty. "The Lessons of Korea." *Orbis*, Spring 1958. Argues that MacArthur's strategic ideas were sound.

Council on Foreign Relations. *The United States in World Affairs, 1950*. Edited by Richard C. Stebbins. New York: Harper, 1951. A very competent review and analysis of the major diplomatic events of the year.

———— *The United States in World Affairs, 1951*. New York: Harper, 1952. Same as above.

Crabb, Cecil V., Jr. *Bipartisan Foreign Policy: Myth or Reality*. Evanston: Row and Peterson, 1958. This is a first-rate analysis of the nature of bipartisanship, the conditions for its operation, and its advantages and disadvantages. In emphasizing the latter, Crabb has rendered a major service, since too many writers in the past have assumed that bipartisanship is good, and criticism of official policy is bad.

Davis, Elmer. "Harry S. Truman and the Verdict of History," *Reporter*, February 3, 1953. A favorable verdict on foreign policy.

Dean, William P. *General Dean's Story*. New York: Viking, 1954. Includes a short account of the military actions prior to Dean's capture.

Department of the Army, *Korea — 1950*. Washington: Government Printing Office, 1952. Briefly records, by text and photographs, the first six months of the war.

DeWeerd, H. "Lessons of the Korean War." *Yale Review*, Summer 1951. Concentrates on the military lessons.

Dille, John. *Substitute for Victory*. New York: Doubleday, 1954. An able presentation of the Administration's conduct of the war by *Life's* correspondent.

Dupuy, Ernest R. and Trever N. Dupuy. *The Military Heritage of America*. New York: McGraw-Hill, 1956. Obviously pro-MacArthur.

Elliott, William Y., and Study Group. *United States Foreign Policy*. New York: Columbia University Press, 1952. An analysis of the obstacles hampering the President's conduct of foreign affairs. Elliott believes these difficulties can only be resolved by fundamental reforms of the American political structure; other members of the group disagree.

Epstein, Leon D. *Britain — Uneasy Ally*. Chicago: Chicago University Press,

1954. An excellent analysis on two levels — national and party — of British responses to American foreign policies in the postwar era.

Fairbank, John K. *The United States and China.* Cambridge: Harvard University Press, 1958. A new edition of this standard work, which includes an analysis of Chiang Kai-shek's collapse.

Feis, Herbert. *China Tangle.* Princeton: Princeton University Press, 1953. An excellent historical analysis of American diplomacy toward China during World War II and the immediate postwar period.

Finletter, Thomas K. *Power and Policy.* New York: Harcourt Brace, 1954. The first major effort to discuss military strategy and political policy in the Atomic Age. Finletter places the major emphasis on strategic air power.

Fischer, John. *Master-Plan, U.S.A.* New York: Harper, 1951. A very able and wittily written presentation of the containment policy and its application in various parts of the world.

Fitzsimons, M. A. *The Foreign Policy of the British Labour Government, 1945–51.* Notre Dame: Notre Dame University Press, 1953. Four pages on Korea.

George, Alexander L. "American Policy-making and the North Korean Aggression." *World Politics,* January 1955. The best analysis yet of the American reaction to North Korea's attack.

Goldman, Eric. *The Crucial Decade.* New York: Harper, 1956. A review and commentary upon the past decade, during which Goldman believes the American people committed themselves irrevocably to the welfare state at home and an active policy abroad. Particularly good for its ability to recapture the flavor of domestic politics during the 1949–1951 period.

Goodrich, Leland M. "Collective Measures against Aggression." *International Conciliation,* October 1953. A United Nations approach to the war: the UN response to North Korean and Communist Chinese aggression, the UN organization and the direction of collective measures, and the UN restoration of peace.

———— *Korea: A Study of U.S. Policy in the U.N.* New York: Council on Foreign Relations, 1956. A much expanded version of the above pamphlet.

Graebner, Norman. *The New Isolationism.* New York: Ronald, 1956. Professor Graebner, taking his interpretation from Arthur Schlesinger, Jr., sees the last five years of American foreign policy as an expression of neo-isolationism, that is, dictated by an extreme concern for a balanced budget, emphasis on air and sea power, disregard for allies, and overconcentration upon a much exaggerated internal Communist threat. A rather oversimplified view, although Graebner does give an interesting analysis of the Republican opposition during the years 1950–1952.

Grey, Arthur L., Jr. "The Thirty-Eighth Parallel." *Foreign Affairs,* April 1951.

Gunther, John. *The Riddle of MacArthur.* New York: Harper, 1951. Gunther attempts to solve the riddle, on the whole successfully. Focuses upon the occupation of Japan.

Haas, Ernst B. "Types of Collective Security: An Examination of Operational Concepts." *American Political Science Review,* March 1955. Haas does a first-class job in relating the concept of collective security to a world of Russo-American conflict and growing Arab-Asian influence.

Hartmann, Frederick H. "The Issues in Korea." *Yale Review,* Fall 1952. An analysis of the alternative courses in Korea in 1951: evacuation, extension of the war, or division of Korea. Hartmann favors the latter course (see also the chapter on Korea in his textbook, *The Relations of Nations,* New York: Macmillan, 1957).

Hillmann, William. *Mr. President.* New York: Farrar, Straus and Young, 1952. A collection of President Truman's personal diary, letters, and principal interviews.

Hoover, Herbert. *Addresses upon the American Road, 1950–55.* Stanford: Stanford University Press, 1955. A convenient collection of Hoover's main pronouncements on American foreign policy.

Huntington, Samuel P. *The Soldier and the State.* Cambridge, Harvard University Press, 1957. This is a very fine book. Provocative in its analysis and beautifully written, its principal value is that it points out that the problems of civil-military relations and effective foreign policies are not primarily a question of institutional arrangements and organizational structures, but fundamentally a question of the values of American society. While Huntington's criticisms of American liberalism are not original with him, his application of these criticisms to the problem of civil-military relations is.

Hunt, Frazier. *The Untold Story of MacArthur.* New York: Devin-Adair, 1954. Nothing that had been untold is included in this polemic.

Jones, Joseph M. *The Fifteen Weeks.* New York: Viking, 1955. An exciting account of the formulation of the containment policy in early 1947.

Joy, C. Turner. *How Communists Negotiate.* New York: Macmillan, 1955. Description of Communist negotiating techniques by the principal allied negotiator.

Kelley, Frank, and Cornelius Ryan. *MacArthur: Man of Action.* New York: Doubleday, 1950. A short admiring biography.

Kennan, George F. *American Diplomacy, 1900–1950.* Chicago: Chicago University Press, 1951. A criticism of American diplomacy for its moral-legalistic framework, which Kennan believes leads most American policy-makers to see the world in terms of black and white, to pursue total objectives, and to subordinate political aims to military victory.

——— *The Realities of American Foreign Policy.* Princeton: Princeton University Press, 1954. Here Kennan, who was reportedly opposed to crossing the 38th Parallel, includes a trenchant criticism of the concept of forceful "liberation."

Kenney, George C. *The MacArthur I Know.* New York: Duell, Sloan and Pearce, 1951. Kenney greatly admires MacArthur, but is not completely uncritical. He brings out particularly well the human side of MacArthur's allegedly cold and aloof personality.

Kissinger, Henry A. *Nuclear Weapons and Foreign Policy.* New York: Harper, 1957. This is *the* major work in the field of military strategy since the end of World War II. It presents a sharply written and withering criticism of American military policy and its almost exclusive reliance on strategic air power. Kissinger offers in the concept of limited war an alternative to the horrible dilemma inherent in a strategy of "massive retaliation": self-destruction (if it is used) or surrender (if it is not). In proposing a more flexible military policy and ending the present divorce between political and military strategy, Kissinger recognizes that one of the basic problems is American liberal philosophy with its penchant for either total abstinence from power politics or total war to destroy its opponent completely.

Lawrence, William. "Truman — Portrait of a Stubborn Man." *New York Times Magazine*, April 22, 1951. Title suggests content.

Lee, Clark G., and Richard Henschel. *Douglas MacArthur*. New York: Holt, 1952. An uncritical and admiring biography.

Levi, Werner. *Modern China's Foreign Policy*. Minneapolis: University of Minnesota Press, 1953. Levi includes a short account of the Chinese "Hate America" campaign just prior to Peking's intervention in Korea.

Lie, Trygve. *In the Cause of Peace*. New York: Macmillan, 1955. Lie recounts his own part in the decision to fight in Korea, as well as his part in the negotiations with the Chinese Communists in the fall of 1950.

Liu, F. F. *A Military History of Modern China, 1924–1949*. Princeton, Princeton University Press, 1956. A former Nationalist officer discusses in the later phases of his book the poor organization and incompetent leadership of Chiang Kai-shek's army during the postwar period.

Lubell, Samuel. *The Future of American Politics*. New York: Harper, 1952 (Doubleday Anchor, 1956). An outstanding analysis of the changing pattern of American politics, particularly of the "myth of isolationism."

——— "Is America Going Isolationist Again?" *Saturday Evening Post*, June 7, 1952. The answer is "no," although there were forces at work in American society which limited the scope and energy of American global participation during the period of the Korean War.

——— *Revolt of the Moderates*. New York: Harper, 1956. Includes a fascinating comparison of the two "politicians of revenge," Anuerin Bevan and Joseph McCarthy.

MacArthur, Douglas. "Text of MacArthur's Statement in Reply to Charges Made by Truman in His Memoirs." *New York Times*, February 9, 1956.

Marshall, Samuel L. A. "A New Strategy for Korea." *Reporter*, March 3, 1953. A recipe for breaking the stalemate.

——— "Our Mistakes in Korea." *Atlantic*, September 1953. Rather vague.

——— *The River and the Gauntlet*. New York: Morrow, 1953. A beautifully told tale of individual heroism in the face of the Chinese offensive of late November 1950. Includes a valuable presentation of the campaign just prior to this full-scale strike.

Martin, Andrew. *Collective Security*. Paris: Kleber, 1952. An excellent analysis of collective security under both the League of Nations and the United Nations.

Masland, John W. and Laurence I. Radway. *Soldiers and Scholars*. Princeton: Princeton University Press, 1957. An excellent presentation and analysis of the soldier's education for his professional duties and higher political and military responsibilities.

McCune, George M. *Korea Today*. Cambridge: Harvard University Press, 1950. Very good reviews of American and Soviet occupation policies in their respective zones.

Military History Section of Eighth United States Army. *A Short (Unofficial) History of the Eighth United States Army, 1944–1954*. (No place, no date.) Concerns itself, despite its title, almost completely with the military operations during the Korean War. Brings out clearly that the Chinese Communist offensive in late November 1950 struck between Eighth Army and X Corps. Maps.

Millis, Walter, ed. *Forrestal Diaries*. New York: Viking, 1951. Contains MacArthur's view on Asia's future role in history, as well as Kennan's famous telegram forecasting the containment policy.

Norman, John. "MacArthur's Blockade Proposals Against Red China." *Pacific Historical Review*, May 1957. Cites Administration witnesses on the proposals' ineffectiveness.

Oliver, Robert T. *Syngman Rhee, the Man Behind the Myth*. New York: Dodd, Mead, 1954. An admiring biography by a close friend.

———— *Verdict in Korea.* State College, Pennsylvania: Bald Eagle, 1952. An unfavorable verdict.

———— *Why War Came to Korea*. New York: Fordham University Press, 1950. The principal reason: Secretary Acheson's failure to include South Korea within the American defense perimeter.

Osgood, Robert E. *Limited War*. Chicago: University of Chicago Press, 1957. Osgood's excellent and well-written book presents, like Kissinger's, a serious criticism of American military strategy and its underlying basis in American liberalism. Osgood also makes two other notable contributions: (1) he analyzes the political, social, and technological conditions which have caused the breakdown of the limited wars of an earlier age into the destructive total wars of the twentieth century; and (2) he analyzes American military policy and the role it has played in the diplomacy of the last decade.

Panikkar, K. M. *In Two Chinas*. London: Allen and Unwin, 1956. The anti-American and pro–Communist Chinese Indian ambassador's recapitulation of his views and activities in Peking during the Korean war.

Parrott, Lindesay. "MacArthur — Study in Black and White." *New York Times Magazine*, April 22, 1951. Title suggests content.

Pelling, Henry. *America and the British Left: from Bright to Bevan*. London: Black, 1956. "A Series of studies of particular controversies in British politics which throw light on the contemporary view of America." Brief on post-Roosevelt era, because of Epstein's excellent analysis of this period.

Poats, Rutherford M. *Decision in Korea*. New York: McBride, 1954. Not particularly valuable.

Reitzel, William, *et al. United States Foreign Policy, 1945–55*. Washington: Brookings Institute, 1956. The purpose of this analysis is "to try to capture the key decisions that were made and the grounds on which one course of action rather than another was chosen."

Ridgeway, Matthew B. *A Soldier's Story*. New York: Harper, 1956. General Ridgeway tells of his rally of the Eighth Army and halting of the Chinese Communist offensives.

Roper, Elmo. *You and Your Leaders*. New York: Morrow, 1957. The subtitle of the book, "Their Acts and Your Reactions," sums up this book neatly. Includes chapters on Truman, MacArthur, and Taft.

Rostow, Walter W. *Prospects of Communist China*. Cambridge: The Technology Press, and New York: Wiley, 1954. Rostow analyzes briefly possible reasons for Communist China's intervention in Korea.

Royal Institute of International Affairs. *Survey of International Affairs,*

1949–50. London: Oxford University Press, 1953. This extremely able area-by-area review of international affairs is probably the best one published.

——— *Survey of International Affairs, 1951.* London: Oxford University Press, 1954. Same as above.

Schlesinger, Arthur M., Jr. "The New Isolationism." *Atlantic,* May 1952. Schlesinger defines what he believes to be the leading characteristics of the "new isolationists," such as Senator Taft — actually "old isolationists" in a new garb.

Schlesinger, Arthur M., Jr., and Richard Rovere. *The General and the President.* New York: Farrar, Straus and Young, 1951. After a speedy review of MacArthur's personality and career, a critical account of the clashes between the President and his field commander. The authors, who wrote this book rather hurriedly, skip vital stages of the Korean War rather lightly. Written with a lively sense of irony, the book is a pleasure to read, even if it is rather one-sided.

Smith, Beverley. "The White House Story: Why We Went to War in Korea." *Saturday Evening Post,* November 10, 1950. An amazingly accurate account written shortly after the event.

Smith, Louis, *American Democracy and Military Power.* Chicago: University of Chicago Press, 1951. Smith discusses the means for maintaining civilian control in rather formal — constitutional and institutional — terms.

Snyder, Richard C., and Burton M. Sapin. *The Role of the Military in American Foreign Policy.* New York: Doubleday, 1954. A very able analysis of the "appropriate role for the military in foreign policy, given democratic values and the necessity for military advice and competence in the preservation of national security."

Stone, Izidore F. *The Hidden Story of the Korean War.* New York: Monthly Review, 1952. Stone maintains that MacArthur, Dulles, Chiang, and Rhee provoked the Korean War without the awareness of Truman or Acheson; and after it had started, the latter could not make peace, because peace spells unemployment, even depression, and thus a Democratic defeat at the polls. What makes this book so fascinating is that Stone attempts to prove these untenable theses by quoting only from the *New York Times,* the *New York Herald Tribune,* and first-class British newspapers.

Taft, Robert. *A Foreign Policy for Americans.* New York: Doubleday, 1951. Concise statement of the late Senator's views on foreign policy.

Thomas, R. C. *The War in Korea, 1950–53.* Aldershot: Gale and Polden, 1954. An extremely brief and superficial coverage of the military campaign and armistice negotiations by a British army officer.

Truman, Harry S. *Memoirs.* Vol. I, *Years of Decisions.* Vol. II, *Years of Trial and Hope.* New York: Doubleday, 1956. A valuable account of the President's thoughts and major policies during his Administration. A substantial portion of the second volume is devoted to the Korean War.

Vandenberg, Arthur H., Jr., and Joe A. Morris, eds. *The Private Papers of Senator Vandenberg.* Boston: Houghton Mifflin, 1952. A very good source for the breakdown of bipartisanship in the period 1949–1951.

Van Fleet, James. "The Truth about Korea." *Life,* May 11, 18, 1953. A criticism by General Ridgeway's successor of the manner in which the Korean War was fought, and how it could have been won.

———— "Catastrophe in Asia." *U.S. News,* September 17, 1954. Similar to above.

Vinacke, Harold M. *The United States and the Far East.* Stanford: Stanford University Press, 1952. Includes a valuable analysis of Chiang's collapse and the Korean War.

Walker, Richard L. *China under Communism.* New Haven: Yale University Press, 1955. A comprehensive presentation of Communist China's foreign policy, focusing closely upon the solidarity of Sino-Soviet relations.

Warner, Albert. "How the Korean Decision was Made." *Harper's Magazine,* June 1951. A not always accurate account of the decision so ably covered by Beverley Smith.

Westerfield, Bradford H. *Foreign Policy and Party Politics.* New Haven: Yale University Press, 1955. An admirable analysis of the relationship of party and Congressional politics to the formulation and execution of foreign policy. Particularly valuable for its presentation of the Administration's conduct of its China policy.

White, William S. *The Taft Story.* New York: Harper, 1954. A very sympathetic, though not uncritical, political biography.

———— *The Citadel.* New York: Harper, 1957. In his favorable presentation of the Senate as the "one touch of genius in the American political system," White discusses the MacArthur hearings and their contribution to the preservation of civilian supremacy over the military.

———— "What Bill Knowland Stands For." *New Republic,* February 27, 1956. Fiscal conservatism and primacy of Big Business.

Whitney, Courtney. *MacArthur: His Rendezvous with History.* New York: Knopf, 1956. The purpose of this book is to record for all time the "titanic influence" MacArthur had upon the course of events in Asia. Written by MacArthur's confidant and receiving the General's endorsement, this book is naturally devoid of criticism of the General. Nevertheless, it is a most valuable contribution for two reasons: it reveals at great length MacArthur's own thoughts and grievances at each stage of the campaign and quotes at equally great length the continuous interchanges between Tokyo and Washington.

Willoughby, Charles, and John Chamberlain. *MacArthur, 1941–1951.* New York: McGraw-Hill, 1955. This biography should have led MacArthur to exclaim, "God, save me from my friends!" For the two authors, the first of whom was MacArthur's chief of intelligence, quote constantly from alleged staff documents, which if true would prove that MacArthur's powers of prophecy are only equalled by God. It has therefore to be read carefully, and in conjunction with Whitney and the *Senate Hearings.*

Wint, Guy. *What Happened in Korea?* London: Batchworth, 1954. A bird's-eye view.

Wolfers, Arnold. "Collective Security and the War in Korea." *Yale Review,* Summer 1954. Wolfers realistically maintains that the American decision to meet force with force in June of 1950 was not dictated by any UN principle of collective security, but by NATO's selective security.

INDEX